Generative Fathering

CURRENT ISSUES IN THE FAMILY SERIES

Series Editor
Timothy H. Brubaker, *Miami University*

The pace of change in contemporary society has had an enormous impact on the workings of its most important institution, the family. This series of volumes explores the various dimensions of societal change and how the family is changing with them. Each edited volume contains the latest theory and research from leading scholars in the family field on a topic of contemporary concern. Special attention is paid to the impact of this research on the work being done by family therapists, family life educators, and family policymakers.

Generative Fathering

Beyond Deficit Perspectives

EDITED BY

Alan J. Hawkins
David C. Dollahite

Foreword by John Snarey

3 Current
Issues
in
the
_{volume} Family

SAGE Publications
International Educational and Professional Publisher
Thousand Oaks   London   New Delhi

For information address:

SAGE Publications, Inc.
2455 Teller Road
Thousand Oaks, California 91320
e-mail: order@sagepub.com

SAGE Publications Ltd.
6 Bonhill Street
London EC2A 4PU
United Kingdom

SAGE Publications India Pvt. Ltd.
M-32 Market
Greater Kailash I
New Delhi 110 048 India

Printed in the United States of America

Library of Congress Cataloging-in-Publication Data

Main entry under title:

Generative fathering: Beyond deficit perspectives / editors, Alan J.
    Hawkins and David C. Dollahite.
            p.   cm. — (Current issues in the family ; v. 3)
        Includes bibliographical references (p.   ) and index.
        ISBN 0-7619-0117-5 (cloth : acid-free paper). — ISBN
    0-7619-0118-3 (pbk. : acid-free paper)
        1. Fathers—United States.   2. Fatherhood—United States.
    3. Father and child—United States.   I. Hawkins, Alan J.
    II. Dollahite, David C. (David Curtis)   III. Series.
    HQ756.G387   1997
    306.874'2—DC2096-35627

This book is printed on acid-free paper.

97 98 99 00 01 02 10 9 8 7 6 5 4 3 2 1

Acquiring Editor:	Jim Nageotte
Editorial Assistant:	Nancy Hale
Production Editor:	Astrid Virding
Production Assistant:	Karen Wiley
Typesetter:	Rebecca Evans
Cover Designer:	Candice Harman
Print Buyer:	Anna Chin

Contents

To our generative parents, Carl and Nelma Hawkins and Mel and Elizabeth Dollahite, for life, fidelity, and wisdom; to our generous wives, Lisa Bolin Hawkins and Mary Kimball Dollahite, for lasting love and intimacy; to our genuinely wonderful children, Caitlin and Brian Hawkins, and Rachel, Erica, Camilla, Kathryn, and Spencer Dollahite, for centering our lives in care; and to our gentle mentors, Nan Crouter, Dave Eggebeen, Bonner Ritchie, Russ Crane, and Kathy Rettig, for persistent faith and abiding friendship.

Foreword

The Next Generation
of Work on Fathering

Veteran players in the study of fathers and families have found it difficult to turn "fatherhood" into a coherent field of practical scholarship. The bases are loaded with intriguing research findings, to be sure, but the game has remained something of a "wait till next year" dream because of the absence of a unifying theoretical framework. In this volume, the editors Alan J. Hawkins and David C. Dollahite have borrowed from and built on Erikson's concept of "generativity" to advance the idea and ideal of "generative fathering" as the developmental work and end point of fathering. They have connected the work of their colleagues from several disciplines and perspectives to construct in this volume a unified framework on which scholars and practitioners can build for the future. Notably, their application of Eriksonian theory is never rigid, stilted, or reductionistic. Rather, "generative fathering" is a broad framework that adds clarity to the craft of fathering from sociological and ethical as well as psychological perspectives.

Generativity

Erik H. Erikson (1902–1994) coined the term *generativity*—caring for and contributing to the life of the next generation—to describe the primary developmental task of adulthood. According to Erikson (1950, 1959), social, psychological, and biological processes interact throughout the life cycle to produce a series of vital psychosocial developmental tasks that intensify to a crisis or turning point in an ordered sequence of eight psychosocial stages. The psychosocial task of middle adulthood,

Stage 7, is the attainment of a favorable balance of generativity over stagnation. The fundamental challenge here is to realize an excess of procreativity,
productivity, and creativity over a pervading mood of personal stagnation
or self-absorption. Most broadly, Erikson (1974) views generativity as
including any caring activity that contributes to the spirit of the generations, such as the generation of new or more mature persons, products,
ideas, or works of art. Most centrally, Erikson (1964, 1980) sees generativity as based on a procreative drive and a need to be needed. Regardless
of the angle of vision, however, generative adults create, care for, and
promote the development of others, from nurturing the growth of another
person to shepherding the development of a broader community.

The favorable resolution of each of the eight crises results in the growth
of a particular ego strength or virtue. The adult virtue that arises from the
successful resolution of the crisis of generativity versus self-absorption is
care—"the widening concern for what has been generated by love, necessity, or accident; it overcomes the ambivalence adhering to irreversible
obligation" (Erikson, Erikson, & Kivnick, 1986, p. 37). Generative care
aims to be inclusively attentive to all that has been created. In contrast,
the ego weakness or vice that results from stagnation and self-absorption
is "rejectivity," a kind of indifference which Erikson (1982) defines as
"the unwillingness to include specified persons or groups in one's generative concern—one does not care for them" (p. 69). Because generativity "is
the link between the life cycle and the generational cycle," the widespread
absence of generative care threatens a society's community life (Erikson
& Erikson, 1981, p. 258).

Generativity is more complex, multifaceted, and differentiated than
any other stage in Erikson's model, in part because it spans a greater number
of years than any of the other stages. It is therefore helpful to note that
Erikson made implicit distinctions between three types of generativity:
(a) biological procreation, (b) parenthood, and (c) societal productivity or
creativity. When speaking of generative fathers, therefore, it is possible
to distinguish between the ways men contribute to and renew the ongoing
cycle of the generations through the care they provide as (a) birth fathers
(biological generativity), (b) child-rearing fathers (parental generativity),
and (c) cultural fathers (societal generativity).

Biological generativity ideally functions to link intimacy to parental
generativity, which, for the couple, represents "a vigorous expansion of
mutual interests" and an "investment in that which is being generated and
cared for together" (Erikson, 1982, p. 67). Parental generativity, in turn, is
the hinge that links biological and societal generativity. It involves carry-

ing out child-rearing activities that promote children's ability to develop their full potential, including realizing favorable measures of trust and then autonomy during the first 2 years of life, initiative and then industry during the early and later childhood years, and identity during adolescence. Here we begin to see that parental generativity provides one of the most basic and beautiful examples of cog-wheeling between life cycles: Generative parents provide important support for their children's development and, in turn, children provide opportunities for parents to satisfy their own developmental need to be generative. In the process of intensive parenting, furthermore, fathers as well as mothers usually develop important competencies for care. Then, as the ability or proclivity to generate new children wanes, the larger society calls for mature adults who are prepared to help establish the next generation of adults and ideas. This synchronization, according to Erikson (1975), provides an opportunity for adults to "apply the energies saved from" their abated parental commitments "to wider communal responsibilities" (p. 243). Parenting children and then adolescents, that is, helps prepare men to care for and mentor younger adults.

Erikson (1974) recounts these developmental processes by noting that after you have learned "what you care to do and who you care to be" (identity), and "whom you care to be with" (intimacy), you are ready to learn "what and whom you can take care of" (generativity) (p. 124). Parental generativity, that is, requires the "significant sacrifices" of love and the generative "commitment to take care of" what "one has learned to care for" (Erikson, 1982, p. 67). These requirements underscore that parenting is a moral endeavor. Many of us in the field of fatherhood studies have come to believe that asking one's self the question, "Am I a good father?" represents one of the most widespread and important acts of ethical self-reflection among men.

Fatherwork

In this volume, Hawkins, Dollahite, and their colleagues employ these and other Eriksonian concepts to bring order to a field generally characterized by an eclectic array of empirical research findings, clinical observations, and subjective experiences. The 15 chapters are equally divided into three parts: theory, research, and practice.

Part I of the book takes us beyond deficit perspectives (Chapter 1) to a framework of generative fathering (Chapter 2), and then elaborates on these ideas in terms of three important current discourses: gender and feminism (Chapter 3), ethnicity and race (Chapter 4), and historical change (Chapter 5). These five chapters challenge the adequacy of what Erikson would term a "negative identity"—an imposed identification of fathers as absent, abusive, deadbeat, deficient, or unnecessary. In contrast, the contributors' coordinated use of an ethic of generative fathering in this volume is evenhanded and positive. The chapter authors capture the experiences and meanings of men's lives by highlighting how fathers meet the needs of their children and sustain a developing ethical relationship with them. In Part II, qualitative and quantitative methods are used to clarify how generative fathering can be understood and encouraged in a variety of challenging circumstances: children with special needs (Chapter 6), teenage fathers (Chapter 7), divorce and remarriage (Chapter 8), single-custodial fathers (Chapter 9), and nongenerative culture (Chapter 10). These five very readable chapters are united by another Eriksonian idea, "generativity chill"—the anxiety resulting from threats to an adult's generativity. This is an important theme because the threatened loss of attachment to one's child is a powerful variable for explaining variations in men's care of their children.

In Part III, principles of generative fathering are applied to the practices of family life education (Chapter 11), clinical work (Chapter 12), scholarship on father involvement (Chapter 13), academic discourse (Chapter 14), and teaching about generative fathering in university courses (Chapter 15). These applied chapters underscore the integrative nature of the book and its potential to influence a wide range of professional practices. This final set of chapters also illustrates the application of "generative ethics"—an ethical position that begins with the next generation in mind. It is this "ethical orientation," according to Erikson (1975), "which makes the difference between adulthood and adolescence" (p. 207) and, we might add, between good-enough and inadequate fathering.

Generative Fathering is a book that reminds us that "good" fathering is less about playing a role and more about the hard work we do to build connections across generations. Generative fathers are men at work. *Generative Fathering* reminds us that fatherwork is also men's most important line of work. Perhaps no other form of labor can offer men such meaning. *Generative Fathering* advances the next generation of theory, research, and interventions for fathers; it encourages scholars and practitioners to see men more holistically and help fathers more effectively. For players in the field of fathering studies, "This is next year."

—John Snarey
Professor of Human Development and Ethics, Emory University

Preface

The purpose of this volume is to help scholars, teachers, practitioners, and students move beyond deficit models of fathering and explore and encourage what in this book we call *generative fathering*—fathering that meets the needs of the next generation across time and context. The concept of generative fathering builds on the foundation laid in Erik Erikson's (1950) theoretical work, especially his concept of generativity—learning to care for the next generation. We are gratified that John Snarey, whose important book, *How Fathers Care for the Next Generation* (1993), reintroduced scholars of fathering to Erikson's work, wrote the foreword for this volume.

A main cord that binds this edited volume together is the commitment to move beyond deficit models of fathering, a plea voiced by Bill Doherty (1991) several years ago. Moving beyond deficit models of fathering, we believe, means acknowledging that most fathers have the desire, ability, and sense of obligation to care effectively for the next generation. A significant reason why we often use deficit models is because we lack a rich, scholarly language to help us talk about fathers' capabilities and contributions. By examining and challenging deficit models of fathering, and by building a generative fathering perspective, we hope to create such a language and advance theory, research, and practice in this important field.

In this volume, we seek to broaden understanding of the many ways fathers care for their children by recognizing fathers' current contributions to the development of the next generation, the constraints under which most fathers labor, the good desires men have to be generative fathers, and their efforts to improve. We emphasize fathers' efforts to progress toward generative fathering while also recognizing the assistance that cultural norms, societal institutions, and professional intervention can provide in encouraging generative fathering and removing barriers that make it difficult.

This volume is a cooperative, multidisciplinary effort to build a useful framework of generative fathering in scholarship and practice. Our chapter authors were trained in and contribute to such diverse fields as family science, psychology, sociology, human development, education, family therapy, and history. The editors and chapter authors worked together to create an integrated, scholarly volume interwoven with various conceptual threads. This was accomplished by inviting each contributor to read preliminary drafts of Chapter 1 (beyond deficit perspectives) and Chapter 2 (an ethic of generative fathering) and in some way create a dialogue with the main ideas in one or both of those chapters. As editors, we encouraged and helped the chapter authors link their ideas to other chapters and to Erikson's ideas. Thus, although each chapter author focuses on specific domains and makes unique contributions, there are also many links between chapters, resulting in an integrated volume that we believe can advance the conceptualization and conduct of fathering in important directions.

We have tried to create a reader-friendly book for professionals and students, avoiding narrow jargon and complex presentations of data to communicate with the widest possible readership. Fathers' own voices, not just those who study or work with them, are heard throughout this volume. In our last chapter, we explicitly attempt to facilitate the presentation, discussion, and learning of the generative fathering perspective for students in university courses.

We hope this volume will stimulate a new generation of concepts and theories; research methods and studies; and practical interventions, programs, and policies aimed at furthering the understanding of what fathers contribute to children, what children need from fathers, and how to strengthen fathers' connections with children. Much work needs to be done to support those fathers who wish to continue—or begin—to turn their hands, minds, and hearts toward caring for the next generation.

Acknowledgments

We are grateful to Tim Brubaker for his generous invitation to two young professionals to edit this volume on fathering for the series **Current Issues in the Family.** We appreciate the helpful advice and careful work on the volume by Jim Nageotte, our editor at Sage. We thank John Snarey, for his belief in our purposes for this volume; he also read an early draft of the manuscript and made very important suggestions for improvement. Many colleagues at Brigham Young University, especially Wes Burr and Brent Slife, gave us important feedback on several chapters, for which we are grateful. We benefited from the helpful suggestions of students in our research practicum on generative fathering: Jen Call, Kathy Froerer, Scott Hall, Stephanie Morris, Jeff Palmer, Jonathan Taylor, and Sara Weyland. We are in debt to Vivian Giles, who industriously and competently assisted in the preparation of the manuscript, and Lisa Hawkins, who carefully reviewed the final manuscript. Most of all, we deeply appreciate the skilled and cooperative scholarship of the all the authors who contributed to this volume.

PART I

Building a Perspective of Generative Fathering

The five chapters in this section provide a conceptual beginning for going beyond deficit perspectives of men and fathering, and exploring how to approach scholarship without assuming men lack interest in or desire to care for the next generation.

The volume editors, Alan Hawkins and David Dollahite, in Chapter 1, "Beyond the Role-Inadequacy Perspective of Fathering," argue that a prominent way of thinking in much scholarship on fathering emerges from a deficit paradigm, and they illustrate deficit thinking in the literature on paternal absence and neglect, fathers' underinvolvement in domestic labor, and clinical literature on the nature of fatherhood. Their critique focuses on one form of deficit thinking, the *role-inadequacy perspective* (RIP), which emphasizes fathers' lack of adjustment to sociohistorical change; resistance to change in contemporary family roles; enjoyment of privilege in the family; and ignorance, incompetence, or sloth in caregiving. Although the RIP accurately and tragically describes some fathers, the authors argue this is not the best place to begin to understand and encourage better fathering, because: (a) the RIP does not give adequate attention to the processes of paternal growth and maturation (it is nondevelopmental); (b) the RIP misconstrues motives, feelings, attitudes, and hopes of most fathers (it is inaccurate); (c) the RIP creates significant barriers to personal transformation (it is unmotivating); and (d) the RIP holds up a constricted standard of good paternal care (it is narrow).

In Chapter 2, "Fatherwork: A Conceptual Ethic of Fathering as Generative Work," David Dollahite, Alan Hawkins, and Sean Brotherson suggest

1

that one way to move beyond a role-inadequacy perspective of fathering is to use the image of fathering as work rather than as a social role (fathering is the work men do, not a role they play). These authors present a conceptual ethic (rather than a descriptive model) of good fathering as generative work and extend a call for fathers to work to meet the needs of their children and the next generation.

The next three chapters discuss generative fathering and moving beyond deficit thinking as related to three important current discourses in family studies: gender, ethnicity, and history. In Chapter 3, "An Institutional Perspective on Generative Fathering: Creating Social Supports for Parenting Equality," Kathleen Gerson presents a feminist perspective on generative fathering. Drawing on her own interviews with fathers, she argues that for generative fathering to exist and thrive, important changes need to take place in public and private institutions to facilitate gender-equitable parenting.

In Chapter 4, "An African American Perspective on Generative Fathering," William Allen and Michael Conner provide an historical and ecological context for discussing the work that African American men do in their families. They demonstrate that African American men have overcome many historical and environmental obstacles to meet the needs of their children. The authors integrate the concepts of generative fathering from an African American perspective and explore factors that promote or hinder generative fathering among African Americans.

In Chapter 5, "Generative Fathering: An Historical Perspective," Robert Griswold provides a fast-paced, historical overview of fathering, from colonial America to the present, to show that men have always occupied a prominent place in their children's lives and cared for their children in important ways, but the terms of involvement, and hence the nature of generative fathering, have changed over time. Emerging forms of generative fathering have their own unique set of challenges, with a tremendous opportunity for contemporary men to develop strong, intimate bonds with their children and become involved in parenting in rewarding ways.

This first part of the book, then, demonstrates that scholarship on fathering that is not based in deficit thinking can be fruitful and accommodate the important discourses of gender, ethnicity, and history in family studies.

1

Beyond the Role-Inadequacy Perspective of Fathering

ALAN J. HAWKINS
DAVID C. DOLLAHITE

A prominent way of thinking about fathering is that it is a *social role* that men generally perform inadequately. This approach springs from a deficit model of men (Doherty, 1991), or a general deficit paradigm, that is evident in much of contemporary family scholarship on men and fathers. Within this paradigm, fathers are willingly uninvolved with their children and unmotivated to change. Not surprising, when scholars and practitioners approach their work with fathers from a deficit paradigm, they are likely to find inadequate role performance. There is, unfortunately, some validity to this general portrait of deficiency; it accurately and tragically describes too many fathers (and perhaps all fathers at times). It fails to describe many good fathers, however. Regardless of the deficit paradigm's descriptive validity, we believe a perspective of fathers as generally deficient in their paternal role is not the best place to begin to understand and encourage better fathering.

In this chapter, we explore the limits of a perspective of fathering rooted in deficit thinking. By so doing, we hope to increase the range of conceptual tools presently available to understand and encourage good fathering. First, we document briefly the existence of the deficit paradigm in scholarly and clinical work on fathering. Then, we delineate the limits we perceive in thinking about fathers from within the deficit paradigm, or more precisely, from a specific form of the deficit paradigm that we label

3

the *role-inadequacy perspective*. This chapter is a product of a constructive discontent through which we invite scholars and practitioners to
examine their assumptions about fathers and fathering. We hope it stimulates serious introspection and discussion among students, scholars, and
practitioners.

The Existence of a Deficit Paradigm

We are hardly alone in a conclusion that a deficiency paradigm exists;
other scholars have also begun to explore biased assumptions and perceptions of men and fathers (Brod, 1987; Cook, 1988; Davidson & Duberman, 1982; Doherty, 1991; Fox-Genovese, 1996; Gerson, 1993; Heesacker & Prichard, 1992; Levant, 1992; Lillie, 1993). These attempts to
examine biases about men and fathers differ from "backlash" writings
(Faludi, 1991); these scholars do not deny the oppression and abuse
women and children too often suffer in families. Rather, these researchers,
in their attempts to view men more phenomenologically, have discovered
that extant theories and perspectives frequently do not adequately capture
the experiences and meanings of men's lives as fathers.

We limit supporting evidence of the existence of a deficit paradigm to
its manifestations in three areas of family scholarship: (a) the "diminishing culture" of fatherhood, (b) clinical literature on the nature of men and
fathers, and (c) fathers' participation in child care and household labor.
We cite only a few respected authors for purposes of illustration rather
than reference extensively the considerable scholarship that comes out of
a deficit paradigm.

The "Diminishing Culture" of Fatherhood

The most demeaning portraits of men sometimes come from social critics
concerned with the decreasing presence of fathers in families and its destructive consequences for children, communities, and society. Blankenhorn's
(1995) impassioned plea for reestablishing a culture of responsible fatherhood in our society is one of the most prominent examples. Although we
share Blankenhorn's analysis that fathers are important to children's
well-being and his desire to promote better fathering, we question the
assumptions he brings to his analysis:

> Because fatherhood is *universally problematic* in human societies, cultures
> must mobilize to devise and *enforce* the father role for men, *coaxing* and

guiding them into fatherhood through a set of legal and extralegal *pressures* that *require* them to maintain a close alliance with their children's mother and to invest in their children. Because men *do not volunteer* for fatherhood as much as they are *conscripted* into it by the surrounding culture, only an *authoritative* cultural story of fatherhood can *fuse* biological and social paternity into a coherent male identity [italics added]. (p. 3)

Blankenhorn only asserts boldly what others quietly assume: Fatherhood is a problem. Men are not biologically suited to responsible fatherhood: "They are inclined to sexual promiscuity and paternal waywardness . . . unwilling or unable to make that vital investment" (p. 3). Creating a culture of responsible fatherhood is our most urgent social problem, he argues. From this perspective, the problem and solution are straightforward: Men are uncivilized brutes, so tame and train them with culture for their unwanted but necessary domesticated role.

The "Emotionally Challenged" Father

Much of the clinical literature on men both contributes to and reflects the deficit paradigm of fathering. A sampling of the labels and concepts used to refer to men and fathers include: incompetent, unaware, underdeveloped femininity, fear of intimacy, distant, infantile, emotional children, emotionally constricted, emotionally constipated, alexithymic, toxic masculinity, hypermasculine, mascupathology, narcissistic, abusive, oppressive. Clinical writings usually trace this paternal pathology to the inadequate or abusive fathering of the previous generation. Emotional distance and physical absence from fathers leave boys "wounded," and without a proper guide they are doomed to repeat this pattern of absent fathering as they search for a connection with their lost selves (Corneau, 1991). Clinicians are divided on whether these emotionally challenged fathers are in need of strong, adult male mentors or a skilled and patient therapist who can guide them through their dangerous inner journeys to healthy, responsible manhood. But there is wide agreement that most men are emotionally and relationally deficient and in need of therapy.

Fathers' "Underinvolvement" in Domestic Labor

The central finding in studies of married fathers' participation in domestic labor is that mothers do two to three times as much housework and child care as fathers do. We do not dismiss this finding, but we are concerned about the meanings and interpretations often attached to it. A phrase often used in the literature to interpret this finding is that married fathers are "physically present but functionally absent." Many fathers should be more involved in domestic work, but the gender disparity in time spent does not mean that fathers are uninvolved either temporally or psychologically. Men's temporal involvement in domestic labor over the last 30 years has not increased by leaps and bounds and is not enough to replace the decreased time spent by women, but fathers do devote time to their children. Pleck (in press), in a thorough review of studies assessing fathers' temporal involvement with their children, estimates that married fathers, on average, spend about 2 hours each weekday and 6.5 hours on Sundays in direct engagement with their children. Recent national data suggest that married fathers report spending about 27 hours a week with their children compared to their wives' reports of 37 hours a week (Galinsky, Bond, & Friedman, 1995). There is still a significant disparity in the temporal involvement of fathers and mothers with their children, but interpreting this disparity as fathers' functional absence from children's lives, we believe, is inaccurate and unfortunate. Fathers do spend time caring for their children. They also spend time with children in valuable ways not measured by studies of the allocation of domestic labor and expend effort on behalf of their children that makes an important difference in their children's healthy development (see Chapter 13, this volume; Pleck, in press).

Similarly, the slow rate of increase in fathers' investment of time in family work (narrowly measured) over the past 30 years often is interpreted to mean that fathers stubbornly and selfishly resist change and greater involvement. But many fathers have made significant changes, and other potential explanations for slow rates of change besides active resistance can be found (e.g., employment barriers, maternal gatekeeping). We suggest the conclusions that married men are physically present but functionally absent and resistant to change are shaped by an underlying presumption of fathers' deficiencies: There are some enlightened fathers who have successfully adapted to changing times, but most are still mired in the mud of outdated ideologies and content to wallow therein. Or maybe they are just immature. Hochschild (1989) suggested directly what others have implied: The problem with men is not that they "have an elaborate idea of fatherhood and then don't live up to it. Their idea of fatherhood is embryonic to begin with" (p. 229). Again, the problem and solution are straightforward: Men are stubborn (or childish), so push (or gently guide) them until they comply (or grow up).

In sum, it appears to us that family scholars and practitioners in this area often approach their work and interpret data within a perspective of fathering that focuses on the deficiencies of some fathers and the struggles of many fathers, ending up with a mind-set within which most fathers are viewed as uninvolved, uninterested, unskilled, and unmotivated to perform their proper paternal role.

A Critique of the Role-Inadequacy Perspective of Fathering

Many scholars and practitioners recognize the value of searching for a conceptual plateau above the swampy perspectives of biological or social deficiency that percolate through much of the fathering literature. Although one can identify in the literature many ways of thinking about men and fathering that emerge from a deficit paradigm, here we examine in some depth one particular form—we call it the role-inadequacy perspective (RIP)—which is concerned with fathers' lack of adjustment to changing family roles. We critique it because of its counterproductive overemphasis on fathers' inadequacies and overreliance on the metaphor of role. We concentrate here on the first dimension of this critique and only touch lightly on the second.

Overemphasis on Fathers' Inadequacies

Cultural Critique Versus Personal Transformation. One brand of the role-inadequacy perspective, which could be called the "progressive family change" position, focuses attention on fathers' lack of adjustment to sociohistorical change; their resistance to change in contemporary family roles; their enjoyment of privilege in the family; and their ignorance, incompetence, or sloth in caregiving. According to the role-inadequacy perspective, society has changed dramatically over the past 50 years and women's roles have been at the epicenter of that change. Specifically, women's greater involvement in the paid labor force has altered women's family roles and created concomitant demands for change in fathers' behavior. But men have not increased much their investment of time and energy in domestic labor (Demo & Acock, 1993), creating what Hochschild (1989) refers to as a stalled revolution—"When women have gone to work, but the workplace, the culture, and most of all, the men, have not adjusted themselves to this new reality" (p. 235).

A competing brand of the RIP, which could be called the "diminishing family culture" position, is focused not on rapidly changing socioeconomic conditions but on the creeping cultural hegemony of hedonistic and individualistic philosophies that threaten the stability of primary family relationships and fathers' willingness to sacrifice for children. From this position, the erosion of a strong culture of fatherhood over the course of the latter half of the 20th century has resulted in dramatic increases in divorce and nonmarital childbearing. In short, the family and fatherhood are in steep decline (Popenoe, 1993). Almost one third of children will be born to nonmarried women and likely will have little significant contact with their biological fathers. A majority of children born to married couples can expect to experience the divorce of their parents and greatly diminished contact and connection with their fathers over time (Cooney & Uhlenberg, 1990; Seltzer, 1991). The diminishment of a strong family culture in the face of a relentless wind of hedonism and individualism is eroding the social soil in which strong families, responsible individuals, and civil societies are nurtured.

Whichever brand is preferred, the role-inadequacy perspective leads to the argument that fathers perform the contemporary paternal role poorly. Yet, the RIP's focus on glaring deficiencies often obscures the possibility that most fathers care deeply for their children and want to be good dads. We assume, and we believe this assumption is consistent with good research (e.g., Snarey, 1993), that most fathers want to be good dads and many bring significant strengths to that work. (Not surprisingly, the contributions to this volume also support this view.) Our aim is to point out the deficiencies of the RIP and its limitations for helping men improve their fathering. Our critique of the RIP centers not on its descriptive deficiencies but its lack of prescriptive potential for helping fathers. The RIP is focused on promoting cultural critique, not personal transformation. It is geared to reengineer the paternal role in society to achieve more social and domestic equality or greater family stability. Thus, the RIP emphasizes macrolevel efforts—social, cultural, economic, organizational, political, legal—to rebuild a more workable father role.

Such efforts are laudable, but they have their limits. These efforts can, for example, include garnishment of the wages of "deadbeat dads" and giving the money to their children, a legal movement we support, but alone such tactics tend to reduce fathering to a minimal economic dimension rather than encourage involvement in children's lives (Blankenhorn, 1995). Social and organizational efforts can help provide more flexibility in structuring employment so fathers can choose to devote more time to family care, which we applaud, but a little more flexibility likely will not be enough to have major impact on how most couples balance their work and family lives (Bohen & Viveros-Long, 1981; Haas, 1990; Haas &

Hwang, 1995). Reevaluation of legislation and judicial policy for their impact on marriages and families yields benefits, but it is easy to overestimate the power of the state to affect highly personal decisions. Macrolevel efforts can help mold the culture of fatherhood to strengthen fathers' ties to marriage and parenting and better serve women and children—and have done so—but their ability to guide fathers in their highly personal paths of transformation is unproven.

The RIP is targeted for broad, macrolevel, top-down efforts at rescripting social roles. And although we support a number of these efforts and hope they persist, there is a critical need for additional perspectives better suited to facilitating personal transformation in men who desire to be better fathers tomorrow than they are today. We argue the role-inadequacy perspective is limited in its ability to facilitate personal transformation in fathers because (a) it does not give adequate attention to the processes of paternal growth and maturation (it is nondevelopmental); (b) it misconstrues the motives, feelings, attitudes, and hopes of most fathers (it is inaccurate); (c) it creates significant barriers to personal transformation rather than encouraging change (it is unmotivating); and (d) it holds up a constricted standard of good paternal care (it is narrow). We elaborate on these points below.

The RIP Is Nondevelopmental. Because the RIP is focused on rescripting social roles rather than on facilitating individual transformation, it necessarily emphasizes sociohistorical transitions over personal developmental ones as critical features for understanding fathering. Hence, it focuses on fathers' need to adapt to external transitions rather than initiate or manage internal ones. We advocate giving greater attention to men's personal development, as transitions, growth, and change are constants in the human equation. Scholarly and applied thinking about good fathering must be responsive to the developmental dimension of men's lives. If our aim is to promote personal improvement in men's fathering, attention to developmental issues is needed.

To explore this developmental dimension of fathering, we have drawn from the late Erik Erikson's theory of human development across the life cycle (Erikson, 1950, Erikson, 1959). Erikson argued that active caring for the next generation, a task he called generativity, was essential for healthy adult development for both men and women. Generativity is the process of expanding one's concern beyond the self and intimate dyad to include one's children and the next generation. "Parenthood is, for most, the first, and for many, the prime generative encounter" (Erikson, 1950,

p. 130). And once a man becomes a father, he must learn to care deeply for and commit to taking care of his children.

This developmental dimension of fathering has a number of important implications for thinking about fathering. One implication is that actively caring for one's children is not only developmentally important to the child, but central to a father's growth and well-being (Hawkins, Christiansen, Sargent, & Hill, 1993). Thus, in most cases, caring for children is not a cultural imposition on fathers—something they do halfheartedly or ineffectively (or not at all) unless cultural forces corral and bridle them. Most men know or learn that good fathering is something necessary to their growth and happiness. Fathering need not be thought of as simply a social role defined and delineated by external forces. Rather, it can be seen as a crucial internal process for a father's development and well-being. To assert that most men resist active involvement in caring for their children is to propose that most men are not interested in their own growth and maturation, much less the development of their children. As adult development proceeds, we believe most fathers come to sense that the quality of their fathering is central to how good a person they are and how happy they, their wives, and their children will be. For most men, we believe, no social playwright is needed to script the contemporary paternal role; good fathering can come from a set of developmental, relational, and ethical motives within men.

Giving attention to the developmental dimension of fathering does not mean ignoring context. Context is critical to healthy development. From a developmental perspective, normative growth usually unfolds in supportive contexts. Thus, to the extent that the conditions (biological, psychological, interpersonal, familial, social, religious, cultural, economic, etc.) under which a man fathers are generally supportive of his active caring, a developmentalist would expect to see him make caring for his children a central feature of his life's work and expect him to strive for competence in this arena. When conditions are less supportive of a man nurturing his children, he may struggle. If too much fathering fits the assumptions of the role-inadequacy perspective, then a developmental perspective suggests the conditions that support good fathering may be weak. Many factors work against good fathering, and most fathers struggle to grow and overcome those barriers. But examining risk factors to the unfolding of good fathering differs from the conceptual starting point of the RIP: the assumption that fathers resist fulfilling a new social role of involved father. If most fathers struggle to become the "good dads" they desire to be, perhaps this is evidence of the hard work of adult development in a less-than-optimal context; it does not summarily convict fathers as inadequate. Indeed, from a developmental perspective, fathers' internal desire to care for the next generation can be a starting point for improvement rather than an end point when cultural forces have done their job.

The RIP Misconstrues Motives and Desires. Almost all fathers' actions are more than occasionally inconsistent with completely committed and caring fathering, but we believe the role-inadequacy perspective of fathering does not accurately account for fathers' motives, feelings, attitudes, and desires regarding fathering and their children. The RIP assumes a set of attitudinal "uns" as it shapes scholars' interpretations of data on men's imperfect parenting: Fathers are *un*caring, *un*interested, *un*committed, and *un*willing. These conclusions are unempirical. Haas and Hwang (1995) recently gathered evidence from various studies to demonstrate that most fathers have strong feelings for their children, believe that their families are more important than their work, and want to spend more time with their children. Although they often struggle and fall short of the high standards such feelings and priorities suggest, these fathers are nonetheless committed to their children. In contrast, the RIP often seems to interpret fathers' behavioral shortfalls as prima facie evidence of their lack of caring.

In other words, the RIP does not accurately portray the motives and desires of less-than-perfect but caring and committed fathers, which we believe constitute a substantial majority of fathers—and the ones most likely interested in improving their fathering. The RIP's broad, negative portrayal of fathers' motives and desires leads to different education and intervention strategies. For instance, a therapeutic strategy that begins with the assumption that fathers cling immaturely to power and privilege will employ different tools from one based on the view of fathers as caring and concerned but struggling to enact their highest aspirations. Similarly, an educational program built from the assumption that fathers are not especially interested in being close to their children until some expert convinces them they should be would differ from one in which fathers are viewed as wanting to be close to their children but facing significant barriers to the achievement of that desire. In both these instances, we believe the RIP distorts fathers' motives and desires and thus is less effective in encouraging good fathering. More helpful perspectives would stress the strong desires most men have to be good dads.

The RIP Creates Barriers to Change. Emphasis on personal deficiencies is seldom a solid foundation on which to build positive change (Doherty, 1991). When scholars and practitioners attend first and primarily to fathers' real or perceived inadequacies, men's defense mechanisms likely engage, and resistance to change becomes an outcome rather than an assumed beginning point. According to Gottman (1994), "One of the great paradoxes in therapy is that people don't change unless they feel accepted as they are" (p. 184). Ultimately, people are less likely to change from a position of imposed guilt and defensiveness than from a personal vision of a better way and a sense of empowerment (Kaufman, 1987). We need to build on strengths more than we harp on weaknesses (Levine, 1993). Moreover, men grow and change because of an ethical commitment to freely chosen goals or in response to feelings for a loved one and a valued relationship (Dollahite, Hawkins, & Brotherson, 1996; Gerson, 1993). An intervention strategy that consists mainly of holding up a mirror to men's faces so they can see their paternal warts more clearly is neither visionary nor empowering. The harsh glare of role deficiency may prompt men to retreat into the shadows of resentment rather than illuminate other paths of personal growth.

Other barriers to change arise from an emphasis on paternal deficiencies. The role-inadequacy perspective may unintentionally invite mothers to expect less from fathers when we interpret data to mean men don't care for their children. After all, if men are so deficient, women have a ready rationale for expecting less from men than fathers are capable of providing. The RIP provides a powerful mental set for maternal gatekeeping. *Gatekeeping* refers to maternal management of paternal involvement, requesting participation but setting the standards and prescribing the process, enlisting "help" but not giving up responsibility. If men's deficiencies are truly so deep, mothers can hardly be blamed for writing their partners' parental lines and continually prompting them with stage directions and cues. The RIP may unintentionally urge mothers to see their partners as supporting actors rather than costars (see Chapter 10, this volume).

Similarly, when professional and popular constructions of men and fathers are so pejorative or condescending, the RIP may have the unintended consequence of lowering the personal standards of good fathering. There is a 20th-century history of poking fun at fathers' incompetency (LaRossa, in press). And when fathers are regularly viewed by professionals as deficient or bumbling, it is not difficult for men to be content simply to rise a step or two above Neanderthal level on the evolutionary ladder of good caregiving. It's easier for them to see themselves as already more involved than their own father or the guy next door, thus inhibiting the process of continual improvement.

The RIP Constricts the Conceptualization of Care. A role-inadequacy perspective also hinders improved fathering because it includes a narrow view of caregiving—that is, the RIP leaves unquestioned the comparison referent for fathering and mothering. Within the RIP is a sometimes subtle but often explicit supposition that fathers are derelict because they are not doing what mothers do, either as much or as well (Day & Mackey, 1989). One scholar has said what others unintentionally imply—that there is really no such thing as fathering, only men that mother (Kraemer, 1991). Another has suggested that we need to "rewrite the parenting scripts" so that fathers parent like mothers (Garbarino, 1993, p. 53). The term *coparenting* is commonly used to refer to spouses sharing equitably in the tasks traditionally associated with mothering. The RIP does not move beyond the presumption that men and women bring talents and capabilities to their care for children that may not overlap completely. The caregiving typically associated with mothering and often emphasized by family scholars and practitioners does not exhaust the range of caring activities needed by children. Fathers are not mothers, and shouldn't try to be. Pruett (1993) argues: "The child doesn't expect it, and the father can't do it" (p. 46). Fathers often bring different assets and skills to their caregiving that add unique benefits to children's well-being. We believe with other scholars (Erikson, 1968; Johnson & Palm, 1992b; Pruett, 1993; Snarey, 1993) that the strengths men bring to caring for children have not been adequately appreciated or explored. If we have a narrow conception of care, we will continue to perceive fathers as less caring.

The question of whether fathers can be competent caregivers to young children was a subject of significant research 20 years ago. The accumulated evidence confirms that men *are* capable and loving caregivers, they respond sensitively and appropriately to children's cues and needs, and that children and fathers attach emotionally to each other (Biller, 1993; Lamb, 1987; Parke, 1981, 1990; Pruett, 1989). This research agenda also revealed consistent differences in the ways that men care for young children, including a greater emphasis on play, physical stimulation, and intellectual development that has positive benefits for children's well-being. Yet, the different strengths that men bring to parenting are understated by this body of research because of its narrow view of care; it is focused on direct, interactive, hands-on, daily nurturing of young children. Although this kind of care is critical to children's development, and fathers should be and often are intimately involved in such care, alone it leaves out a wide range of tasks and responsibilities also essential to the well-being of the next generation. The result undervalues the good that many fathers do and ignores a foundation on which to build increased efforts to encourage even better fathering.

In other words, the RIP often implies that to be good fathers, men must become like mothers (Ehrensaft, 1990; Garbarino, 1993). A sex role change operation is neither appealing to most fathers nor respectful of their lives, experiences, and skills. We advocate adoption of perspectives that would be more respectful of men's lives. We encourage scholars and practitioners to view men as capable fathers instead of deficient mothers and to raise the standard of good fathering rather than fit men into the mold of mothering.

Moreover, the RIP's conception of care is also culturally narrow. The notion of good fathering implied in the RIP arises from one cultural ideal and is imposed on all men regardless of race, ethnicity, culture, religion, and socioeconomic situation. Men from diverse backgrounds facing various challenges are judged deficient by parenting standards tailored to fit a white, Western, educated, upper-middle-class ideology. Generative, nondeficit perspectives of fathering would allow for diversity of style, approach, and values, while condemning sloth and oppression. Facilitating better fathering would begin by recognizing the healthy variety of ways men in different contexts care for the next generation.

Overreliance on the Metaphor of Role

Our critique of the role-inadequacy perspective thus far has been focused on the "inadequacy" part, that is, on its counterproductive emphasis on men's inadequacies in the contemporary paternal role. Integrated throughout this critique has also been a concern with the RIP's overreliance on the metaphor of role. Before concluding, we briefly wish to make explicit our concern with the "role" part of the RIP as well.

The concept of role is one of the most pervasive, frequently used conceptual and analytical tools in the social sciences (Nye, 1976; Rogers & White, 1993), and the family literature on fathering depends heavily—if not exclusively—on it. Indeed, in the fathering literature, the concept of role has become nearly reified. Rather than being employed from time to time as a useful metaphor to understand fathering, the concept of role has become the only analytic tool with which to think about fathers. With only this tool, scholars and practitioners are likely to forget that it is just a metaphor. Indeed, they may never be conscious of using a role meta-phor. But metaphors shape our thinking in profound ways (Rosenblatt, 1994). For instance, a role metaphor leads us to think about fathering as an external persona that men choose to or are compelled to put on or take off. The metaphor of role encourages us to conjure up an image of fathering as relatively passive, narrow, distinct, and interchangeable—passive because it suggests a father's lines are already culturally scripted and his move-ments blocked, narrow because it can imply fathering is only a reduced fraction of the whole that constitutes most men's experiences, distinct because it tempts us to think that the various roles men play are easily separable, interchangeable because we can think of other men being substituted or hired to fill the part ("father figures"). Indeed, it allows us to ask whether fathers are fungible, or readily replaced (Hawkins & Eggebeen, 1991). Admittedly and unfortunately, the fathering of some men is adequately described as passive, narrow, and interchangeable. But most fathers do not see their labors in such a limited way. Activities in which we make deep investments merge with our personality; they be-come an inseparable part of us rather than external dimensions (Turner, 1978). Even as fathers struggle to achieve a broader and deeper concep-tualization of fathering, they know that good fathering is active, creative, all-encompassing, irreplaceable, hard *work,* not simply a role they *play.*

Conclusion

In this chapter, we critique one form of deficit thinking about fathering, the role-inadequacy perspective, which emphasizes fathers' lack of adap-tation to sociohistorical change, their lack of involvement in caring for children, and their lack of interest in changing the status quo. The RIP fills a need for a tool for critically examining societal constructions of gender roles, but it is lacking as a compass to guide fathers and the professionals who assist them in men's personal paths of transformation. Because the RIP gives little attention to the processes of men's adult development, it fails to locate parenting at the center of men's lives, which is where many fathers put it and where most fathers know it must be; because the RIP misconstrues many fathers' motives and desires toward their children, it places transformational forces outside of, rather than within, fathers; because the RIP generally paints pejorative images of fathers, it is defi-cient in presenting empowering messages to inspire better fathering; because the RIP has a narrow conception of care, it blinds users to the many ways that fathers care deeply for the next generation and discourages respect for fathers' lives and experiences as distinct from those of mothers; and because the RIP relies on the metaphor of a role, it leads us to think about fathering as a passive, narrow, and interchangeable part of adult men's lives rather than the core of their adult experience.

We encourage scholars and practitioners to move beyond the deficit paradigm in general and the role-inadequacy perspective in particular toward new frameworks that simultaneously emphasize the desires men have to do the work of good fathering, the capabilities they bring to their parenting, and the ethical responsibilities they must assume to care for the next generation. The next chapter points us in this direction.

2

Fatherwork

A Conceptual Ethic of Fathering as Generative Work

DAVID C. DOLLAHITE
ALAN J. HAWKINS
SEAN E. BROTHERSON

In this chapter, we move beyond the role-inadequacy perspective of fathering discussed in Chapter 1. We present a conceptual ethic of fathering as *generative work* and a synonymous, but more succinct and user-friendly term, *fatherwork*. In the first part of the chapter, we briefly introduce some of the ideas that form the backdrop for our framework and the ways we are thinking about it in relation to other forms of conceptual models. Next, we discuss why we use the concept of fathering as work rather than as a social role. We then devote the major portion of the chapter to the conceptual ethic and discuss ways that it can be used to resolve important issues in understanding and encouraging good fathering.

Our approach in developing this framework was to try for both conceptual clarity and practical utility. We wanted a set of ideas and ideals that could suggest to scholars and practitioners important areas to attend to in trying to understand and encourage good fathering, but also translate as directly as possible into clinical interventions and educational programs. To work effectively with fathers, practitioners must attend to the different ways they learn and change (Dollahite et al., 1996; Minnesota Fathering Alliance, 1992); we believe our approach is well suited to these issues.

We employ language, terms, and concepts consistent with our general purpose to call scholars, practitioners, and family members to understand, encourage, and practice good fathering. We also hope that the conceptual ethic will be helpful to scholars trying to move beyond a deficit paradigm and to practitioners attempting to call forth positive change from those they teach and counsel.

By "conceptual ethic," we mean a framework that is intended not primarily to model or describe reality but to suggest what is possible and desirable. Many readers in the social sciences are more comfortable with conceptual attempts to map reality and less comfortable with efforts to suggest what can be ("idealism") or ought to be ("moralizing"). Our framework is not intended to be value neutral or objectivist. Indeed, we question whether scholars and practitioners can or should be value neutral in their work (Doherty, 1995; Slife & Williams, 1995). Rather, we propose an ethically grounded, intervention-oriented approach to viewing good fathering as generative work that builds on our scholarly understandings, clinical and educational experiences, and deeply held beliefs about the importance of good fathering for the next generation.

That said, we believe it is important for the reader to be aware of some of the values and ideals that influence our work. As fathers, we have experienced personally the challenges and rewards associated with caring for our children. As family scientists and family practitioners, we are committed to using scholarly tools not simply to understand but also to assist. In our shared religious faith (as members of The Church of Jesus Christ of Latter-day Saints), fathering is regarded as one of the most important kinds of work that any man can do (Hawkins, Dollahite, & Rhoades, 1993). These experiences, values, and commitments will certainly be reflected in this chapter.

Guiding Assumptions of a Conceptual Ethic of Generative Fathering

Our conceptual ethic of generative fathering is an approach to theory, research, and intervention designed to better understand fathering and encourage generative fathering (Snarey, 1993). By *generative fathering, we mean fathering that meets the needs of children by working to create and maintain a developing ethical relationship with them.* We believe the concept of generative fathering can serve as a constructive point of departure in framing a broad theoretical model of responsible fathering. That our approach is a conceptual ethic means that we believe ethics precede and ground all scholarly understanding of fathering and professional practice with fathers. An ethical framework allows for the conceptualization of better ways of parenting: more appropriate ways of caring, more helpful ways of relating, and more empowering and respectful forms of guiding.

Assumptions are imbedded in all behavioral theories (Slife & Williams, 1995). To make explicit the guiding assumptions underlying our conceptual ethic of generative fathering, we assume (a) fathers are under the obligations of an ethical call from their children and their communities to conduct the multidimensional work of caring for the next generation in ways that attend to the fundamental conditions and constraints of children's lives within families, (b) generational ethics rather than adult relational ethics should be preeminent when considering the needs of children, (c) fathers have contextual agency in their relationships with the next generation, and (d) a responsibilities-based and capabilities-based perspective according to which fathers should and can care for their children in meaningful ways.

The Ethical Call to Fathers. We believe that fathers are "called" by the next generation to meet their needs and labor for their well-being. This assumption is grounded in the ethical imperative to respond to the needs of "the other" (Levinas, 1985, 1987) and in Snarey's (1993) assertions that the relationship between fathers and children has "moral significance" because "fathers directly experience the moral claims of their children and are personally obligated to their children" (p. 357). This places an ethical obligation on fathers that must be attended to for the sake of both fathers and children (Elshtain, 1993; Erikson, 1950; Snarey, 1993). Thus, a generative ethic calls a father out of convenience and comfort to the challenging and rewarding labor of caring and responding to a face-to-face relationship with another human being across generations (Levinas, 1987; Snarey, 1993).

Generational Ethics. By generational ethics, we mean a set of expectations for care that fathers have for themselves and communities have for fathers in relation to the next generation, particularly, but not exclusively, their own children. Forming and maintaining a healthy and loving generational connection between parent and child is in itself an ethical challenge (Boszormenyi-Nagy & Sparks, 1984; Erikson et al., 1986; Snarey, 1993). But it is imperative that fathers also broaden their sense of responsibility beyond their own children and beyond young children to include the next generation of humanity. Snarey (1993) points to such an ethical interest as "the challenge to adults to create, care for, and promote the development of others, from nurturing the growth of another person to shepherding the development of a broader community" (p. 19). Much of the family literature is focused on adult expressive individualism and adult gender equity as the issues of main emphasis (Bellah, Madsen, Sullivan, Swidler, & Tipton, 1985; Demo & Acock, 1993; Fox-Genovese, 1996). Less attention has been devoted to specifying what children need and how fathers can use their time, talents, and resources to work in ways that meet those needs.

Contextual Agency. Slife and Williams (1995) argue that the vast majority of theories in the behavioral sciences are based on "assumptions of necessity." All behavior is assumed to be necessary (or determined), given the biological, physical, social, emotional, relational, and economic causes of that behavior. The ethic of generative fathering makes an *assumption of contextual agency*—that is, fathers make choices within a context of influence from a variety of factors (Slife & Williams, 1995; Williams, 1992). We believe fathers will respond better to this approach, which emphasizes their ability to choose to become the kind of fathers their children need.

Responsibilities and Capabilities of Fathering. An ethic of generative fathering assumes that men have both the obligation and the ability within themselves to be good fathers. We assume that most men can and want to become the kinds of fathers their children need for them to be (Biller, 1993; Cohen, 1987; Pruett, 1989). This will not necessarily come naturally or easily for most men, but we think that scholars and practitioners should not assume that men are inherently deficient and that only strong cultural pressures or effective clinical interventions will force them to father well (Blankenhorn, 1995; see also Chapter 1, this volume). The positive capabilities that men have to care for their children must be appreciated and emphasized to encourage generative fathering.

Fatherwork: Fathering as Generative Work

In this section, we discuss the advantage of using the metaphor of *work* to understand and encourage good fathering, and present the conceptual ethic of fathering as generative work, or what we term *fatherwork*. From our perspective, father*hood* seems like a good term to describe a cultural or social construct concerned with what fathers are expected to do and be. Father*work* is our term to describe the conduct of generative fathering. Fatherwork (like housework and homework) refers to an activity that involves a person in sustained effort. Fatherwork can be a useful term, as it sounds less scholarly than generative fathering and may appeal to practitioners as well as fathers themselves. Throughout the rest of the chapter, we use the terms fatherwork and generative fathering interchangeably.

Generative Work Versus Social Role

We agree with Ruddick's (1989) critique of contemporary thinking about fathering. She argues that social scientists tend to view fathering as more of a "role determined by cultural demands [rather] than a kind of work determined by children's needs" (p. 42). In our framework, we conceptualize fathering as generative *work,* rather than as a social role embedded in a changing sociohistorical context. We employ Bellah et al.'s (1985) meaning of work as a *calling* in which "work constitutes a practical ideal of activity and character that makes a person's work morally inseparable from his or her life" and which "links a person to the larger community, a whole in which the calling of each is a contribution to the good of all" (p. 66). This meaning of work connotes one's "life's work," or "mission," or "labor of love" rather than one's job or career. Of course, fathering, like mothering, involves routine tasks and so-called dirty work. But fathering also includes the element of joy in doing important work well and in meaningful connection with the next generation. Hence, the concept of fatherwork includes the notion of joyous labor. Indeed, often one of the most valuable ways fathers work with and for their children is through play (Snarey, 1993, p. 35). Thus, the concept of fatherwork involves a blending of Freud's and Erikson's concepts of love and work (Erikson, 1950, 1982) and conceptually links what are often conceived of as opposing spheres of commitment.

In Chapter 1, Hawkins and Dollahite briefly discussed the limitations of the social role metaphor when conceptualizing fathering. Using the metaphor of work in our thinking about fathering rather than the image of social role has some conceptual advantages. The first advantage is that it reconnects the concepts of family and labor for fathers as well as mothers (Ahlander & Bahr, 1995). Feminist scholars have reclaimed day-to-day domestic labor as real work (Thompson, 1991), making what was once invisible to family scholars highly salient to their studies. Similarly, we seek to enrich scholarship in fathering with the metaphor of work. For various reasons, our society tends to think of work only as something that is done away from home and family and compensated with money (Ferree, 1990). The argument that industrialization severed the connection between work and family care can be misleading. A more accurate statement of this line of reasoning is that economic work and family work are not as intricately intertwined as they once were (Cowan, 1987). But it does not suit scholars simply to divide the world conceptually into economic and domestic spheres with work as the exclusive activity of the former and nurturance as the only activity of the latter.

A second advantage of thinking about fathering as work is that it places fathering in a familiar context for men. Both paid employment and unpaid domestic labor are encompassed by the concept of fatherwork. It is important to acknowledge that paid employment is an important arena for father's generative work and that most men and women across time and culture see this as a central way that fathers contribute to their children's well-being. Earning money is not the only thing contemporary fathers are expected to do, however. Levant (1992), in his essay on the reconstruction of masculinity, stresses that paid work is what men have traditionally been encouraged to do and they have done it well. He argues, however, that the breadwinner ethic has passed and asks, "Now . . . what do men do?" (p. 393). We suggest they should still work. Fathers should work with and for the next generation, both in providing for their material well-being and in helping them develop and flourish in all aspects of life.

The nature of fatherwork does differ from market labor in important ways: (a) market work is product oriented whereas fatherwork is people oriented; (b) market work is usually limited by time and place whereas fatherwork is not; and (c) market work is an economic activity to earn income, whereas fatherwork is an ethical activity to provide for, be with, and care for family members. Yet, economic work and fatherwork are also similar in some fundamental ways: (a) both are what fathers must do and what most choose to do; (b) both are burdensome and ennobling, draining and energizing; and (c) both call for active, conscious, creative, adaptive effort. This is a reality that men understand and appreciate. Working hard is central to most men's lives and something that most fathers are committed to do well (Levant, 1992). Thus, thinking of fathering as work—generative work—may help men see more clearly the connection between their personal responsibilities to care for the next generation and the capabilities that fathers have within them and can continually develop.

A third advantage of thinking of fathering as work is the more helpful, transformative images invoked compared to images summoned by the role-inadequacy perspective of fathers critiqued in Chapter 1. For example, thinking of fathering as a social role suggests a set of externally prescribed behaviors that when followed facilitate the smooth functioning of a group or community. The metaphor has the weakness of being both deterministic (fathers simply do what their role demands of them) and relativistic (good fathering is based simply on changing social norms rather than on abiding needs of children). A role is a passive, interchangeable image. Thus, thinking of fathering as a social role does not invoke strong images of choice, flexibility, creativity, growth, or change. In contrast, thinking about fathering as work can produce different and more active images: sweat, daily toil, perseverance, problem solving, attention to detail, decision making, creativity, choice, skills training, education, competence, improvement, development, adjustment to change, commitment, and loyalty. When these images color our conceptions of fathering, it is easier to think about ways of strengthening fathers, valuing the good work they do, raising the standard of their work, and promoting improvement.

Of course, there are other images and metaphors that could be employed to facilitate our understanding and encouragement of good fathering, and there are advantages and disadvantages to any metaphor (Rosenblatt, 1994). The image of work may be more effective with some fathers than others. (For instance, see Allen & Connor, Chapter 4, this volume.) We encourage scholars and practitioners to develop other images and metaphors. Thinking of fathering as generative work has been a fertile beginning for us in our efforts to understand and cultivate good fathering.

A Conceptual Ethic of Fathering as Generative Work

The broad outlines of our framework are summarized in Table 2.1. Overall, in this conceptual ethic we focus on the conditions and constraints of the generative context, necessary categories of generative work, the responsibilities of and capabilities that fathers bring to their generative work, and the intended consequences of generative fathering.

Conditions and Constraints of the Generative Context

Any attempt to understand and improve fathering must be grounded in real situations and deal with the real challenges fathers face. This makes

Table 2.1 Conceptual Ethic of Fathering as Generative Work

	I *Conditions and Constraints of the Generative Context*	II *Corresponding Necessary Categories of Generative Work*	III *Responsibilities and Capabilities of Generative Work*	IV *Intended Consequences of Generative Fathering*
			Fathers Should and Can:	
A	DEPENDENCE Biophysical and Psychosocial	ETHICAL WORK ensure secure environment respond to needs and wants	*Commit* *Choose*	MORAL Fathers and Children
B	SCARCITY Material and Temporal	STEWARDSHIP WORK provide resources provide opportunities	*Create* *Consecrate*	PRODUCTIVE Fathers and Children
C	CHANGE Systematic and Chaotic	DEVELOPMENT WORK maintain supportive conditions adapt to varying situations	*Care* *Change*	MATURE Fathers and Children
D	INTERDEPENDENCE Interpersonal and Emotional	RELATIONSHIP WORK facilitate attachments encourage understanding	*Connect* *Communicate*	LOVING

theoretical sense, as opportunities and capabilities do not exist without barriers, constraints, and challenges. This approach also makes practical sense because when practitioners attempt to work with fathers it is more likely that their interventions will be received and effective if they explicitly acknowledge these factors. We propose four fundamental conditions and constraints that exist for all fathers who engage in generative fathering: (a) biophysical and psychosocial *dependence* (of the child on the parents), (b) material and temporal *scarcity*, (c) systematic and chaotic *change,* and (d) interpersonal and emotional *interdependence* among all family members. We think that most significant issues and challenges fathers face fit conceptually into one of these groups, although there may be other conditions and constraints that fathers must deal with as well. Most challenges are a result of more than one of these conditions or constraints.

Dependence. Children are brought into existence by a father and a mother. They are then dependent (biologically and materially) on adults (usually their parents) for continued existence and well-being for several years. Most continue to benefit from receiving social, emotional, economic, and other resources from their parents throughout life (Biller, 1993; Lamb, 1981). The dependency of children places moral and ethical obligations on both parents (Snarey, 1993) to provide for the next generation. In every society, parents are expected to sacrifice much for their children to ensure each child's health and well-being. The ethical response to others' needs lies at the heart of all human relationships (Buber, 1970; Lee, 1976; Levinas, 1969). The condition of dependence creates the need for what we call the *ethical work* of generative fathering.

Scarcity. Fatherwork takes place under real constraints on resources (Lamb, Pleck, & Levine, 1986). These include material resources (e.g., money, land, housing space), human resources (e.g., energy, knowledge, skills, creativity, patience), and time (Rettig, 1993). Fathers cannot give children everything they may want to. Fathers must negotiate with their partners, their children, and others and must prioritize obligations and decide on options. They must daily use scarce time, money, energy, and space that may involve choosing between self and child, partner and child, one child and another child, work and home, community and family, extended family and children, recreation and work, and so on (Dollahite & Rommel, 1993). Conditions of scarcity engage fathers to become good stewards, to produce and obtain necessary resources for a family's welfare, and to allocate such resources wisely and well to strengthen the family. This necessitates permanent commitment from parents to children as well as daily choices about allocation of scarce resources. The condition of scarcity creates the need for what we call the *stewardship work* of generative fathering.

Change. Change is constant and complex. In a sense, one does not parent the same child throughout that child's life, for the child grows, develops, and matures; goes through stages, phases, and transitions; and is constantly evolving into what he or she will become (Snarey, 1993). Development continues across the life cycle and across circumstances (Erikson, 1982). Family structure and processes change over time and families are subject to changes in the broader social, political, economic, occupational, and cultural contexts in which their members live and work (Becvar & Becvar, 1993). Thus, good parenting is complex and dynamic; there are no simple formulae for success. A framework for understanding and encouraging fatherwork, therefore, must involve helping fathers learn the principles of promoting positive change, attending to the child's development, and competently and creatively adapting to changing environmental conditions (Biller, 1993). Fathers must support the child's developmental growth and make personal adjustments as the relationship evolves. Any conceptualization or intervention that does not include change as a fundamental consideration and developmental ideas as basic components will not provide much understanding or assistance (Hawkins, Christiansen, et al., 1993). The condition of change creates the need for what we call the *development work* of generative fathering.

Interdependence. The biological and material circumstances of birth create dependence of children on parents. As Erikson (1964) suggested, however, there is as much interdependence as dependence in families, because family members depend on one another for social and emotional well-being; we all "need to be needed" (p. 130). Therefore, fatherwork takes place in a complex, dynamic, and influential web of relationships, including parental, spousal, sibling, intergenerational, and extended relationships. A framework intended to promote understanding and facilitate improvement of fathering must encourage scholars and practitioners to attend to a number of relationships and relationship issues (Grossman, Pollack, & Golding, 1988). The relationship between the mother and father resulted in the child's life so it must receive significant ongoing attention. The relationship between mother and child is usually a powerful physical, psychological, social, emotional, spiritual, economic, and legal bond that influences the child and the father-child relationship in ways that cannot be understated (LeMasters & DeFrain, 1983). The relationship between the child and his or her siblings, grandparents, aunts, uncles, friends, teachers, and others impact the relationship between the father and child (Cowan & Cowan, 1992). Fathers must create and maintain good relations with their children and with those people who are important to the child's growth and well-being, and also facilitate the creation and maintenance of good relationships between their children and those people (Cherlin & Furstenberg, 1986). Relationship issues that must be attended to include (among others) attachment, understanding, communication, love, and continuing to care for children if spousal relationships sour. The condition of interdependence creates the need for what we call the *relationship work* of generative fathering.

Categories of Generative Work

From the four conditions and constraints fathers face, we derive four critical areas of generative work having to do with ethics, resource stewardship, development, and relationships. These four areas are not assumed to be the only things that matter in caring for children over the individual and family life cycles, but together they are considered to be essential to understand and promote good fathering. Along with a brief discussion of each of the four categories of generative work, we also mention how the term *generative*, applied to the work of fathering, applies to each of the four types of work. The term is grounded in Erikson's (1950, 1982) concept of generativity, but has extended meaning as we use it. These four categories of concepts are inseparable in reality, and research on this framework suggests that they often overlap or combine in actual lived experiences (Borrows, 1996; Brotterson & Dollahite, Chapter 6, this volume; Brotherson, 1995; Dollahite et al., 1996). For the purposes of explanation and conceptual distinction, we discuss each of them in turn.

Ethical Work. Ethics permeates all areas of fatherwork, but we want to give it emphasis with its own category. Ethical work is a necessary part of fatherwork because of the prolonged biological and economic dependency that exists in human offspring. Ethical work involves a commitment to *ensure a secure environment* for the child for as long as the child needs it and choosing to *respond to the needs and wants* of the child (Biller, 1993; Elshtain, 1993). The core principle of ethical work might be expressed as acting as a moral agent for the benefit of the next generation. The ethical dimension in the concept of generative work flows from the premise that caring for the next generation is not simply a lifestyle choice or a desirable activity, but rather an ethical imperative (Erikson, 1964; Lee, 1976; Levinas, 1985; Snarey, 1993). Thus, we assert that fathers are moral agents who have ethical obligations for which they are accountable. The joy in ethical work comes from choosing to do what one has committed to do for one's children and in assisting members of the next generation in becoming moral people.

Stewardship Work. Fatherwork must be understood and promoted in a context of real material needs, tangible limits, and complex decision making. In most cases, material resources must be procured by work, and other resources (time, opportunity) by creative ingenuity. Stewardship work is a necessary part of fatherwork because of the constraint of scarcity in the family's and the father's resources (e.g., money, energy, time) and the corresponding need of children for investments of individual and family resources to help them survive and thrive (Dollahite, 1991; Dollahite & Rommel, 1993). Stewardship work involves creative, dedicated effort to *provide resources* for children and family and *provide opportunities* for children to develop and learn to care for their own and others' physical and psychosocial needs (Lee, 1976). The ethical aspect of stewardship work involves creating and maintaining a relationship with others who depend on the work of the father and keeping a sense of ethical responsibility to deal justly with the resources and the people who need them. The core principle of stewardship work might be expressed as providing resources and opportunities and dedicating one's energies for the benefit of the next generation. The resource stewardship dimension in the concept of generative work is captured by its root *generate,* which implies active creation of resources and opportunities. The joy in stewardship work comes from dedicated, creative enterprise to meet the material needs of one's children and in assisting members of the next generation to become productive people.

Development Work. Development work is a necessary part of fatherwork because of systematic and chaotic change in children, fathers, families, and other systems children interact with. Development work involves adaptive, caring effort to *maintain supportive conditions* for children's healthy growth and development (Erikson, 1988), and to *adapt to varying situations* across time and circumstance (Snarey, 1993). The core principle of development work might be expressed as promoting and supporting growth in the next generation. The developmental dimension in the concept of generative work comes from Erikson's (1950) concept of generativity, or caring for the next generation, which is the central psychosocial developmental task of adulthood. Moreover, fatherwork requires careful attention and response to the constant changing needs of children, and thus fatherwork must be understood and promoted with a sensitivity to developmental issues such as growth, transitions and stages, developmental tasks, and context (Hawkins, Christiansen, et al., 1993). The father can and should give care to the child and change as needs arise during the child's development to establish a mature relationship. The ethical aspect of development work involves helping children learn to "live truthfully" in the world, that is, become persons of integrity (Williams, 1992). The joy in development work comes from seeing one's children grow in healthy ways and in assisting members of the next generation to become mature people.

Relationship Work. Relationship work is a necessary part of fatherwork because of the condition of interdependence between parents and children. It involves devoted effort to *facilitate attachments* between the child and the people in his or her life, *encourage understanding* between the child and others, and help the child understand the needs of people around him or her (Gilligan, 1982). The core principle of relationship work might be expressed as building healthy relationships and fostering love among and between the generations in a way that attends to the deep and abiding needs that children of all ages have to be knit together with previous generations. The term generative work also highlights the obvious intergenerational relationship nature of fathering. Strong bonds are a necessary feature of parenting. Fatherwork involves relational work between unique individuals rather than simply a socially prescribed or biologically determined role, and it must be understood and promoted with sensitivity to the relational issues inherent in how unique individuals are connected to and communicate with each other across generations. Fathers can form lasting and supportive attachments with children (and others) and facilitate a child's communication with parents and other persons. The joy in relationship work comes from establishing and maintaining healthy connections with children and in assisting members of the next generation to become loving people.

Responsibilities and Capabilities in Generative Work

The central concepts in our model are the responsibilities of generative work and the corresponding capabilities that fathers bring to this generative work. These responsibilities and capabilities flow from the conditions and constraints fathers face and lead to the intended consequences of fatherwork: moral, productive, mature, and loving fathers and children. These responsibilities and capabilities represent essential things that fathers *should do, want to do, can do,* and *actually do* for their children. We believe that the needs of children call fathers to use their fathering capabilities to meet those needs (Levinas, 1985). Thus, the model assumes that fathers are able to choose (within certain constraints and contexts) to do this work.

We conceive of eight fundamental responsibilities and capabilities, which, as a heuristic for assisting practitioners and fathers to remember and use the concepts, begin with the same letter. We suggest that fathers have the ethical imperative, the desire, and the ability to *commit,* to *choose,* to *create,* to *consecrate,* to *care,* to *change,* to *connect,* and to *communicate* to meet the needs of the next generation. Certainly, these eight responsibilities and capabilities are closely related; they also have noteworthy distinctions. Similarly, although these eight responsibilities and capabilities overlap considerably and can be associated with each of the four domains of generative work, we specifically associate each domain with two responsibilities and capabilities (e.g., commit and choose with ethical work).

Commit. The responsibility and capability to commit involve the call and capacity to accept and fulfill the obligations inherent in the intergenerational relationship with a child (Bahr, 1992). Fatherwork means promising to care for, connect with, and provide for a child throughout his or her life. It means that fathers pledge to themselves, to their partners, to their children, and to their community that whatever circumstances may arise, they will, as much as possible, provide a secure environment for the next generation (Elshtain, 1993). Commitment is highlighted by both the physical support a father provides and his mental awareness and involvement with a child over a lifetime.

Choose. The responsibility and capability to choose involve the call and capacity to make decisions in day-to-day life that meet the needs of children. Fatherwork means being able and willing to determine what the child needs and then to do what is possible to provide for that need. It means that fathers must elect to forego many selfish personal opportunities to do what is best for children and refuse to let other things distract them from choosing what leads to the long-term happiness of the next generation (Gerson, 1993). Vital aspects of this concept include choosing responsibly to make hard decisions for a child's welfare and choosing how one's time and energy as a father is given to children (Brotherson, 1995).

Create. The responsibility and capability to create involve the call and capacity to meet a child's needs through work that produces or procures resources and opportunities for the child. To create for one's family is a multidimensional concept. A father who creates for his family not only creates resources for material well-being but also creatively solves problems and constructs opportunities for emotional and overall well-being (educational options, learning activities, etc.). Fatherwork means working to make space for the child in the home and family, to make money for the child's needs, to make time for the child in one's schedule. It means that fathers do not simply live with things the way they are or take what life gives to them for their children. Rather, they use their creative energies and abilities to fashion a world that their child can flourish in (Dollahite, 1991).

Consecrate. The responsibility and capability to consecrate involve the call and capacity to dedicate one's time, talents, resources, and energies to the well-being of the next generation. Consecration involves sacrifice and dedication to providing sustenance for that child; fatherwork means sacrificing to give the child what he or she needs to live and grow to maturity. It means that fathers define their most important work as *being* for the next generation and give it their best effort and energy. Thus, consecration implies more than simply to provide; to consecrate means that the father creates and maintains a deeply meaningful and, indeed, sacred or spiritual relationship with the child that transcends normal obligations and connections. For many fathers, this kind of bond with the next generation flows from religious beliefs or covenants in which children are seen as a gift from God with attendant paternal accountability for their nurturance and consequences for families and communities if fathers fail to turn their hearts to children (Hawkins, Dollahite, et al., 1993; see Malachi 4:6).

Care. The responsibility and capability to care involve the call and capacity to do for children what they need done at different stages in their development and in varying situations (Erikson, 1982). Fatherwork means attending to the important transitions in a child's life and working to provide supportive conditions that facilitate optimal growth. It means that the father does all he can to work together with his partner (or former parnter) to build a strong parenting alliance that enables them to care mutually for their children (Gerson, 1993; Snarey, 1993). Care is often signified by the physical presence and active involvement of the father, and can be seen at every stage of a child's life.

Change. The responsibility and capability to change involve the call and capacity to adapt as children grow and as the father matures in his ability to care for his children (Snarey, 1993). In other words, fathers are called to adapt to become what their children need for them to be at varying times and in different circumstances. Fatherwork means adapting to situations that arise in family life and in the broader community that may impact on one's child's welfare. It means adapting one's parenting patterns to practice developmentally appropriate ways of relating, teaching, disciplining, and working together (Lamb, 1981). It can mean making shifts in one's job or lifestyle for more time and energy with children.

Connect. The responsibility and capability to connect involve the call and capacity to form healthy, lasting attachments with a child (and his or her mother). Fatherwork means creating good relationships with children that change over time in ways that meet children's evolving needs. It means that the father does all he possibly can to maintain a happy, mutually supportive relationship with the child's mother and also to ensure that the ties that link one generation to another are maintained— even in the event of the legal or residential dissolution of the father's relationship with the child's mother. Fathers can connect with children especially through participating in various activities together, and in providing them needed support and love (Brotherson, 1995).

Communicate. The responsibility and capability to communicate involve the call and capacity to relate with children by sharing meaning with them both verbally and nonverbally (Nydegger & Mitteness, 1991). This can involve conversation, written communication, touch, and especially the ability to listen and attend to children empathically and responsively. Fatherwork means working to maintain an ongoing, evolving, improving, meaningful dialogue with one's children throughout their lives. It means fathers teach and are taught, tell and hear stories, give and receive counsel, and regularly communicate their love for their children and their pride in them (Dollahite et al., 1996). It means employing positive and helpful communication when administering discipline or discussing painful subjects. It also means simply expressing support and love.

In summary, we suggest that men have the desire, the imperative, and the ability to do fatherwork. This work involves the call and the capability to *commit* to, *choose* on behalf of, *create* for, *consecrate* oneself to, *care* for, *change* for, *connect* with, and *communicate* with the next generation.

Intended Consequences of Generative Fathering

It usually helps to know the desired goal of one's work to give it direction and to specify standards for its execution. Our framework suggests four important outcomes of fathers' generative work: moral fathers and children, productive fathers and children, mature fathers and children, and loving fathers and children. These four desired outcomes of generative fathering correspond to the four conditions and constraints fathers face. By *moral,* we mean ethical, honorable, principled, and generative in the sense of being fully committed to the well-being of others and willing and able to make the hard choices in day-to-day life that come from this commitment. By *productive,* we mean energetic, resourceful, creative, and generative in the sense of working hard and sacrificing personal comfort and wants to provide for the needs of others. By *mature,* we mean steady, balanced, resourceful, adaptive, and generative in the sense of looking beyond one's own changing needs to the well-being of others and helping others to grow. By *loving,* we mean caring, devoted, understanding, warm, and generative in the sense of creating and maintaining meaningful relationships with other people and giving of oneself for others' social and emotional needs.

To summarize, generative fathering involves (a) committing and choosing to act in ways to ensure a secure environment responsive to the needs of the next generation (ethical work), (b) dedicating one's creative efforts to provide resources and opportunities for the next generation (stewardship work), (c) caring for the next generation by maintaining supportive conditions and adapting to varying situations (development work), and (d) connecting and communicating with the next generation by facilitating attachments and encouraging understanding (relationship work)—all done with hopes of facilitating the creation of moral, productive, mature, and loving fathers and children.

Concerns and Conclusions

There are numerous approaches that can flow from a nondeficit, generative ethic. We have suggested one framework that appeals to us, namely, viewing fathering as generative work. We invite inspection and evaluation of the framework, however. We anticipate the need to inspect, add on, and remodel. For instance, children's need for meaning and purpose suggests the possibility of another category of fatherwork, perhaps called spiritual work, involving counseling a child for a meaningful purpose in life and resulting in integrity for father and child. We hope our approach is a beginning for collaborative work by scholars united in their desire to move toward an ethic of generative fathering.

One concern we have is that our framework will somehow limit the generation of other helpful approaches to understanding and encouraging good fathering. We do not believe that the metaphor of fathering as generative work is the only metaphor that could be used in moving beyond a deficit perspective. In our approach, we emphasize the sense of obligation and engagement in fathering. Others may want to stress, for example, a sense of joy and gratitude at being able to be a father or a deep sense of spiritual connection with one's child. In short, we hope scholars and practitioners will develop different approaches to understanding and encouraging good fathering that share many of the purposes of our ethic of fathering as generative work but emphasize different aspects.

Another concern that could be raised about our framework is how social scientists and practitioners can employ an avowedly ethical approach. With our approach, we seek to instill in scholars, practitioners, and fathers a sense of high expectation and moral accountability and call for the best fathers can give to the next generation. An ethical stance can seem judgmental and naive, however, in an age and culture of diminishing expectations, demands for complete tolerance, increasing forms of freedom and choice, and expressive individualism. Of course, the postmodern critics of positivist science and intervention have challenged both the possibility and the desirability of complete objectivity in the social sciences and social practices. Unfortunately, many strains of postmodernist thought leave us with no sense of any real standards or values we can hold fathers up to. So, we are left only with the vapid scholarly task of cataloging preferences and the solipsistic educational and intervention work of encouraging people to be true to themselves.

The conceptual ethic of generative fathering moves beyond this relativism to a place where scholars and practitioners can talk about the ethical imperatives involved in caring for the next generation, not with rigid, dogmatic "moralism" but with a clear call to generative responsibility with a recognition of the conditions and constraints that make fatherwork challenging. Grounding this conceptual ethic in what children require places fathering on the firm foundation of the needs of the next generation rather than on the shifting sands of societal role expectations, the fragile fault line of adult gender relations, or the engulfing quagmire of expressive individualism. We agree with Snarey (1993) that ethics and good fathering are inextricably linked and with Doherty's (1995) position that social practitioners must acknowledge and embrace the ethical and moral aspects of their work. The conceptual ethic of fathering as generative work should spur scholars, practitioners, policymakers, and fathers to ask much of men on behalf of the next generation. We believe that most fathers want to do right by their children and are up to the challenge (Snarey, 1993).

With such high expectations, the concern also could be voiced as to whether our conceptual ethic of generative fathering simply raises the standard of fathering or defines good fathering in a way that places more fathers in a position of deficiency. In other words, we might be accused of reinforcing deficit perspectives by adding to the list of obligations for fathers, increasing the distance between the actual conduct of fathering and the emerging culture of fatherhood (LaRossa, 1988). We hope this is not the case. It is true that an ethic of generative fathering can be used to clarify some of the demands and complexities of good fathering, thus making it more obvious that this is no simple task that anyone can do well with little effort or commitment. Still, with our conceptual ethic we clearly recognize the great potential and important strengths that most men bring to their fatherwork. We build our framework on a foundation of potential and encouragement that does not require a denial of gender identity or compliance with external role demands. The framework is respectful of fathers' motives and works to encourage them to act on these intentions. And because empirical literature, clinical intervention, and personal experience demonstrate that many fathers actually do these things, the framework builds on existing strengths and holds out the hope of examples of excellent fathering to assist others in their efforts to improve.

We believe that fathers from varied backgrounds and in various circumstances will respond willingly to an approach based on moral imperatives grounded in the needs of the next generation. We hope this conceptual call for fathers to bless and keep, to serve and sacrifice, and to provide for and play will nourish scholars and practitioners in their generative labors to turn the hearts of fathers to their children and to create families and communities of care.

3

An Institutional Perspective on Generative Fathering

Creating Social Supports for Parenting Equality

KATHLEEN GERSON

With the approach of a new century, vast changes in family life and gender relations have called into question some of our most deeply entrenched and long-held beliefs about men as fathers. No longer are most fathers the sole or primary breadwinner in their families. As mothers have strengthened their attachment to paid work, and divorce and out-of-wedlock childbearing have become increasingly acceptable options, men have faced new challenges about whether and how to care for a new generation. Never has there been more need for men to develop committed, caring, involved relationships with children that extend beyond the limited vision of fathers as only economic providers.

Yet conceptions of fatherhood, and the theories on which they rest, have remained curiously mired in images of the past. As demonstrated in Chapter 1, both popular beliefs and scholarly paradigms continue to stress a limited, deficit-driven model of fatherhood. In these models, men are portrayed as uninterested in parental involvement and resistant to establishing close, intimate bonds with children. Fathering is defined by what men lack rather than what they possess.

Recent research suggests that there is another, more felicitous story to tell. Numerous studies have demonstrated that many, perhaps most, fathers possess both the desire and capacity to nurture children (Coltrane, 1989; Lamb, 1979; Levine, 1976; Parke, 1981; Pleck, 1985; Pruett, 1988; Risman, 1986; Snarey, 1993). For these men, the problem is not what they lack personally but what society fails to offer them—viable avenues for developing, expressing, and enacting nurturing aspirations. Some men are able, by the sheer force of their will and commitment, to become thoroughly involved in the full range of child-rearing tasks despite the obstacles in their path. Yet, there is little doubt that social and cultural obstacles, such as the rigid "40-hour plus" workweek or the high demands of breadwinning and career building, make their task harder and discourage other fathers from following in their path. Similarly, the rise in divorce and out-of-wedlock childbearing has created new avenues for men to become estranged from their offspring. There is more reason to be optimistic about the motivations of individual fathers than about U.S. society's commitment to creating institutions that foster men's involvement.

In this chapter, I present an institutional perspective on fathering. I argue that generative fathering (Snarey, 1993) extends well beyond providing economic support to include full, and ideally equal, sharing in the whole range of emotional and physical activities of child rearing. ("Equal" does not mean "identical," but it does imply that fathers shoulder a fair and equitable share of the work of child rearing. What constitutes equitable sharing differs, of course, in different family situations.) I presume that there are substantial benefits—to women and children as well as to men—when fathers become generative (Erikson, 1959; Snarey, 1993). And I argue that most men possess the ability and desire to become committed, nurturant, and involved parents. From this vantage point, the central problem is not to describe how men are deficient as parents, but rather to explain how and why their parental involvement is either promoted or suppressed by institutional arrangements. Why is most men's participation in child rearing more limited than it could be, and what social arrangements foster more extensive involvement among a small but growing group of fathers?

Generative Fathering and Social Institutions

At first glance, the connection between generative fathering as a psychosocial concept and large-scale social institutions may seem tenuous and far-fetched. If parental attachment is such a deeply experienced bond, how can organizations far removed from the intimacy of family life, such as the workplace, make a difference? And why should changes in social institutions outside the home, such as the availability of parental leaves, flexible work schedules, or equal opportunities for women workers, affect such a fundamental relationship as that between a father and a child? As noted in Chapter 1, the ability of "macrolevel efforts" to "guide fathers in their highly personal paths of transformation is unproven, (p. 9)." What's more, the authors of Chapter 1 argue, this approach often becomes coercive and pessimistic, focusing on less responsible men and externally imposed efforts to rescript social roles.

By starting from quite different assumptions about the nature of manhood and the process of parenting, however, it is possible to construct a more humanistic and optimistic version of the institutional approach. Such an approach offers a way to integrate a generative vision of fathering with a socially grounded perspective on human behavior. Although in my approach I stress the role of institutional arrangements in shaping the degree and type of men's parental involvement, I nevertheless share a number of assumptions with the perspective articulated in Chapter 2 (see also Erikson, 1950, 1968, 1982). Like the perspective of fathering as generative work, my institutional perspective stresses men's capacities for responsible, engaged parenting rather than their lack of such capacities. I stress men's moral and ethical responsibilities to others, including women as well as children, and I focuses on the active, often-unexpected process by which men develop, or fail to develop, strong parental bonds. Yet, I propose to add another dimension to this argument. Without ignoring the lives of individual men, we also need to discover the social contexts that either encourage or thwart men's desire and ability to develop nurturing attachments, to make ethically responsible choices, and to construct mutually fulfilling bonds with their children. Without this social dimension, any theory of generative fathering is incomplete. It will neither explain developing patterns in society nor prescribe effective solutions to the problems men, women, and children increasingly face.

The Social Foundations of Generative Fathering

To paraphrase an often-stated argument about mothers, "good enough" parenting, whether by a woman or a man, cannot be coerced. For a man to become a generative father, two conditions are needed. First, he must *want* to do so. If a man does not wish to become an involved, nurturing, committed parent, then no amount of coercion will succeed. Once the desire to be deeply involved in child rearing has emerged, however, a man must be able to *act* on these wishes. At both stages in this process, social circumstances play a crucial role. They can make the difference between an aspiration suppressed and a desire fulfilled.

In my research on how men develop commitments to family and work, I found that most men experienced significant change in their orientations to fatherhood over the course of their lives (Gerson, 1993). In my detailed interviews with 138 men from various backgrounds, mostly in their 30s and 40s, I found that among men who grew up expecting to become family breadwinners with limited involvement in daily care for children, only about a third actually did so as adults. Another third avoided child-rearing involvement altogether, either by deciding not to have children or by becoming estranged from their offspring in the wake of a divorce or breakup. The remaining third of men developed a strong desire to be highly involved, or generative, fathers, a proportion strikingly similar to Snarey's (1993) four-decade study.

A similar process of change occurred among men who, as children, hoped to avoid marriage and parenthood. Only a minority of these men actually remained single and childless. Some became traditional family breadwinners who stressed the importance of providing economic support to their children but downplayed the significance of other types of parental involvement. These men expected their wives to perform most of the daily tasks of child rearing and to provide the lion's share of nurturance and emotional support as well. A substantial proportion of these men, however, like those who planned for traditional breadwinning, became involved fathers.

About a third of the men thus became oriented toward involved, generative fathering. These men did not divide domestic labor into mother's work and father's work. Rather, they defined good fathering as involving an intense emotional bond and a high level of participation. These men became, or planned to become, thoroughly involved in all aspects of their children's lives—from the day-to-day tasks of child care to the less tangible work of providing emotional support and sustenance. They were similar to the fathers with strong commitments to coparenting reported by Dienhart and Daly in Chapter 10, this volume.

Although deeply involved in their children's lives, most of the men in my research did not assume equal responsibility for child care. They made great efforts to share parenting with their partners, often in the face of considerable constraints, but they also remained "mothers' helpers" who relied on women as the primary parental caretakers. Yet, a notable group of men (slightly more than a third of the involved fathers, or about 15% of the entire group) did become "equal" or "primary parents"—they assumed equal or primary responsibility for the daily care of their children. The findings from my research underscore the contention that many men are becoming generative fathers. Whether as "equal parents" or as "mothers' helpers," these men are involved in the lives of their children to an extensive, and perhaps unprecedented, degree. The findings also show that other men are moving in another, less auspicious direction, however—away from even the limited form of fathering embodied in the breadwinning ethic. Why did some men move toward generative fathering while others moved away from it? Because these men shared similar childhood backgrounds, at least on the surface, adult experiences and opportunities likely account for their disparate developmental paths. I do not dismiss the real possibility that childhood experiences influence the development of paternal generativity (Snarey, 1993), but *adult* events and circumstances also clearly influenced both the desire to become an involved father and the ability to fulfill that desire. Although change is always experienced in a deeply personal way, such individual transformations still occur in a cultural and structural context.

Developing a Generative Orientation

Generativity is developed over the course of the life cycle (Erikson, 1959); neither males nor females are born with it. And although some men may be attracted to nurturing early in life, few men are socialized as children to view involved fathering as necessary or desirable. Indeed, in my research, less than 8% of the men developed a generative orientation in childhood, and about half of these men did not sustain that outlook over time. A strong desire to nurture and be involved thus emerges, or is suppressed, in response to developmental experiences over the course of a man's life, as he confronts his options and faces unexpected obstacles and opportunities.

What explains the emergence of a generative orientation? What has led a growing group of men to yearn for involved, nurturant bonds with children? I found that three social conditions, either alone or in combination, are especially important in nourishing a generative orientation. First, such an outlook tends to emerge when a man becomes committed to an egalitarian relationship. Although not all involved fathers are in such relationships, those who are face opportunities and pressures that do not generally obtain for other men. Work-committed women expect to share child rearing with their partners and create a context that encourages and supports a father's full participation. When a man becomes committed, often unexpectedly, to a woman who has developed strong ties to work outside the home, involved fathering comes to represent not only an emotional commitment to the relationship but also a moral commitment to fairness and gender justice. Juan, a social worker, found his own values and self-image changing as he grew more committed:[1]

> This relationship has helped me to care for other people. I think through life I've been selfish a lot, thought too much of my own well-being, and I think I'm becoming a better person, more careful with people, more understanding.

And Joe, a construction worker and aspiring actor, worked the night shift so that he could spend the days with his newborn daughter while his wife pursued a dancing career. He viewed this choice in moral, not just rational, terms:

> We agreed in the beginning that as much as possible, we share fifty-fifty. What other way can you go nowadays, the whole economy being what it is? But that's also the way it should be. Even if I had the money to take care of things myself, my wife has a calling, a vocation that she needs to fulfill and I want her to fulfill.

Commitment to a woman with strong ties to a vocation or avocation outside the home provides one type of "push" toward generative fathering, but it is not the only condition that promotes such an outlook. An involved orientation also tends to emerge when a man's paid work provides room for other avenues of personal fulfillment and expression. This can happen in two very different ways. For men with limited work opportunities, the desire to nurture can be frustrated in the workplace. Blocked mobility can prompt men to look for other sources of meaning and fulfillment, and child rearing offers a rich alternative. These men look to parenting as a form of productive labor, and like the proverbial proud mother, they come to see children as their primary identity and even a source of vicarious identity. Despite his professional commitment, Michael, a therapist who became a custodial father when his wife left to pursue a career, placed parenthood above everything else:

I can't imagine not being a father. It's the most important component to my identity. If somebody were to ask me who I am, I would happily say a single-parent dad first and then a therapist.

And Dean, having grown disillusioned with his job as a driver for the park service, developed an identity increasingly lodged in parenting, where he could see the direct effects of his contributions:

Brendon's extremely bright, and I tend to think I had something to do with it since I spent the early part of his life with him. I've had teachers tell me, "We don't know what you did, but you did something right," and to me, that's more important than the fifteen years I spent with the job. Basically my work is just a job, but Brendon is really my greatest accomplishment.

Work, however, need not disappoint to promote involved fathering. Men who turn away from highly demanding jobs to work at less time-consuming endeavors also enjoy the opportunity to become more involved fathers. Often, these men have chosen more intrinsically satisfying work over more highly paid occupations. They have sacrificed income to pursue other work goals, such as personal satisfaction in the work itself. By rejecting income maximization as the purpose of work, they begin to stress time rather than money as the essential ingredient in good fathering. Clarence, a self-employed career counselor, began to change his definition of good fathering as he became increasingly involved with rearing his girlfriend's son:

I don't want work to consume so much time that I won't have time for the family. I'm willing to make a little less money in order to have a little more time to dedicate myself to raising a kid. In other words, I'm working so that I can be with the family. The work is a means to the end. The end is a family. My primary goal is to be with the family.

There is a third and equally important circumstance that, like egalitarian commitment and a less exclusive emphasis on paid work, tends to promote a generative orientation. The desire to nurture also grows out of opportunities to develop satisfying relationships with children. Although most men are sheltered from such experiences, a growing group are facing situations in which they are allowed, encouraged, and even expected to take on expanded nurturing responsibilities. Some men move directly from the delivery room to diapering, feeding, and soothing their own newborns. Others find themselves caring for other people's children, such as nieces, nephews, and stepchildren. Whatever the setting, early and intense involvement in the care of children can trigger desires and attachments that were never contemplated nor anticipated. The opportunity to participate in a nurturing relationship thus allows men to discover generative skills and to seek gratification in developing them. This puts an interesting twist on Erikson's (1982) idea that generativity is learning to take care *of* what we come to care *for.* These men, through early and intense involvement, have been surprised by how much they come to care *for* those in their daily care. For Vincent, a self-employed businessperson, tutoring in adolescence provided an opportunity to discover nurturing skills:

> In high school, I was a tutor and just teaching those kids was an incredibly worthwhile experience. There was a great deal that came back to me. It became a common joke that a number of the girls said they would like me to be the father of their child because I was so good with kids. I learned I had something for kids, and I expect that to happen with my own, too.

When Clarence, the career counselor, became the stand-in father to his girlfriend's young son, he discovered emotional depths and resources that he had not known he possessed:

> I never envisioned having kids, but a seven-year relationship with a woman and her son got me to thinking along those lines. We became a family, and I was instrumental in raising her son. I questioned myself for the first year, but then there was a kind of rapport that developed between us, and I really felt good about the all the things we'd do everyday. I found myself going into his bedroom when he was sleeping and kissing him, looking at him in the dark for fifteen minutes. I just had to admit how much I loved him. I derived as much satisfaction out of my relationship with him as I did with just about anything in my life.

And despite earlier fears and doubts, Tom, an editor, experienced a love and devotion for his infant son that he had not anticipated. When his wife returned to work and he became the primary caretaker, he discovered unexpected competence and joy in parenting:

> Once my son was born, I was just totally crazy about him. Then Lynn went back to work after two or three months, which was just about the time I was finishing the school year. So, I spent the summer being a househusband, taking care of him every day. And that was a great experience. It just knocked me out. There was something about being a father that I suddenly discovered appealed to me. I just liked having someone that I would be in that relationship with.

These circumstances—commitment to a partner with strong ties to the workplace, work that allows and encourages more emotional and actual investment in family life, and satisfying experiences with children—tend to foster a generative orientation. Any one of them can trigger a process that leads to intense involvement in child rearing. These experiences nourish a vision of fathering that extends well beyond breadwinning to encompass all of the psychological and physical tasks required to meet children's needs. Men who did not undergo at least one of these experiences did not become involved fathers.

Although these circumstances promote a generative orientation, none guarantees that, once developed, such an outlook will be realized. Even when the desire to be involved is strong, men still face considerable social and personal obstacles to realizing fully such a goal.

Becoming an Equal Parent

There are many kinds of generative fathers, and there is surely no one correct way to achieve or implement involved, nurturing fathering. Similarly, generative fathers need not do exactly the same things or participate to the same extent as mothers. Generative fathers are thus not necessarily equal parents. Nevertheless, a father who shares fully and equally in the hardships as well as the pleasures of child care is surely an important kind of generative father. As pointed out in Chapter 2, generative fathering is *work*. It entails active labor that is often, but not always, enjoyable. Generative fathering implies extensive sharing of the burdens as well as the joys of parenthood. It is thus important to understand how and why some men become not just generative fathers but egalitarian parents as well.

There are at least three dimensions to equal parental sharing. First, it means *equal participation in the routine, prosaic work* (such as house cleaning and diaper changing) as well as the "fun work" (such as playing) of child rearing. Jack, a sanitation worker with three children, explained that genuine involvement means refusing to draw boundaries in dividing daily tasks with his wife, a chiropractor:

We've always shared breadwinning and caretaking right down the middle. That's from washing the floor, changing diapers, washing clothes, cleaning the house. I don't draw any lines as to what is men's work and women's work; work is work. When something has to be done, it has to be done.

In addition to equal participation, egalitarian fathering implies *assuming equal responsibility* for children and their care. This means moving beyond helping out and being available to feeling equally accountable for seeing that things get done. Sandy, a physical therapist, explained how he felt responsible to share decision making for the care of his young daughter:

> I felt very responsible. I wanted to be there for the good times and the bad times. I wanted to share in making decisions, which was good for my wife, too. She didn't want to make decisions by herself, and I want to be a part of those decisions. I don't want her to decide on a nursery school; let's decide together. So I don't see it as her responsibility. I see it as *ours,* because how can I say I want children and not take that kind of responsibility?

And third, egalitarian fathering means *making equal sacrifices,* such as career and leisure sacrifices, for the well-being of children. Sandy explained how he sacrificed some career opportunities for close involvement with his daughter:

> Careerwise, I've sacrificed and not pushed for certain things—things that might have required more traveling, more nights, and more time away. Sometimes, I feel like if I didn't have the family, maybe I would have pushed more. So maybe I traded off for my family. But I never second-guessed. I certainly would rather have what I have than trading off the family for a career.

Rick, a junior high school teacher, was well aware of the leisure—and sleep—he lost to be involved equally:

> It's worth it because I get something out of it, [and] the really hard part ends early. It doesn't seem like it at the time, when they get up five times in the middle of the night crying, or when you're constantly having to diaper, or when you're exhausted and you still can't go to sleep. . . . I don't feel so good about having done the laundry or gone to the grocery store sixty thousand times, but there's nothing you can do about it, and it doesn't last forever.

Men who participate fully in all of these dimensions of child rearing are rare, and not all genuinely generative fathers become equal parents. Among men oriented toward generative fathering, only around a third developed equal or primary parental ties. This should come as no surprise, as this arrangement poses demonstrable disadvantages to men and the social supports for it are notable by their absence. Although it may be easy to understand why most involved fathers do not become equal parents, the greater challenge is to discover what leads some men to do so. Why do they share the less desirable as well as the more pleasurable tasks, and why do they assume the costs as well as the benefits of nurturing? Equal parenting emerges from and depends on unusual circumstances. Most parents, whatever their wishes, face situations in which greater maternal involvement is easier and makes more sense. An economic structure that tends to pay men more than women, for example, makes it difficult for fathers to loosen their ties to paid work. So do workplaces organized around an ideal 40-hour-plus workweek and an uninterrupted male career. Divorces that typically result in maternal custody reinforce the presumption that only women can and should be primary parents. The path of least resistance leads most parents to primary reliance on the mother, even when fathers wish to be involved.

For men to become equally involved coparents, the incentives and obstacles that prevent most men from doing so need to be overcome or reversed. Three such circumstances are especially important in fostering equal parenting among men. Indeed, I found at least one of these circumstances to exist in every case of parenting equality.

One situation that fosters coparenting is the economic and emotional support of a work-committed partner. Given the pressures for working mothers to perform more of the caretaking as well, equality in parenting is more likely to emerge when the mother faces not just equal opportunities for work success but even better opportunities than the father. When a man's partner enjoys relatively higher job prospects than he, it makes more sense for him to invest an equal or greater amount of time at home. Economic incentives provide a rationale for this arrangement, but a woman's moral support is also crucial. Motivated fathers are given the opportunity and the prodding to become equally involved. Hank, a paramedic married to a hospital administrator, knew that his wife's chances of pursuing an emotionally rewarding and well-paid career exceeded his own:

> I'm a jack of all trades, a master of none, and Connie is a master at something. Financially, she makes more than me, and she has more potential. She has more degrees, and she's going for another one now, so she'll always have that potential. So if I can make arrangements—because financially we're not there yet—I'll stay home and raise the kids.

Hank knew that staying home with a child depended on his wife's support—which in turn depended as much on her preferences as his own:

I want to be there. I definitely want to be involved. And if it made me happy, she'd go for it, and she knows the kids would be looked after. But if she feels the need to be home with Junior, then she'll be home with Junior. I'm only jealous because she has that option.

Another circumstance that fosters equal involvement is the option to choose flexible work arrangements. Rigid work schedules and demanding jobs that allow little letup during the early stages of child rearing prevent even the most motivated fathers from becoming deeply involved in all aspects of caretaking. A man need not give up a high-powered career in a demanding profession to become an equal parent, nor does he need to sacrifice security and commitment in blue-collar and nonprofessional fields. Regardless of his occupation, however, he needs sufficient flexibility and autonomy at work to create the time and space for equal parenting. Only when the opportunity for flexible scheduling is available can a man, no less than a woman, integrate the competing demands of work and caretaking. Such flexibility includes at least some control over the time and place in which work is performed as well as discretion about how to balance work and family effort over the course of a career. Few men enjoy this option, but those who do are more likely to become equal parents. For Rick, the teacher, more flexible hours and summers off allowed him more family time than his wife:

I always got out of work earlier. I got out sometimes at noon, sometimes at one o'clock, two o'clock, three o'clock, and she always worked till between five and six. So I took care of the kids the lion's share of the time. I also was the one who did most of the grocery shopping and the laundry and straightening up.

Joe, the construction worker, chose the night shift so he could spend his days with his newborn daughter while his wife pursued a dancing career:

The night shift was my preference now that we have a child. We're lucky. We can trade off as far as taking care of her. If we were both working a daytime schedule, I don't know what we'd do. So I take care of her in the morning and until I have to leave for work. I wake up with the morning ahead of me, and all I have to do is look at that little face, and I feel good.

Although equal parenting remains rare, even among generative fathers, special circumstances make it more likely. Those who enjoy such opportunities tend to feel lucky. But their luck is based on specific, if unusual, social contexts.

Beyond Blame: Reconstructing Theories of Fathering

In a world of diminishing economic opportunities, where most men do not earn enough to support a family alone, generative fathering offers men new opportunities for fulfillment. As important, with most mothers of young children working outside the home and many marriages ending in divorce, involved fathering offers the best hope for meeting the needs of children and solving the dilemmas of employed mothers.

Despite these apparent advantages, the case for generative fathering has not received the attention or support it deserves. Critics across the political spectrum have tended to either ignore or denounce the possibilities for male involvement in child rearing. For some social critics, opposition to generative fathering stems from a deep distrust of so-called nontraditional family forms. These critics argue that only patriarchal families, constructed around breadwinning fathers and full-time caretaking mothers, provide the conditions necessary for raising healthy, morally conscientious children. Moreover, they assert that men, if left to their own devices, "naturally" prefer independence from family commitment and thus must be forced to assume their moral responsibilities as family breadwinners (Blankenhorn, 1995; Himmelfarb, 1994; Popenoe, 1988; Wilson, 1993).

Even many feminists do not consistently support generative fathering as an alternative to the patriarchal family. Many feminists (myself included) stress the liberating potential of equal parenting, but some feminists argue that involved fathering merely replaces one form of male dominance with another. These opponents fear that men will misuse parental involvement to deprive women of their parental rights and reassert unwarranted power over children (Chesler, 1986; Segal, 1990). Ironically, many critics on both the right and the left share a vision of men as untrustworthy, deficient in moral faculties, and in need of coercion and control, as discussed in Chapter 1.

Yet, my research suggests that these arguments rely on truncated and misleading views of men. As I have shown, many men are willing and able to be generative fathers. These men do not aspire to become control-obsessed patriarchs or deadbeat dads. Moreover, I found that the line that separates distant fathers and absentee dads from involved, generative fathers is very thin. Were it not for a different set of circumstances, many involved fathers would have traveled another path. Similarly, more distant fathers might have become deeply involved if circumstances had nourished such a stance. Nowhere is this more evident than in those cases where a man is estranged from one child (due, for example, to a bitter divorce) but closely involved with another (due to a new, more egalitarian marriage). A contentious divorce left Joe, the construction worker, estranged from a 12-year-old son, and a subsequent marriage brought him deeply into the process of rearing a second child. Close involvement with his daughter left him rueful about his distance from his son:

> When I see her going through new stages, it reminds me of him—being cheated at not having him at the breakfast table or helping him out. . . . It's sad that there will never be a way to repay him for any of the pain of the separation and that sort of thing.

There is thus strong evidence that under the right circumstances most men are capable of becoming involved, nurturing parents. One of those circumstances is egalitarian commitment. Rather than undermining gender equality, generative fathering both promotes more egalitarian relationships and grows out of them.

There is, moreover, good reason to believe that children benefit from egalitarian parenting. Far from disrupting the moral order, men's involvement in caretaking gives children a more moral vision of manhood and a wider range of adults from whom to learn responsibility and caring. Just as it is misleading to adopt a deficit model of fathering, it is also faulty to assume that all women and women only possess some special capacity to care for children. Once we cease idealizing mothers, we will be better able to recognize the benefits of shared, flexible parenting. Children get the dedicated attention of two caretakers. As Larry, a limousine driver, explained:

> Having spent a lot of time with both of us, she's not really dependent on either one of us. Mommy's like daddy; daddy's like mommy. At times I *am* her mother. It's good to switch roles. [She] don't run to mommy or run to daddy. She runs to both of us.

Children also learn that both men and women possess a wide range of abilities and interests, and they can more easily envision a variety of future options for themselves. Simon, a paramedic, thus concluded that his two sons would ultimately become more responsible husbands and fathers because they had seen their father participate at home:

They feel closer to the two of us. Maybe when they get old enough and get married, they'll start helping out in the house. They'll see mommy and daddy both did it, not just mommy or daddy.

And Sandy decided his involvement created a better domestic environment for his daughter:

> The sharing—it's a good role model for her. She sees me cook. So I'm hoping she sees that it's split and not that just the wife does this and man does that. . . . The roles here, hopefully, show her that regardless of whether I'm the father or the mother, I do different things. . . . And I hope she has a career. I hope she finds something she really likes and works for it. At least to teach her to make her own decisions.

Generative fathering entails some challenges, but it is integral to a humanist vision of equality. Such a vision rests on the recognition that the capacities men and women share as *humans* far outweigh the differences that separate them, that genuine equality entails equal rights *and* equal responsibilities, and that those opportunities and obligations must be equally accessible to *both* women and men. To create the conditions for involved fathering (and parenting equality), men and women alike must cede some previous advantages; these are more than offset by the gains— to men, to women, and most of all, to children.

Promoting Generative Fathering: Where Do We Go From Here?

Generative fathers are made, not born. They require many of the same supports that allow and encourage generative mothering. Some of these are highly personal and individual, of course. There is no one route to this end and no single form that it may assume. Nevertheless, most generative fathers depend on supportive social arrangements to nourish their desires and ease their way. Among these are financial security, time and positive incentives for caretaking, and the backing of institutions and individuals who respect the needs and responsibilities of parenthood.

If we are seriously committed to fostering generative fathering, we need social policies that encourage individual transformations and make parental involvement an attractive option for a larger group of men. To make room for daddy in the home and at the workplace, "carrots" will be more effective than "sticks." Among the many ways to nurture generative fathering, three institutional strategies stand out as especially important.

First, more flexible workplaces free of penalties for involved parents of either sex will help men and women to integrate their nurturing and breadwinning responsibilities. Second, equal economic opportunities for women will give fathers and mothers more choice about how to share and divide parenting tasks. And third, equal parenting opportunities for men will encourage strong father-child bonds so that generative fathering can develop whether or not a child's parents are married and live together.

For men to forge new paths toward parental involvement, they must overcome many obstacles along the way. Given the size and pervasiveness of these obstacles, the growth of generative fathering is more remarkable than the fact that it still remains an atypical pattern. If we wish to nurture involved fatherhood and the men who would choose it, we cannot afford to ignore the social supports on which it rests. Indeed, if we fail to build supportive institutional arrangements, generative fathering will remain a limited option chosen only by a minority. In that case, children will not be the only ones to suffer.

Note

1. The case examples quoted in this chapter are discussed in more depth in Gerson (1993).

4

An African American Perspective
on Generative Fathering

WILLIAM D. ALLEN
MICHAEL CONNOR

In this chapter, we explore the crucial work that African American[1] men perform in their families and for the next generation. We begin with a brief summary of historical factors that contributed to the current picture. Next, we outline several components of African American fatherhood and develop an Afrocentric perspective on generative fathering (Snarey, 1993), making numerous links to the conceptual ethic of fathering as generative work as presented in Chapter 2 of this volume. Our proposal includes specific challenges that African American men face and meet in their lives as family members. Finally, we briefly discuss implications of this perspective for those involved with African American families and suggest directions for future research and intervention.

Although we speak about African American fathering throughout this chapter, our interest is not limited solely to either biological or parental generativity (Snarey, 1993). Being a father is but one of several potential experiences that African American men have in families. In addition to being fathers and partners, these men are sons, brothers, and members of kin networks. Each of these experiences provides opportunities for African American men to perform generative work by engaging in supportive, nurturing family relationships. For some, being a biological father may not be the most important fathering work they do in their lives. This does not detract from the significance of being a father in the African American community. Rather, it requires us to widen our view of what constitutes generative fathering and who is able to do it. It is impossible to discuss African American fathers without placing them in the broader context of familial roles they occupy over the courses of their lives. Ethnicity (like gender and generation) is an organizing principle in family life. *How* African American men view their family experiences, *what* they are able or willing to do as family members, and even *when* they decide to do it are often directly affected by ethnicity. In this chapter, we assume that any discussion of fatherhood and generative fathering must be embedded in an ethnocultural context. This requires a basic knowledge of the history, culture, and philosophy of both the United States *and* the nations of Western Africa. Our discussion of ethnicity must also address the balance between the differences from and similarities with other ethnic groups. African American men operate from a unique historical and sociopolitical context, yet they share aspects of their past and present with men in other ethnic groups. Maintaining this balance when discussing the adaptations that African American men have made interpreting their family roles is essential if we are to avoid erroneous conclusions or inappropriate comparisons.

To borrow from Harriette McAdoo's (1988) writing about African American families, there is no such thing as *the* black family, only *black families*. This is also true of the family experiences of African American men. There is a great deal of variety in these men regarding their involvement in fathering work. Taken as a group, they are as different as they are similar. In this chapter, we hope to sensitize readers to how these similarities have combined to shape the men and their families. We also hope readers gain an appreciation of how the differences help to explain why many African American family men are quietly doing so well, although a relative (albeit more publicized) minority do so poorly.

Theoretical Frameworks Used in This Chapter

We believe that more than one theoretical perspective is necessary to fully explore generative fathering among African American males. In this chapter, we use theory in two ways: (a) to *guide* inquiry and discussion, and (b) to *explain* what we find. In studying African American families, we must avoid evaluating African American men solely based on comparisons with other ethnic groups or by pathologizing their differences from cross-ethnic referents (De Anda, 1984; Peters, 1988; White & Parham, 1990). *A culturally relevant perspective* (Allen, 1976) involves examining

African American men, their behavior, and psychosocial development in their own cultural context (e.g., Afrocentricity).

Human ecology theory facilitates our understanding of the variety of roles African American men undertake in their families (McAdoo, 1993). It suggests that these men also operate as members of larger kin networks and communities. The health (or disrepair) of these larger systems has a direct impact on men's ability to nurture and provide for their families. In addition, symbolic interaction theory is useful in uncovering meaning systems that shape family interactions. Most African American men develop a meaning for fathering work through experiences with their own fathers and father figures, engaging in paternal behaviors themselves, and through interactions with extended family and kin. They are also influenced by societal interactions (e.g., other fathers) and interpretation of cultural images (e.g., mass media). Although we do not explicitly refer to this theoretical framework throughout the chapter, we mention it here in the hopes of heightening the readers' awareness of ethnic differences in the meaning of generative fathering. Even when discussing the broad outline of what constitutes generative fathering, it is important to keep in mind the minute, interpersonal exchanges that combine either to promote or hinder this type of fathering over time. Finally, we weave a number of Eriksonian concepts into the chapter, acknowledging an intellectual debt for the term *generative fathering*.

Historical Context

Unique historical forces have acted to separate or exclude African American men from family life. Few of these have been as powerful as the combination of forced immigration and the institution of slavery during the colonial period in the Americas. The consensus of black scholars is that although the traditional family and community customs of these forced immigrants were seriously affected by slavery, their need (and desire) to develop close familial relationships endured (Billingsley, 1993; Staples & Johnson, 1993). Research demonstrates that early African American families exhibited elements of both constituent ethnicities. Thus, they included preferences for committed, monogamous relationships (e.g., marriages), biparental nurture and socialization of children, and inclusion of extended-family members (Blassingame, 1972; Guttman, 1976). As husbands, fathers, brothers, and sons, African American men often risked severe punishment for their efforts to maintain family ties

(Genovese, 1974). Slave fathers were known to have bought their wives' freedom before their own, to ensure that their children would inherit the mother's free status (Kaplan & Kaplan, 1988). Such actions were profoundly generative, in Erikson's (1950) terms, in caring for the life and freedom of future generations.

During the post–Civil War years, most long-term African American couples sought to legalize their "informal" marriages, and two-parent households represented the norm (Billingsley, 1993; Billingsley & Greene, 1973-1974; Harris, 1976). As African Americans began to migrate from the agrarian South to the urban, industrialized North, increasing numbers of men experienced temporary separation from family and kin networks as they established new roots. This voluntary migration represents another example of a potentially separating influence. The African American population of several Northern cities swelled during the period from about 1870 through 1930, with some black communities doubling in size in a single decade (Lemann, 1991). Although African American women often fared better in the new job markets due to the demand for unskilled and domestic female labor, men typically found themselves competing with recent European immigrants for jobs as skilled and manual laborers (Genovese, 1974). Thus, even in this "Great Migration," the dreams of many African American men for their family's economic independence ("off the farm") faded under the pressure of economic competition in ethnically polarized, urban industrial centers (Billingsley, 1993).

The first half of the 20th century proved to be particularly difficult for African Americans as various levels of government often supported their systematic exclusion from society. Even in locations where segregation was not legally mandated, African American men, women, and children found barriers to full participation in education, employment, and access to social services. Many of the men who served in segregated military units overseas to "make the world safe for democracy" found little improvement in their own prospects to provide for their families when they returned. By the 1930s, the United States was in the grip of the Great Depression with unemployment rates among Americans of European descent as high as 25% (in 1933). During this national calamity, the potential impact of constant, unresolved male unemployment on families became evident as reports of individual and collective despair, family disruption, widespread homelessness, and even suicides were not uncommon. Society (particularly European Americans) came face to face with the devastating impact of poverty on a global scale and the direct and indirect effects that lack of work coupled with hopelessness could produce in families.[2] Although it might be assumed that the socioeconomic environment for African Americans was even more precarious at this time, there is little evidence their family relationships were differentially *worse* than those of other ethnic groups (Billingsley, 1993; Staples & Johnson, 1993). On the contrary, it was not until the post–World War II period that the historically high rates of marriage and two-parent households among African Americans began to decline, and low rates of out-of-wedlock birth and consensual relationship dissolution began to increase (Glick, 1988).

By 1950, the tide of northward migration had begun to ebb, but there were new problems. African American veterans of World War II returned to a shortage of single-family homes in most large, Northern cities. This, coupled with discriminatory housing practices, forced many families to move into crowded tenements and housing projects. Inadequate education, lack of employment opportunities, and lack of political clout combined to disenfranchise thousands of African American men eager to find work that could help them establish and support households. In the South, ethnic tensions were more overt. The consequences for African American men who attempted to improve the lives of their families "too much" could be extremely harsh (e.g., retribution from vigilante groups such as the Ku Klux Klan). In the face of these pressures, African American families adapted, and men's involvement in family life looked surprisingly similar to that of men in other ethnic groups. In the majority of households, family members' ability to share roles flexibly and to incorporate extended family members enhanced stability and cohesion. Typically, African American men and women both shared in child-rearing duties and were employed outside the home.

This ability to adapt became increasingly crucial as the United States shifted from an industrial to a service economy during the second half of the 20th century. The African American workforce made this transition more slowly than its European American counterpart primarily due to relative lack of vocational prerequisites (e.g., educational level or special skills) and to discriminatory hiring and promotion practices. As African American men increasingly competed for fewer manufacturing jobs, African American women were relatively more successful in gaining entry-level access in the growing service economy. The net effect of decreasing male employment in predominantly blue-collar industries and increasing female participation in the service sector was increased pressure on African American families. The technology-driven transition that produced wealth for some became a major cause of expanding unemployment, household disruption (e.g., divorce, single-parent households), and hopelessness for others (Billingsley, 1993). This continues to be particularly true for young, urban men who find themselves caught between their own (and society's) expectations of establishing and caring for families and scarce opportunities to do so. Older, more highly educated men who had the requisite skills to enter white-collar and professional careers could move their families precariously into the emerging black middle-class. Even here, though, it typically took at least two wage earners in a family to maintain middle-class status.

The civil rights movement of the 1960s created new educational and employment opportunities for African Americans at a time when the national economy was also expanding. Socioeconomically diverse communities with vibrant spiritual and recreational resources were initially able to weather the storms of street crime, drug abuse, and juvenile delinquency. Some observers have blamed the flight of the black middle class for the general deterioration of many of these African American communities across the nation. In fact, the concomitant decline of blue-collar employment (particularly for men) has been at least as important not only in the erosion of these communities but in the quality of life for the families who live in them. Families in which men were chronically unemployed or underemployed might achieve some measure of stability if a female partner could work. Relationship conflict and financial distress in such families tended to increase over time, however, as evidenced by disproportionately dramatic increases in marital disruption among African Americans from the mid- to late 1960s through the late 1980s. In his book *Climbing Jacob's Ladder,* Billingsley (1993) writes: "It is perhaps ironic that the traditional family system that slavery could not destroy during 200 years may be dismantled in a few short years by the modern industrial transition" (p. 135).

Overview of the Current Situation

Methodological Issues

In the past, researchers tended to have (a) homogeneous views of blacks, (b) an obsession with abnormality and dysfunction, and (c) a predisposition toward inappropriate cross-ethnic comparisons (Jackson, 1974). Their emphasis on making global inferences based on "the most economically deficient, socially vulnerable, [and] problematic black families" (McAdoo, 1981, p. 234) produced many harmful stereotypes. The "matriarchal" black family with its "absent father" was the predictable focus resulting from a poverty of investigative concepts and methodology applied to the study of African American family life. It also is a consequence of the relentless focus on the failings of African American men to the exclusion of their accomplishments (Crawley & Freeman, 1993).

Given the obstacles that African Americans have overcome over the last four centuries, one might expect there to be more interest in the successful adaptations they have made in their family life and relationships. Recently, increasing numbers of studies have explored strengths and success in African American families (Crawley, 1988; Oliver, 1989). Researchers have begun to document the unity, stability, and adaptability of the African American family (Mirande, 1991). Despite these increases in the quantity and quality of research on African American family life (Taylor, Chatters, Tucker, & Lewis, 1990), the various familial experiences of African American men have remained largely unexplored. One explanation for this phenomenon is that family researchers have typically focused on the experiences of women and children, and women's reports of family life. Attempting to explicate paternal involvement by asking mothers what the fathers do (or do not do) seems an incomplete strategy, at best. This is not because women are unfamiliar with their families or the dynamics within them. It is because a male perspective on the family, even if different, *is equally valid*. A comprehensive understanding of family life requires both perspectives.

In exploring the experiences of African American men in families, researchers must also avoid two conceptual errors concerning the impact of ethnicity (Mirande, 1991). The first error is to ignore the potential effect of ethnicity, assuming that all fathers are alike—"a father is a father." This approach negates the possibility that there might be *unique* positive or negative consequences of ethnic-group membership. Conversely, the second type of error is the assumption that ethnicity has the *same* effect on all members of a given ethnic group. This problem has been discussed as the "theoretical myth of sameness" (Hardy, 1989). Researchers who make sweeping comparisons of ethnic groups using sophisticated statistical analysis run the risk of missing subtle but significant intragroup differences. These differences may hold the key to discovering differential outcomes for different fathers in the same ethnic group.

The lack of research on the family experiences of African American men is particularly problematic considering the general public's lack of knowledge about African American families. Without accurate information, negative stereotypes depicting African American men as neglectful, abusive, dependent, or absent proliferate. In the social sciences, the reluctance to undertake credible scholarship about African American fathers may be the result of many researchers' misconceptions about African American men. Researchers' misgivings about black men's suitability for or interest in family life often emerge from the deeper societal ambivalence about ethnicity and "race relations."

The Construction of African American Manhood and Fatherhood

One departure point for an exploration of how African American men think of fathering work is to examine their definitions of manhood. Hunter and Davis (1993) have hypothesized three major components of African American men's sense of manhood, components implicitly linked to Erikson's (1950) concept of generativity: *identity or self-development, spirituality,* and most important for this discussion, *family.* Family is further distilled into the sense of responsibility and connectedness, a desire for equity in gender relations, and a commitment to fulfilling family role expectations. The finding that African American men view families and family relationships as central to their definition of manhood is not unique. Research in a variety of geographic locations (Connor, 1986; McAdoo, 1986), economic circumstances (Allen, 1981; Bowman, 1993), and across the life span (Connor, 1995; Allen & Doherty, 1995) also cite the family as a primary source of meaning in African American men's lives.

Hunter and Davis (1994) found that the central challenge of manhood was what these men expected of themselves, as much as family role expectations of others, their worldview, and their sense of spirituality. Significantly, family responsibility and economic viability were "linked," suggesting that providing economically is based on family or kin group promotion rather than individual achievement. This suggests that African American men must balance societal gender norms (e.g., aggressive, individualistic) with culturally specific expectations (e.g., cooperation, extended-family orientation). This balance creates a tension that illustrates a key element of ethnicity's impact on the family life choices African Americans make.

McAdoo (1993) uses human ecological theory to describe four major aspects of paternal generativity among African American men. These include being a provider, being a decision maker, child socialization, and being a marital partner. Being a provider for the family is foremost among these and refers to supplying both material and emotional resources. The majority of African American men list economic support of their families as an essential component of fathering, despite structural barriers to full participation in the workplace (Comer, 1989; Taylor, Leashore, & Toliver, 1988). These barriers are both direct (e.g., job discrimination, lower pay) and indirect (e.g., provider role strain, family economic distress).

McAdoo also identified fathers' involvement in socialization of children as a primary task for these men. This theme has been cited by others describing the importance of African American children developing the skills to facilitate their survival in a predominantly European American society (Willie, 1976). Along with this "bi-cultural socialization" (Crawley & Freeman, 1993), fathers provide their children with Afrocentric socialization on issues such as the validation of collectivity versus individualism (Asante, 1987; Oliver, 1989). Several studies have shown African American fathers to be warm, supportive, and emotionally expressive with their children (Price-Bonham & Skeen, 1979; McAdoo, 1981). This is true for men across SES levels (Allen, 1981; Bowman, 1993) and across the life span (Allen & Doherty, 1995; J. McAdoo, 1988).

These men also view child care as a responsibility to be shared by both parents (Cazenave, 1979; Hyde & Texidor, 1988). Egalitarian decision making also seems to be important to many African American men (Connor, 1995). Greater involvement in decision making and child socialization appear to promote men's effectiveness at fathering (McAdoo, 1993). Moreover, many of the middle-class fathers in these studies perceived themselves as more expressive, involved, and egalitarian than their own fathers. These perceptions may confirm broader socioeconomic and generational shifts in the culture (and conduct) of fatherhood (LaRossa, 1988).

An Afrocentric Perspective on Generative Fathering

In this section, we present an Afrocentric perspective on generative fathering and our thoughts on its significance for practice and policy. We use the Eriksonian concept of generative fathering generally, and more specifically the ethic of fathering as generative work discussed by Dollahite et al. in Chapter 2 of this volume as a starting point. We believe that generative fathering among African Americans has four major components. The first of these is a set of *prerequisites* that men must acquire and maintain. These include the *motivations* to be in a family, to provide for its material and emotional needs, and to nurture and socialize the next generation. These motivations are linked to African American men's belief in the centrality of family membership and stewardship mentioned earlier. Other prerequisites are the *skills* that promote healthy family interaction and parenting, such as maturity, patience, and the abilities to tolerate and resolve conflict. The ability of many African American men to enter into egalitarian decision making with their partners is an example of such a skill. Note that even in situations in which the partners do not remain in a committed relationship, this set of skills is vital for effective, respectful coparenting and the well-being of children (as well as the adults involved). Finally, *energy* is a prerequisite without which little effective parenting of any sort can take place. We think of energy primarily in terms of the capacity to engage other family members in nurturing, mutually enhancing relationships, but we might also consider the material resources that men provide to their families as potential forms of energy (e.g., a paycheck can be converted into food, clothes, or shelter) or the spiritual resources they bring to the family (e.g., belief in a supreme being or a general sense of agency and optimism).

The second component is the development of *patterns of involvement.* Lamb, Pleck, Charnov, and Levine (1987) have described paternal involvement as a combination of *interaction, availability,* and *responsibility.* In an Afrocentric model of generative fathering, we place particular emphasis on responsibility, and being responsible for one's family transcends providing for their material needs. Paternal responsibility also means remaining emotionally available for one's partner even when beset with work or community-related problems, or finding unconventional ways to interact with a child if not in the household. As one group of young African American fathers summarized it, the challenge of developing patterns of involvement is the challenge of "being there" (Allen & Doherty, 1995).

The third component is the sense of *competence.* Fathers, stepfathers, grandfathers, uncles, or brothers who feel confident of their value to their family and kin develop self-confidence in their ability to provide and nurture. The more African American men labor with and for their families, the more they develop a sense of competence (Erikson, 1950). Conversely, it should not be surprising that when these men are unable to provide for their families or are frustrated in their efforts to nurture their children, they feel and become increasingly incompetent. We believe this is true for the entire spectrum of family work and roles that African American men do and take. Competence is also a *dynamic* component in that changes in family structure and circumstance call for new competencies to match these changes.

The final component, *commitment,* is both a prerequisite and a product of competent involvement over time. Commitment is related to motivation, as in African American men's sense of familial responsibility discussed earlier. We now add to this the element of "calling" (see Chapter 2) to arrive at our idea of commitment. Unfortunately, even when ethnic influences promoting collectivity and kin group promotion are strong, social (e.g., prejudice) and structural (e.g., unemployment) barriers can frustrate African American men's attempts to realize their paternal and family aspirations. This is when a sense of commitment, as in a willingness to sacrifice, and a faithfulness or fidelity to a self-chosen value system (Erikson, 1964) become crucial. Men who understand the sacrifices of their ancestors and who have thought seriously about what kind of ancestors they themselves want to be can make a commitment to generative fathering.

The four components are related in a circular fashion. The prerequisites facilitate the development of men's family involvement. This involvement in turn leads to an increasing sense of competence. Finally, as levels of involvement and competence rise, African American men potentially experience a synergy between their ideals for family life and their achievement as custodians of their families. This synergy enhances their sense of commitment to generative fathering. That commitment has the power to motivate, to stimulate acquisition of new skills, and to replenish energy. Along with the link between commitment and motivation, there is a potential link between competence and skills. Men who feel competent about their work in families may be more likely to attempt to acquire new skills or adapt old ones. As they master these, they continue to enhance their sense of competence.

Challenges for African American Men

The use of the metaphor of work, suggested in Chapter 2, in connection with an Afrocentric perspective on generative fathering requires some caution, however. Many black men have come to associate work with social vulnerability (e.g., to ethnic and class bias) and inevitable cultural conflict. Regardless of their socioeconomic standing, work for these men often conjures up images of hassles with "the man" and having to "play the game." Thus, if we use work as a descriptor of African American generative fathering, we must be sure to incorporate African American men's family aspirations in the description. The work of men in families must be understood as the actualization of their innate desire for family involvement, as opposed to some externally defined or imposed social role. Otherwise, many African Americans will see the use of this term as a trivialization of the sacred obligations that bind family members to each other.

Staples (1994) discusses the conflict between black family ideology and actual family arrangements. Socioeconomic conditions can impede the actualization of Black aspirations for a traditional family life and roles, and in some cases push African American men out of their families. LaRossa (1988) describes an asynchrony between the culture and conduct of fatherhood as a way of understanding the apparent contradiction between what U.S. men believe fatherhood means and what they actually do as fathers. As with fathers in other ethnic groups, this divergence can be seen in the culture and conduct of African American fathers. Their conduct (what they do) is more susceptible to limitations imposed as direct or indirect results of ethnicity, however. To provide for the material needs of a family, one must be able to qualify for a job, secure a position, stay employed, and eventually be promoted to gain higher income. At each of these four stages, ethnicity can become a critical success factor, and ethnicity's effect on the conduct of fatherhood may be more pronounced as economic or familial resources are reduced. Therefore, it should not be surprising that the African American men who appear to show the widest asynchrony between their culture and conduct as fathers are often the impoverished, struggling in the nation's inner cities.

The probability of consistently providing economically for children is directly related to employment opportunities and adequate compensation for that employment (Leashore, 1986). Fundamental changes in the U.S. workplace have jeopardized disproportionately more African American men's ability to provide for their families (Billingsley, 1993; Wilson, 1987). This is due to historical trends of oppression resulting in diminished educational and employment opportunities for African Americans, coupled with the decline of high-paying jobs for unskilled labor. Increased "provider ability" (and provider role capability) have been demonstrated to lead to more effective provision of familial support (Connor, 1986; McAdoo, 1993). Conversely, decreased or frustrated ability to provide leads to role strain and vulnerability to personal distress and family (relationship) problems (Bowman & Saunders, 1988). In other words, *men who can provide for their families are more effective fathers.*

Factors That Promote (or Hinder) Afrocentric Generative Fathering

Several factors affect African American men's ability to perform generative fathering. *Biculturalism* can be a key asset for men living in an ethnically diverse society. We define biculturalism as the ability to embrace and profit from membership in two divergent cultures. Biculturalism does not mean abandoning one culture or absorption into another; the ideal is for both constituent cultures to be accessible and useful. African American men who are comfortable being bicultural gain an advantage in social situations that require social exchange between members of different ethnic groups. They are also better prepared to teach their children how to cross cultural boundaries successfully.

We also believe that the work of generative fathering is inhibited when African American men adhere too tightly to Eurocentric standards of masculinity, as stereotypically defined by individualism, accumulation of wealth, and power (Sum & Fogg, 1990; Wilson & Melendez, 1986). African American men must also incorporate Afrocentric standards such as collectivity, awareness of African heritage, and belief in the continuity of life (Asante, 1989; Oliver, 1989). It is probable that the African American fathers who have been most successful at meeting the challenges posed by parenting in a multiethnic society are those who have effectively used strategies suggested by their African heritage. Thus, a father whose sense of family or kin group obligation is stronger than his sense of individual autonomy may more readily seek help from his primary partner and extended-family members. The more "autonomous" father, though seemingly acculturated to Western values and priorities, might choose to leave a family under emotional or economic duress. Such action may stem from a misdirected sense of personal agency ("I'd be better off without them") or to relieve his family of the burden created by his inability to provide for their needs ("They'd be better off without me").

Consistent with Eriksonian theory, the relationship between a father and the mother of his children is potentially a major determinant of his ability to perform generative fathering. One of the reasons for this is that African American men's self-esteem and relationship satisfaction appear to be affected by the quality of the marital and parental relationship (McAdoo, 1993). Another reason is that a father's problematic relationship with the mother of his child can hinder or preclude father-child interaction (McLoyd, 1990). Such adult relational conflict may also have negative consequences for the self-esteem and relationship satisfaction of his partner (Broman, 1988) and provide a poor model of intimate relationships for his children. Thus, African American men interested in generative fathering must develop intimate, or at least cooperative and respectful, relationships with the mothers of their children if they are to realize their aspirations of being nurturing, supportive fathers.

Generative fathering is often difficult work because fatigue and self-doubt can become constant challenges. The constant drone of negative messages about ethnic heritage and one's ability to be involved in family life represent additional obstacles African American men must overcome. Such messages erode self-confidence and simultaneously devalue the potential of other African American men to care for their families (Connor, 1986). To counter this, African American men have developed adaptive strategies that enable them to experience success as members of families and kin networks (Harris, 1992). "Cool pose" (Majors, 1987) is an example of an intracultural support mechanism that has often been misinterpreted as "hypermasculinism" although it more accurately represents an adaptation to oppression and prejudice. These and other adaptations bolster our view that African American men are crucial resources for each other. The fellowship experienced in fraternities, business associations, barbershops, or 12-step groups can promote generative fathering because these peer interactions can facilitate mutual support, mentoring, and renewal.

Fellowship also provides opportunities for transgenerational interaction. Elders are our closest links with our ancestors, and they keep us aware of past sacrifices that enable present achievements. Older African American men often bring historical perspectives to contemporary challenges owing to their greater experiential base. Many elders develop a sense of integrity (Erikson, 1950) with their ability to balance hope and wisdom against despair, combining optimism with pragmatism. Men who acquire this skill provide effective role models to children who must deal with the ambiguity that is inherent in ethnically polarized societies. These men are able to discuss ethnocentrism with their children in ways that avoid imposing a depressing sense of futility. In this generative activity, the teaching of important lessons nourishes both fathers and children (Erikson, 1964).

Generative African American fathering is an ethic with an emphasis on agency over victimhood. It fosters empowerment through love and nurture as opposed to devitalization through cynicism and bitterness. Men who embrace this ethic exude a sense of pride about work and responsible provision. The first author's father was a blue-collar machinist, a member of a trade union who never went to college. Yet, he never spoke with anything but pride about what he did or about his ability to feed, clothe, and provide shelter for his family of eight. This sense of pride in work and making a way for oneself was impressed on each of his six children. Each of them went to college, became gainfully employed, and continues to be successful. A similar situation exists for the second author, whose father was educated through the eighth grade and worked as a janitor. He also took pride in his work and shared his philosophies that "No work can hurt you" and "You can learn about life and yourself from whatever work you do." All of his children possess advanced university degrees.

Implications for Clinicians and Social Service Providers

There are several strategies based on this model of generative fathering that workers involved with African American families will find useful. Practitioners working in the mental health services need to examine their aptitude for working with African American men before either accepting referrals or attempting to acquire new skills in "multicultural" therapy. Crawley and Freeman (1993, p. 28) have posed several trenchant questions for professionals working with African American men, which we paraphrase here:

1. Are my interactions and interventions informed by the traditional psychosocial paradigms or am I using a schema that encompasses the realities of African American men's experiences?
2. Are my interactions and interventions informed by paradigms that suggest pathology, deviance, or inferiority or, rather, a search for strengths and positive attributes from an Afrocentric perspective?
3. What aspects of my interaction facilitate or block African American men's opportunities for empowerment (e.g., encouraging ethnic pride and racial self-identification)?
4. Do I help African American men identify opportunities to learn from each other (e.g., young and older males across and within cohorts) about survival and thriving as African American men?

Along with the issues raised by the questions above, we would emphasize the continuing need for service providers to increase their understanding of ethnicity's role in family life and development. This should include an awareness of one's own ethnicity, so that ethnocentric biases do not get in the way of promoting healthy models of male family involvement for African Americans. Although women and children typically seek (or are referred to) therapy initially, men are usually involved in these families as well. Conversely, men may come to or be mandated to attend therapy to address issues not directly related to family relationships (e.g., work-related problems or chemical dependency). It is crucial that service providers make the connection between these specific presenting issues and their broader ramifications for family relationships if they are to be helpful to African American men *and their families*. This approach can be summed up in the question, *"To what extent do my clinical interactions with African American men promote or hinder generative fathering from an Afrocentric perspective?"*

Implications for Educators and Managers

The worlds of academia and employment have not always been welcoming to African Americans. Although structural barriers for entry into these worlds continue to erode, educators and managers need to be aware that some African American men have had to make adaptations to survive institutional racism. Sometimes, these adaptations highlight real differences in value systems and priorities between African American men and those in other ethnic groups. Too often, however, intraethnic support mechanisms such as "cool pose" (Majors & Billson, 1993), "machismo" (De La Cancela, 1994), or *"la cara de palo"* (Thomas, 1987) have been misinterpreted as aggression, hostility, and mental instability by teachers, managers, and others in a position to evaluate and promote African American men. These misinterpretations, in turn, have had deleterious effects for these men's prospects in school and in the workplace. They have also negatively affected the quality of life for the men's families. We believe that educators and employers must understand and accept the reasons African Americans have had to make such adaptations. In doing so, they may gain greater insights into how African American men can be motivated and encouraged to be successful without having to resort to the adaptations in the first place.

Implications for Public Policy Makers

Government policies, particularly those related to employment and education, can have disproportionately greater impact on African American men. Seemingly minor changes in the tax code or in social service funding can wreak havoc in the lives of African American men supporting families. For example, raising the age of eligibility for retirement with full benefits from 65 to 67 could have more negative consequences for

African American men because of their shorter life expectancies (Hill et. al., 1993). Because many such men would not live long enough to collect full benefits, their families would also be affected.

Recent attacks on the nation's affirmative action programs highlight another ill-considered and potentially destructive change in public policy. Although there are legitimate criticisms of its implementation, history clearly shows that by removing prejudicial barriers in education and employment, affirmative action has provided opportunities to many African American men that would not otherwise have been provided. These opportunities have been leveraged by African American men and their families to a more equitable footing with the rest of society based on true merit and social justice (rhetoric about "quotas" and "reverse discrimination" notwithstanding). Without an honest approach to the continuing problem of ethnocentrism, and particularly the societal consequences of institutional racism, the dismantling of affirmative action will simply serve to jeopardize the lives of black families and the moral health of the nation.

Conclusion

In this chapter, we have presented an Afrocentric perspective on generative fathering. Although biological fatherhood is the most prominent type of such work, we hope that readers have gained an appreciation for the wider contributions that this description suggests African American men can make to their families. Further research is needed to increase our knowledge of what promotes generative fathering and how best to assist men to do more of it. In studying men's involvement in families, it is crucial that a male perspective be incorporated. This is especially important if we intend to draw deductions from the data that would prescribe how such involvement could be improved. Researchers must endeavor to reach a wider variety of subjects, not just men who are most accessible to study (e.g., clinical populations). Researchers should also incorporate a greater awareness and understanding of ethnicity, particularly when crossing ethnic boundaries. Collaboration between researchers and disciplines may be useful in this respect. Finally, the search for theories and models of successful adaptation should continue to replace the search for explanations of failure. All of these may increase the cost of research, but the resulting insights will more accurately reflect the subjects' lived experiences and their potential for generative fathering.

The African American community is primarily responsible for socializing, educating, and energizing its young men to function as productive family members and citizens. The rest of society must share in that responsibility, however, as these communities are embedded in a national context. Moreover, as various levels of government and the private sector have participated in and profited from the systematic oppression of African Americans, these institutions must become part of the solution to the social problems that inhibit generative fathering. During this time of calls for personal responsibility, others may object to our holding society responsible for its role in many of the current problems African American men face. Whether we like it or not, all of us (regardless of our ethnicity) are bound together by the challenges and opportunities we face as a nation, and by our common destiny. Thus pragmatism, if not morality, should motivate us to address the social problems that hinder African American men's family generativity.

We do not believe that our definition of generative fathering places additional burdens on African American men. Rather, we may need to reexamine what we as black men do in our family lives to promote generativity. This reappraisal might involve doing less of certain things we are currently doing and more of others. It might require developing even more confidence in our ability to be generative fathers and an increased capacity to support each other as men involved with families in the face of contradictory social stereotypes and media messages. Our definition is based on the assumption that African American men have both the individual and collective prerequisites to develop patterns of family and community involvement. These patterns have the power to promote resiliency in children as surely as they can reclaim neighborhoods. We choose in our definition to emphasize the competence of African American men, prosperous and poor, young and old, over the past 400 years. Without this competence, so many of us and our families would not be doing as well as we are. At the same time, given this collective, almost archetypal, competence, it should be considered a national disgrace that so many African American families are doing so poorly. We believe this situation speaks to the continued potency of institutional racism that some have dismissed as no longer important.

Finally, our definition of generative fathering is buoyed by the commitment that African American men feel to their partners, children, and kin. Regardless of one's views of the organizers, the 1995 march in Washington, D.C., of "a million black men" was, in a tangible sense, a testament to this sense of commitment. We believe that the African American men from all backgrounds and economic circumstances who participated in this event were eager to demonstrate a commitment to what has been described in these pages as generative fathering. As was pointed out by several of the event's speakers, this commitment was evident irrespective of participants' affectional orientation, their current paternal or relational status, or the level of satisfaction in past or present family relationships. The concern for and need to be involved with the next generation is an integral component of the definition of African American manhood. The Afrocentric perspective teaches us that it takes an entire village to raise children. Therefore, generative fathering is crucial work for all men, African American and otherwise, now and in the future.

Notes

1. We use the terms *African American* and *black* interchangeably in this chapter. We have a slight preference for the former because it captures the essence of our dual heritage, but because several of our referents use the latter, we have chosen to use both.

2. It is unfortunate that ethnic prejudice and a diminished sense of history prevent us as a nation from being alarmed at rates of unemployment among African American men that typically hover around 12%, but that for young men (aged 15-25) are consistently reported in the 25%–27% range (Larson, 1988). These same young black men are the husbands and fathers of tomorrow's black families.

5

Generative Fathering

A Historical Perspective

ROBERT L. GRISWOLD

In the May 2, 1925, edition of the *Saturday Evening Post*, the former boxing great Gentleman Jim Corbett contributed a piece titled, "If I Had a Son." After lamenting that he and his wife had never had children, he outlined his vision of the father he would like to be. To his mind, affection, commitment, and companionship made up the essence of good fathering: "By all means in your power," wrote Corbett, "get him to feel that he can always talk to you about things that trouble him, as man to man, and not in a shamefaced way." Ultimately, even the most personal of matters might be discussed between father and son: "If he has learned that he can talk freely and frankly with his dad maybe he will also bring his problems of the body to you. And he should be able to learn about them from you with greater safety than he can from the boys at the corner" (quoted in Griswold, 1993, p. 88).

Corbett clearly had in mind what is being termed in this volume as generative fathering (Erikson, 1950; Snarey, 1993; see also Chapter 2, this volume). Nor was he alone: In the closing decades of the 19th century, a new conception of masculinity called men to the home and to active fathering. Influenced by the emergence of more companionate family relations and new assumptions about manhood, as well as by changing class and residential patterns, middle-class men at the turn of the century finally had the income and the leisure to construct a new conception of fathering. The emphasis was on mutual companionship, growth, and enrichment: Men would learn the joys of nurture, children the joys of fatherly solicitude and good cheer. Friendship and play, not obedience and discipline, would define the ideal paternal relationship with children. It had not always been so. Although men have always occupied a prominent place in their children's lives, the terms of involvement, and hence the nature of generative fathering, have changed over time. Historically, fathering has had less to do with companionship and personality formation than with breadwinning, vocation training, and religious instruction. Such obligations and responsibilities shaped men's relationships with their children, provided a coherent sense of masculine identity, and fashioned the lineaments of family authority for both men and women as well as parents and children. This vision of fatherhood, although never static, changed decisively in the late 19th and early 20th century as family experts—drawn from social work, sociology, psychology, home economics, and psychiatry—articulated a new vision of fathering that emphasized father-child companionship and men's contributions to the development of their children's personality and sex role identity. This conception of generative fathering, in turn, lasted until the 1960s, when a massive influx of women into the labor force coupled with the rise of feminism once again transformed the nature of generative fathering, this time in directions that offered unique opportunities—intimate day-to-day relationships with children and a sharing of hands-on child care with spouses—as well as troubling challenges that ranged from balancing work and family obligations to conflicts between parents with different ideas of how to care for children.

Colonial America

The prominence of men in their children's lives is not difficult to find in colonial America. Although the experience of Puritans, Anglicans, whites, blacks, rich, and poor cannot be conflated, historians agree that fathers played a crucial role in the lives of colonial children. Puritan fathers, of whom we know the most, supported their children materially but also spiritually and intellectually. A man who neglected the educational and religious life of his children disqualified himself as a good father. Nor could a good father leave the discipline of children to his less trusted, more pliant and emotional wife. Indeed, Puritans' fiercely ambivalent views about women meant that fathers played the critical role in New England child rearing. It was fathers who led the family prayers and

Bible readings; who taught sons and daughters lessons on death, damnation, and salvation; and who began to teach sons at an early age the importance of finding their vocational "calling." As children grew older, fathers helped them find apprenticeships, places of service, and ultimately marriage partners. Through it all, fathers had a clear duty to show by example how the family was truly a "little commonwealth," the foundation of society and a cornerstone of all rightly constituted authority (on colonial fatherhood see Frank, 1995, chap. 1; see also Demos, 1982; Griswold, 1993; Pleck, 1987; Rotundo, 1985; on 19th-century manhood see Rotundo, 1993).

Space prohibits a detailed discussion of variants to the New England pattern, but research suggests that colonial fathers played an active part in the lives of their many children and that the Puritans likely had less openly affectionate relationships with their children than those men of more moderate religious temperaments. Although Puritan evangelicals emphasized the venality of children and the need to crush the will, others, especially among the literate and genteel, increasingly saw children as malleable innocents whose character needed shaping, not breaking. By the 18th century, in fact, family life was undergoing fundamental changes that would reshape the nature of fatherhood. The paternal dominance and evangelical authority that infused the Calvinist vision of family life in the 17th century gave way in the next century to an emphasis on more affective, less instrumental family relationships. Hierarchy and order, the watchwords of older forms of paternal dominance, gave way to a growing emphasis on mutuality, companionship, and personal happiness (see Mintz & Kellogg, 1988).

The deepest roots of the "new fatherhood" likely emerged sometime in the mid-18th century among relatively affluent colonists. Toys, books, games, naming patterns, even the structure of homes reflect new concern for children, now conceived not as "infant fiends" but, as Isaac Norris of Philadelphia wrote in 1746, "little Babes [who] have yet no Characteristick but their innocence" (quoted in Griswold, 1993, p. 12). Southern men echoed such sentiments and emphasized the delight they took in their children's antics. Isaac Avery's pride in his 4-month-old son's accomplishments and good looks came through in a letter to a friend: "Thomas Lenoir Avery, a young gentlemen . . . can sit alone, laugh out loud and cut other smart capers for a fellow of his age and is the handsomest of all [our] . . . children" (quoted in Griswold, 1993, p. 18; see also Smith, 1980). Other evidence suggests that 18th-century Southern fathers shared with their Northern counterparts a delight in the playfulness of their children, lamented separation from them, frequently gave them gifts, worried about their health, celebrated their accomplishments, and looked after their academic preparation. Although important differences existed between the two regions—principally in the Southern emphasis on the inculcation of honor—middling-class men from both regions increasingly lived in child-centered families.

The 19th Century

The story of generative fathering from the close of the 18th to the end of the 19th century is anything but simple. As economic changes marginalized men's place within families, cultural forces simultaneously heightened their standing. On the one hand, the American Revolution and the rise of a commercial, industrial economy generated a series of social and ideological changes that politicized motherhood and marginalized fatherhood. On the other, cultural developments that began in the antebellum period but accelerated toward the end of the 18th century underscored men's importance to their children. By the close of the century, a new mode of generative fathering was clearly emerging.

The Revolution and its aftermath certainly helped to shift the cultural focus from fathers to mothers (Bloch, 1978). During these years, the prepolitical woman became the "republican mother" entrusted with the socialization of children, especially sons, to proper republican adulthood. Mothers, not fathers, were entrusted with molding the character traits in children on which a free nation depended: By serving their families, mothers would serve the state (Kerber, 1980; Norton, 1980). Although republican motherhood waned in the early 19th century, the centrality of mothers to family life did not. They became the target of an outpouring of child-rearing advice that emphasized mothers' crucial role during infancy, the joys and importance of breast-feeding, the danger of wet nurses, and the malleability of the child's character. Antebellum moralists entrusted mothers, not fathers, with creating a loving, affectionate environment in which their children's essential goodness unfolded. The century of the mother was at hand.

The rise in the North of a commercial, later industrial, society likewise undermined paternal influence. The relative decline of farming and artisanal work coupled with the rise of factory employment and office work meant that increasing numbers of men became breadwinners who commuted to work while their wives assumed direction of the household. From this perspective, men's absence from the home for long hours at a time became the mark of modern fatherhood, and though men might try to forge emotional, companionate bonds with their children, their work sabotaged such efforts. Whether one was a deskilled artisan who could no longer pass his craft to his son, a hard-pressed farmer driven into a mill town to survive, or an upwardly mobile office manager trying to squeeze a few more work hours out of the day, the changing economy of the 19th century might well have worked against generative fathering.

Or so it seems. Yet, although breadwinning became crucial to male identity and women became ever more identified with the home, fatherly nurture—generative fathering—secured cultural space in which to develop. It found expression as early as the 1830s and 1840s, as the historian Stephen Frank (1995) discovered, in the ideal of "Christian fatherhood" and later in the century in the works of medical writers who connected fatherhood to manliness and biological well-being. In the first variant, moralists called men back to the home and lamented their long hours in factories and offices, their excessive involvement in politics, and their proclivity to spend leisure time in the company of other men (Frank, 1995; on male absence from home, see also Carnes, 1989; Griswold, 1982). A good father, went their advice, provided for his family; helped the mother shape the character of the children; and prepared his offspring, especially sons, for adult life. Along the way, a father should take time to enrich his children's education and to play with and become his children's companion. All of this, the moralists made clear, would redound not only to the benefit of the children but would also help invest a man's life with meaning. Thus, as early as the mid-19th century, social thinkers saw generative fathering in therapeutic terms.

The second variant emphasized men's biological impact upon their children and affirmed that fatherhood was the sine qua non of real manhood. To fail to become a father struck 19th-century doctors and moral advisers as unnatural, self-indulgent, and immature. Fatherhood even shaped sexual desire. The influential physician William Acton, for example, described in his book *The Functions and Disorders of the Reproductive Organs in Childhood, Youth, Adult Age, and Advanced Age* how men's sexual desires changed once they reached their mid-20s: "The natural longing is there still, but is no longer toward mere sensual indulgence only (it will be remembered that I am speaking of the continent man), but is deeply tinctured with the craving for wife—and home—and children" (quoted in Frank, 1995, pp. 86-87). Begetting children, went the argument, ultimately made men less selfish, more refined, and better disciplined. In Frank's words, "Fatherhood was the crowning reward for the self-restraint, self-culture, and self-mastery central to Victorian conceptions of masculinity" (p. 89).

Thus, despite men's seeming marginalization within the family culture of the 19th century, moralists and doctors found a place for what we would call generative fathering. That their conceptualization was, at one level, an effort to fortify patriarchal authority should be clear; after all, fatherhood brought true virility, and it was this sense of virility, Acton argued, that gave men the sense of their rightful place as "head and ruler" within the family. But on another level, the two variants of generative fathering suggest the recognition that fathers have vital work to do in families and that fathering has a crucial place in the lives of men. The task now is to explore the behavioral dimensions of generative fathering among men in the last century.

A detailed analysis of 19th-century men's involvement with their families is well beyond the scope of this chapter; moreover, variations by race, class, ethnicity, and region complicate the story. Bearing in mind these qualifications, several important points deserve mention, starting with the question of paternal availability. Although most historians agree that the industrial revolution took men out of the home, it is by no means clear that fatherly availability precipitously declined as a result. As Frank (1995) has pointed out, many rural fathers left home for long periods of time and thus were less available to their children than their industrial counterparts. So, too, rural teenage children often left home in search of work, thereby placing themselves beyond sustained contact with their fathers. Nor was the industrial world necessarily hostile to father-child contact. The separation of home and work wrought by industrialization appeared slowly and unevenly, and in some factory communities, families worked as a unit and fathers played a decisive role in recruiting their own children as coworkers. Nor is it clear that fathers' absence from home diminished their influence; Alice Stone Blackwell, daughter of women's rights activists Lucy Stone and Henry Blackwell, often commuted from her suburban home into Boston with her businessperson and journalist father to visit the library, the Athenaeum, and on occasion, his office. The children of Amos Lawrence, an influential Boston merchant, visited his office regularly and ate the noon meal with their father at home (Frank, 1995, p. 121). The point is that fatherly availability may or may not have declined with the rise of industrialization. It is an issue that will only be decided with more research.

The evidence that we do have, again drawing from the research of Stephen Frank (1995), suggests that middle-class fathers did value the time they spent with their children. Frank found that men became increasingly solicitous of their wives during pregnancy and often helped tend to their needs in the birthing chamber. Once the child was born, men's breadwinning obligations made them "part-time" fathers, but the evenings and Sundays they spent with their children took on an almost ritualistic importance. At the dinner table or the fireside, fathers quizzed, played games with, read stories to, or simply talked with their youngsters. Such men push to the edges of the cultural canvas the stereotype of flinty, withdrawn Victorian fathers and center our focus on men who expressed intense interest in the mental, moral, and physical development of their children and "frolicked" with them in every conceivable way. If moralists idealized the home for men as a place of refuge from the workaday world, how better to recharge one's batteries and reground oneself morally than by entering actively into the lives of children. Throughout the 19th century, writers on domesticity underscored fathers' role as play partner, and middle-class men's diaries and letters confirmed that many fathers took such advice to heart.

As their children grew older, fathers became less frolicsome and more concerned about securing a place in society for their sons and daughters. Farm fathers inducted their sons into the work of rural life at an early age, an obligation that could breed both respect and resentment. In contrast, fathers in towns and cities became increasingly attentive to the education of their children, especially those in the burgeoning middle class. Properly educated children, in fact, became a marker of social class, a sign that one had taken the time and made the necessary sacrifices to position one's children for economic success in the changing social structure of the 19th century. John Davis, a Massachusetts lawyer and congressman, expressed such sentiments in an 1830 letter to his wife: "If it were not for the education of the boys I should not strive much more for money, but they will be a heavy item on my hands that will call for constant exertion and I shall cheerfully devote my labor to them" (quoted in Frank, 1995, p. 299). As young men used their educations to secure a place in the middle class, they often continued to live under their father's roof until well into their 20s, a situation rife with possibilities for affection as well as conflict (Frank, 1995).

Nor were 19th-century fathers oblivious to the needs of their daughters. Emotionally, fathers appeared to establish closer relations with daughters than with sons. In private documents, for example, daughters tended to focus on their fathers' companionate side whereas sons underscored their fathers' exercise of authority. Fathers made the same distinction in their private correspondence with their children: Letters to daughters evinced more expressive language than those to sons. Fathers also felt free to advise their daughters about pregnancy, childbirth, weaning, wifely duties, household furnishings, morality, intellectual development, and in the case of Stephen Foster and his 16-year-old daughter, the importance of good conversational abilities: "This is the faculty which charms; & you must remember that to charm is to captivate & that to captivate is to command. This, then, is the chief source of power, especially to your sex" (quoted in Frank, 1995, p. 321). Fathers' attention became especially focused when their daughters considered marriage, and here, too, men felt obliged to offer counsel that was sometimes sought and sometimes viewed as meddlesome.

As the 19th century came to a close, town and city fathers began to explore the boundaries of a new mode of generative fathering. Although many men still conceptualized the father-child relationship in contractual terms and emphasized the mutual obligations between fathers and their children, a growing number of men highlighted the expressive, affective dimension to the relationship and underscored fatherly self-sacrifice for the well-being of their progeny. It is to this variant that we now turn.

The 20th Century

At the turn of the 20th century a new conception of masculinity emerged, calling men to the home and to child rearing. Over the next three decades a fully articulated vision of this mode of generative fathering took shape. This new mapping of masculinity and fatherhood—"masculine domesticity," as one historian (Marsh, 1988, 1989, 1990) called it—prevailed as a cultural ideal until the late 1960s and reshaped patriarchal relations, helped delineate class boundaries, and became part of the therapeutic management of interpersonal relations (see Griswold, 1993, chap. 5). In other words, the "new fatherhood" of the 20th century was, indeed, a form of generative fathering, but it cannot be understood apart from wider cultural developments, nor can the ironies, limitations, and politics of the new fatherhood escape scrutiny.

The new fatherhood of the early 20th century reflected changes that had deep roots. Quite clearly, 19th-century men had forged important ties with their children, but what emerged in the late 19th and early 20th centuries was the appearance of an entire class of men with the incomes and leisure to live out this form of generative fathering and a group of intellectuals and social scientists who gave this relationship intellectual meaning and academic respectability.

Although new fathers came from cities and farms, the archetype was of a suburban dweller, who with his family affirmed a new class identity by their purchasing power, the homogeneity of their surroundings, and their social and physical distance from the working class. Here lived those who forged the modern, child-centered, companionate family characterized by romance, companionship, sexual fulfillment, mutual respect, and emotional satisfaction. This new vision of middle-class fathering emerged when older sources of male identity were disintegrating and a "crisis in masculinity" was at hand. As work became increasingly bureaucratic and segmented, as cities swelled and face-to-face relationships declined, as religious doubt and feelings of fragmentation and emptiness grew, middle-class men became increasingly concerned about the quality of their private lives and about their lives as fathers (see Lears, 1983). Men could find meaning in the private realm as fathers, a task elevated and shaped intellectually by an increasingly self-conscious group of family professionals drawn from social work, sociology, psychology, home economics, and psychiatry.

The emergence of these professionals gave intellectual coherence to fathers' place in the new century. These were the men and women who analyzed modern fatherhood, examined the connection between fathers and personality formation, set new standards for fatherly behavior, and explored the relationship between that behavior and class identity. Central to their theory was the belief that family bonds had been weakened by industrialization and urbanization; that fatherly functions and authority had diminished; and that the key task for men now was to help foster the healthy personality development of their children by building families characterized by tolerance, strong emotional bonds, diffuse authority, and companionship. Men needed to become role models for both their sons and daughters, and the only way to do that was to spend time with their children. By the 1930s, such ideas had crystallized into a full-blown theory of sex role socialization predicated on the belief that fatherly involvement with children would help to counteract a dangerous drift toward excessively feminized homes. Sustained fatherly contact and admiration promoted good personality development by guiding a son into manhood and helping a daughter "transfer her emotional focus from her mother to her father as an intermediate step preparatory to its final resting in her husband" (quoted in Griswold, 1993, p. 97).

Popular writers echoed these ideas. Fathers must take time from their busy schedules to engage in sports, hobbies, and other diversions with their children, and if they did so, proper sex role development would be enhanced and mutual companionship, affection, and trust would be assured. These writers recognized that the idea of father as buddy clashed with traditional views of patriarchal authority, but the error was on the side of tradition, not modernity, a point made by one father in an article tellingly titled, "It's Fun Being a Father," published in 1927: "We are a gang. And I don't insist on being the leader of the gang more than my share of the time. . . . We don't have any heavy father and subservient son stuff. No sirree, not in *our* family" (Kelland, 1927, p. 146). The modern middle-class father was now seen as a kindly, nurturing democrat, who shared rather than monopolized power, a sharing that ultimately redounded to the psychological well-being of both men and their children.

Without challenging the gender-based division of labor and the ideology of male breadwinning, these professional and popular writers staked out a new vision of generative fathering that would prevail until the late 1960s. It is also true that affluence, suburbanization, job security, and increased leisure gave millions of U.S. men the time and money to focus on the private dimensions of their lives. In fact, the historical record suggests that millions of U.S. men throughout the 20th century conscientiously strove to be more competent, better informed fathers. Middle-class men in the 1920s and 1930s, for example, often read literature, listened to radio shows, or attended child study groups about child rearing. More often than their working-class counterparts, middle-class fathers read or told stories to their children and took an active role in disciplining their children. Researchers in the mid-1930s discovered a connection between father-child closeness and well-adjusted personality development and praised fathers who became the confidants of their offspring (White House Conference on Child Health and Protection, 1934). Other evidence confirms men's interest in child nurture: Hundreds of men wrote in the 1920s and 1930s to Angelo Patri, an Italian-born educator, principal of a New York City junior high school, and author of a nationally circulated newspaper advice column on child rearing. They sought advice on virtually anything related to bringing up children. Some worried about their child's sex role development, irrational fears, or lack of attentiveness; others had questions about medical problems, homework, appropriate movies, nightmares, stubbornness, sexuality, or most commonly, poor school performance (on fathers' allegiance to the values of the "new fatherhood" in the 1920s and 1930s, see Griswold, 1993).

Evidence from World War II and the postwar years likewise reveals men seeking to establish close relations with their children. During the war, experts worried about what impact the drafting of fathers would have on social order, and fathers who served overseas lamented missing the early years with their war-born children. Meanwhile, psychologists asserted the psychological indispensability of fathers to family life and counseled mothers on how to keep their absent husbands present in the lives of the children. For their part, mothers actually did try to help young children remember absentee fathers.[1]

As men began new families or returned to their old after the war, the responsibilities of fathers became even more elaborate. Breadwinning remained critical, but experts in the 1950s and 1960s insisted that fathers imbued with a democratic, permissive, nurturing sensibility could produce well-adjusted offspring capable of resisting the new dangers of the age—authoritarianism, juvenile delinquency, schizophrenia, and homosexuality. In a culture beset by a variety of cold war and sexual anxieties, the nurturing, companionate father constituted an important line of defense against social disorder. Such nurturing, moreover, not only reduced social disorder by fostering children's sex role adjustment but became an important marker of social class and a sure sign of "maturity," "responsibility," and manhood itself (for extended discussion of these themes, see Griswold, 1993).

The 1950s and 1960s were, indeed, propitious for middle-class fatherly absorption into private life. Everything from television programming to consumer spending habits to fertility patterns suggest that the affluence of the postwar years gave a boost to generative fathering. Men, especially middle-class men, if survey evidence is reliable, tried to build companionate relations with their offspring. In a 1957 study, for example, researchers found that 63% of some 850 fathers had a positive attitude toward parenting (the same figure for mothers was 54%) (Verhoff, Douran, & Kulka, 1981), and an examination of New York City fathers discovered that 76% mentioned companionship as one of the chief satisfactions they derived from being a father (Tasch, 1952). These same men recorded an abiding interest in their children's emotional health and personality development. On the other side of the continent, fathers at Stanford affirmed their belief in the importance of father-child companionship and their desire to spend time with their children. One father, the son of a baker, remembered that his own father's long working hours prevented the two from knowing each other. He pledged to do things differently: "I feel this is not the way it should be, and so I purposely attempt to spend time with the children" (quoted in Griswold, 1993, pp. 204-205).

Such efforts are to be applauded, but they should not be allowed to obscure the political meaning of this mode of generative fatherhood or the barriers men have encountered in trying to enact it. It is well to remember that the focus on generative fathering in the early 20th century arose at a time when masculinity and domesticity were both in crisis. Traditional sources of male identity in work, religion, and community had slowly declined during the second half of the 19th century; meanwhile, the emergence of the "new woman" and feminism posed basic challenges to assumptions about men's and women's place in society. The new fatherhood emerged within this context, part of a reconception of marriage and home that gave new meaning to men's lives while containing women's desires for autonomy and independence. Just as women were to find meaning within the home, so too, in part, were men, and by becoming a crucial element in this redefinition of family relationships, the new fatherhood helped to enlarge the cultural significance of the domestic sphere at a time when it was under attack from a variety of quarters. This enlargement came, it is important to point out, without in any way challenging the basic division of labor between men and women. This new mode of fathering was about companionship, play, and personality development, not about diapering, feeding, dressing, nursing, and the myriad other tasks that keep families running. From this perspective, the new fatherhood's progressive rhetoric obscured its conservative consequences.

Nor do the contradictions and complexities of the new fatherhood stop here. Men who struggled to meet the demands of the new fatherhood found that the therapeutic assumptions of modern fatherhood might erode paternal authority. After all, the standards for the new fatherhood were psychological and emotional, set by confident, university-trained experts who rarely exhibited self-doubt despite obvious limitations in their theoretical understanding, empirical evidence, or therapeutic recommendations. Becoming a new father ultimately increased one's dependence on the very experts who had first mapped this new paternal terrain, a point dramatically made by the middle-class men who wrote to ask Angelo Patri's advice about the simplest of matters. Patri's answers, sometimes brief, other times lengthy, left little doubt that competence was meeting incompetence. Where the fathers exhibited weakness, he showed strength; where they evidenced confusion, he demonstrated clarity; where they gave up in frustration, he offered an answer (for a full discussion of these ideas, see Griswold, 1993).

Faced with the bewildering complexity of modern child rearing and apparently bereft of independent standards for rearing children, fathers who approached the therapeutic culture and tried to become generative fathers did so at the risk of deferring to the specialized knowledge of doctors, psychologists, and educators. Those who relied on common sense and tradition lost out in a different way. While experts and mothers built the parent-education movement, most men remained outsiders and many resented the collusion between their wives and the experts in the rearing of the young. In the 1950s, sociologists noticed this resentment and found that husbands considered the experts "as inadequate men who have not been able to make the grade in the *really* masculine world" (Seeley, Sim, & Loosely, 1956, p. 194; see also Breines, 1992; Griswold, 1993).

The "really masculine world" in this view was the world of bread-winning, but winning bread has impeded generative fathering in both simple and complex ways. Obviously, earning a living takes fathers away from the family; time spent at the workplace is time not spent with children. But the culture of consumption that has developed in the 20th century has also given new meaning to and made new demands on men's breadwinning obligations. Faced with the seemingly insatiable and increasingly individuated wants of their wives, children, and themselves, men as early as the 1920s, as Robert and Helen Lynd (1956) observed in Muncie, Indiana, "seem to be running for dear life in this business of making the money they earn keep pace with the even more rapid growth of their subjective wants" (p. 137). Advertisers helped keep men running as they invaded the family and reshaped its desires, promising vitality and the good life to those who bought the right brand of automobile, the more modern refrigerator, the most up-to-date radio or television.

Nor has more leisure and a shorter workweek necessarily made fathering easier. Over the course of the last century, leisure, like consumption, has become increasingly segmented and individuated. The leisure of both fathers and children has been reshaped in directions that tend to separate rather than unite the generations, a separation deepened by the development of a massive, diverse youth culture that pulls children away from their fathers' influence and toward the authority of the young themselves. As the lives of children have become increasingly marked by segmented leisure, prolonged schooling, peer associations, the ubiquitous automobile, and consumerism, men have found themselves struggling to maintain contact with their children.

Toward the Future of Generative Fathering

The struggles described above are real and made worse by the difficulties facing divorced fathers and the experiences of men who never know the children they have fathered. For a variety of reasons, these men struggle to establish generative relationships with their children. It is both a personal and in the eyes of some critics a social tragedy that is rendering the United States increasingly "fatherless." We must also recognize that millions of men's relationships with their children will be structured by more or less traditional breadwinning responsibilities coupled with their desire to shape the intellectual, moral, psychological, physical, and spiritual development of their children. This older mode of generative fathering has deep roots in the culture, and its resilience and importance should not be underestimated. Nor should we ignore the fact that the much-ballyhooed new fatherhood is not without contradictions; paeans to its promises sometimes mask many men's well-documented ability to resist the demands of daily child care and housework and obscure therapeutic assumptions that have less to do with caring for dependents and more to do with personal growth and self-esteem. So, too, the difficulties that come when two parents try to balance work and family demands are made worse by the unwillingness of corporate leaders to change the working environment in "parent-friendly" directions. We may even admit that the new fatherhood functions as a marker of social class in a society beset by a host of middle-class status anxieties and that fatherhood has lost cultural coherence and become fragmented and politicized. We may concede all of this and more and yet still hold out optimism about the future of this new mode of generative fathering.

Such optimism stems from a variety of sources. The long-range direction of change suggests that millions of men will continue to establish generative relationships with their children. "Deadbeat dads" will not disappear and out-of-wedlock birthrates will likely remain high, but other changes since the end of World War II—most notably the transformation of the household economy, the rise and triumph of equity feminism, and changing expectations about the adult life course—have already reshaped and will in the future further change fatherhood. In fact, no force will reshape day-to-day fathering more significantly than the movement of mothers into the labor force. As they do so, and as they earn a significant share of the household income, they will feel more entitled to help with child care and housework and men will feel more eager to give it. In other words, women's wage work has decisively refashioned the nature of generative fathering and offers men a unique historical moment to become more involved in the day-to-day care of their children. Millions of men already recognize this fact; sometimes eagerly, sometimes less so, men are taking on new tasks and becoming more involved in day-to-day child rearing. In fact, the evidence suggests that as mothers work more hours outside the home and earn more of the total household income, fathers tend to share more housework and child care; so, too, as fathers value family involvement over rapid career advancement, they spend more time with their children. In one recent study, for example, researchers found that 74% of men would rather have a "daddy-track" job than a "fast-track" job. In another study, 48% of the respondents reduced their working hours to spend more time with their children and 23% passed up a promotion for the same reason (Levine, 1991). A new mode of the new fatherhood is clearly at hand.

Moreover, an ideological consensus has emerged in the last two decades that highlights the importance of generative fathering to social well-being. Since the 1960s, liberal feminists have decried the assumption that child care is primarily a maternal responsibility and have repeatedly called for increased child care options, restructured jobs, flexible working hours, and the expansion of maternity and paternity leaves. The feminists' underlying assumptions about the need and importance of fathers as caregivers has been endorsed by politicians, journalists, psychologists, social workers, and health care providers and has sparked books, newspaper articles, newsletters, radio and television programs, workshops, and classes of every stripe dedicated to making fathers better caregivers. If there are those who worry about this change, who see it as part of an androgynous drift that renders fatherhood culturally superfluous, there are more, I think, who see this new mode of generative fathering as a positive development that opens up new possibilities for father-child connections.

It is undoubtedly a fruitless and misguided task to suggest that one mode of generative fathering is better than another. Each arose at a given historical moment and each has given way under the advent of new circumstances. The hard-pressed Kansas farmer of the 1870s may have offered his children more stability than intimacy, more religious instruction than companionship; the middle-class Kansas City teacher of the 1990s, by contrast, may offer more intimacy than authority, more time as a confidant than as a vocational instructor. The lives of these two men could not be more different, and yet each profoundly shapes his children's lives and cares for the next generation. At the same time, the egalitarian assumptions of the latest mode of generative fathering have become deeply embedded in U.S. culture and will grow stronger as women's status and economic standing become more equal to that of men. In short, we are at a unique, perhaps decisive, moment in the history of fatherhood.

Building egalitarian parenting relations on a foundation laid over a century ago, millions of fathers are exploring new modes of generative fathering that are reshaping assumptions about family life and male identity. Despite the reality of fathers who will continue to drift away from or flee their children, millions more will find a more vital place in the lives of their children. As they do so, male dominance will decline, men will become more important to their children, and a more egalitarian social order will likely emerge (Coltrane, 1996).

Note

1. For a full treatment of fatherhood and World War II, see Griswold (1993). Even the aims of the war had less to do with high ideals than with personal matters. U.S. men, as Robert Westbrook (1990) has explained, "were not called upon to conceive of their obligation to participate in the war effort as a *political* obligation to work, fight, or die for their country" but rather "to defend *private* interests and discharge *private* obligations" (p. 588). Some of the themes, as well as some passages, in this essay draw from Chapters 5 and 6 of my book, *Fatherhood in America: A History*, copyright © 1993 by BasicBooks, A Division of Harper-Collins Publishers, Inc. and are used with permission.

PART II

Exploring Generative Fathering in Challenging Circumstances

Even in the best of circumstances, fathering is hard—but rewarding—work. Yet, so much of contemporary fathering is done in circumstances that challenge the best of efforts. The authors of the five chapters in this section address a few of the challenging circumstances fathers and children face. Sean Brotherson and David Dollahite, in Chapter 6, "Generative Ingenuity in Fatherwork With Young Children With Special Needs," look at a challenging circumstance faced by millions of fathers—caring for children with, for example, physical handicaps, developmental delays, or serious or chronic medical challenges. They use the conceptual ethic of fathering as generative work presented in Chapter 2 to frame narrative data collected during interviews with fathers of special needs children, showing how these fathers engage in "generative ingenuity" to meet the various needs of their children.

In the following conceptual and policy-oriented chapter, "Teen Dads: A Generative Fathering Perspective Versus the Deficit Myth," Lyn Rhoden and Bryan Robinson contrast the common, deficit perspective of teen dads based on stereotypes and myths with a newer perspective of generative teenage fathering. The authors encourage policymakers, educators, clinicians, medical professionals, clergy, and parents who work with teenage mothers and fathers to adopt a perspective of generative adolescent fathering and acknowledge these young fathers' desires to be responsible and involved parents, their abilities to be important supports to mother and child, and the many significant challenges they face in accomplishing this (e.g., developmental, educational, economic, attitudes of others).

Kay Pasley and Carmelle Minton in their chapter, "Generative Fathering After Divorce and Remarriage: Beyond the 'Disappearing Dad,'" address one of the most significant challenges fathers face in a society with high rates of divorce and remarriage—remaining involved with their children during marital transition. Drawing on their extensive interviews with fathers, Pasley and Minton explore the very real barriers—legal, economic, social, psychological, and interpersonal—men in marital transition face in their efforts to remain connected and available to the children they care deeply about.

A small but increasing proportion of fathers in marital transition retain custody of their children. In Chapter 9, "Single Custodial Fathers and Their Children: When Things Go Well," Alfred DeMaris and Geoffrey Greif explore the positive experiences of men who take on the day-to-day work of raising their children after marital disruption. They use quantitative data from 1,132 single custodial fathers raising children to examine factors that influence why some have more "successful" parenting experiences than others.

In the final chapter of this section, "Men and Women Cocreating Father Involvement in a Nongenerative Culture," Anna Dienhart and Kerry Daly address no single challenging circumstance but the broader cultural context in which contemporary fathering takes place. They argue that the culture of fatherhood in contemporary North America is not always conducive to the conduct of generative fathering, supporting their arguments with in-depth interview data from 18 couples from a variety of family and work structures in which the partners were committed to involved fathering. The data supports the authors' contention that there are subtle and obvious ways in which private, public, and work cultures join together to create obstacles to involved fathering. In this chapter, Dienhart and Daly give voice to the fathers trying to be generative when there is much around them in their culture that discourages this commitment.

Many other difficult circumstances that challenge the generative work of fathers in contemporary society are not addressed in this section. But these five chapters demonstrate that research can investigate fathering—even fathering in circumstances in which men face formidable barriers to generative fathering—without reverting to deficit perspectives.

6

Generative Ingenuity in Fatherwork With Young Children With Special Needs

SEAN E. BROTHERSON
DAVID C. DOLLAHITE

I learned that I would die for this person. I learned that from this moment
on we will be linked forever. This child is my responsibility forever,
to guide, to direct, and to nurture.

—A father at the birth of his daughter

It would be difficult to find a sentiment that captures more expressively
than the one above the essence of what is meant by *generative fathering*.
It reflects ethical concern, generational commitment, and caring responsibility. It suggests that in the relationship between father and child is the
substance of what it means to be moral and to be human. In this chapter,
we focus on the generative work done by fathers who have children with
special needs and how this reflects the main themes in the ethic of
generative fathering, or *fatherwork*, as discussed in Chapter 2.

Generative Fathering and Children With Special Needs

The challenge encountered by most fathers today, as in the past, is to
develop the skills and knowledge necessary to care for the next generation—

a concept Erikson (1950, 1982) termed *generativity*. Snarey (1993) framed generativity as being "any caring activity that contributes to the spirit of future generations" (p. 19). More specifically, he had in mind those caring activities that aid in establishing physical, social, and spiritual health and well-being for children of the next generation. Erikson (1964) wrote, "Parenthood is, for most, the first, and for many, the prime generative encounter, yet the perpetuation of mankind challenges the generative ingenuity of workers and thinkers of many kinds" (p. 130). In Chapter 2, the concept of generativity formed a beginning point in formulating a conceptual ethic of generative fathering.

Generative fathering is defined in this conceptual ethic as fathering that meets the needs of children by working to create and maintain a developing ethical relationship with them (see Chapter 2). With an ethic of fathering as generative work, we embrace the ideal of fathering as disciplined and joyful moral *work,* and suggest that fathers are engaged in four broad categories of such work: *ethical work, stewardship work, development work,* and *relationship work.* In Chapter 2, Dollahite and his colleagues also use the term *fatherwork* to refer to generative fathering.

Generativity chill and generative ingenuity are two additional Eriksonian concepts relevant to the particular challenge of being a father with a disabled or terminally ill child. *Generativity chill,* a concept advanced in Snarey's (1993) four-decade study, refers to an anxious awareness of the self as finite arising from the threatened loss of one's child, creation, or creativity. The impact of this major threat to a father's psychosocial generativity varies, depending on how a man copes with the significant and unique form of anxiety resulting from threats to his generativity. *Generative ingenuity,* Erikson (1950) notes, provides a perspective on how men cope with generativity chill as well as with the more typical challenge and responsibility of perpetuating those values and behaviors that bind a family together from generation to generation. In this chapter, we define generative ingenuity as *the capacity to commit to and care for another person and enhance his or her personal growth through exercising creativity, wisdom, and love in the relationship.* Caring for a child with special needs, whether it be on account of a learning disability or a terminal illness, challenges any parent's creative capacities to provide for that child's concerns and to cope with his or her own generativity chill. Yet, a parent's resourcefulness in giving needed care to such a child can be a critical difference in that child's development and happiness *and* in his or her parent's well-being. Indeed, some of Erikson's ideas about generative care take on further meaning when considered in light of fathering special needs children. The especially important and poignant ethical obligations to care for a child with significant disabilities is captured by Erikson's (1964) statement, "Care is the widening concern for what has been generated by love, necessity, or accident; it overcomes the ambivalence adhering to irreversible obligation" (p. 131). Erikson (1969) also stated generativity means to "'take care of' that which needs protection and attention, and 'to take care not to' do something destructive" (p. 53).

Previous Research on Fathers of Special Needs Children

Only minimal research on fathers who have a disabled or special needs child has been conducted (Bristol & Gallagher, 1986; Pedersen, Rubenstein, & Yarrow, 1979), which is not surprising because fathering as a research topic has blossomed only within the last two decades (Biller, 1993; Snarey, 1993). In fact, Lamb and Meyer (1991) state, "Fathers of children with special needs have been conspicuously ignored" (p. 153). As a result of this lack of extended research on fathers with developmentally or physically disabled children, what little information that does exist is limited in both scope and applicability. Scholars in this area have called for researchers to address fathers' reactions to child disability, how much time these fathers spend with their children and how the time is spent, the effects of paternal involvement on the child's development, the direct and indirect processes of influence fathers have in families with a disabled child, and the needs and patterns of fathers in accessing support resources (Bristol & Gallagher, 1986; Lamb & Meyer, 1991). Bristol and Gallagher (1986) point out, "Assumptions of pathology should be superseded by studies of factors relating to successful adaptation by fathers and families" (p. 95). An additional consideration in such research should be approaching the study of fathers of children with special needs from a capabilities paradigm rather than from a deficit perspective of father-child interaction (Doherty, 1991; Chapter 1, this volume).

Researchers on fathers and children with special needs have examined both the effects of parenting such a child on the father and the father's impact on the child's development (Bristol & Gallagher, 1986; Meyer, 1986); the majority of this research focuses on the influence a disabled or special needs child has on the father. Diagnosis of a child's disability has been seen as a critical juncture for parents (Wikler, 1981), and this experience is almost universally regarded as negative and troubling for parents (May, 1991; Stoneman & Brody, 1982). The stress for fathers may be exacerbated when physicians or support systems personnel fail to recognize and include the father's interest in the concern (May, 1991). Some research shows that the father's acceptance or rejection of a disabled child most strongly affects how other family members cope with this challenge, and is especially important to the mother's coping and marital satisfaction (Bristol, 1984; Peck & Stephens, 1960). Thus, how fathers cope with generative chill has an important mediating effect on others that will influence the child's well-being. Particularly important here may be the father's commitment to caring for the child and his willingness to choose positive and helpful attitudes (Brotherson, 1995).

Although the initial response of parents to learning of a child's disability or other need can be very stressful, research suggests that in most cases parents and families adapt maturely (Lamb & Meyer, 1991). Some researchers have proposed that having a disabled child dramatically affects many fathers' self-esteem (Cummings, 1976; Meyer, Vadasy, & Fewell, 1982), but others indicate no significant difference between these and other fathers (Gallagher, Cross, & Scharfman, 1981). Fathering a special needs child brings increased challenges to engaging with and productively interacting with the child (Turbiville, 1994). This is particularly true when the child is a boy, as fathers tend to have higher achievement expectations for their sons, and this may make the father's adjustment more difficult (Grossman, 1972; Frey, Greenberg, & Fewell, 1989). Many fathers respond creatively in caring for and playing with their children who have special needs, however (Brotherson, 1995). A disabled child may increase marital strain and divorce rates (Lonsdale, 1978), but this has also been contested widely, and in the long run, such a challenge can strengthen a marriage (Darling & Darling, 1982; Krause-Eheart, 1981). It does seem clear that the response of the father to a child's disability has an important mediating effect on how the mother gauges her marital happiness and copes with this parenting challenge (Lamb & Meyer, 1991).

Studies exploring the influence fathers have on their special needs children are few, but increasing efforts have begun to provide a more coherent picture of fathers in such circumstances. Research on fathering in general has shown that fathers wield an important and lasting influence on their children (Biller, 1993; Lamb, 1981a; Snarey, 1993), and it has been suggested by inference that fathers also have a significant impact on special needs children (Lamb & Meyer, 1991). Fathers influence their children through both direct and indirect processes (Bristol & Gallagher,

1986). Those few studies in which the direct influence of fathers on disabled children is directly addressed have shown conflicting results, and reviews of over 85 studies on parents' dealing with a child's disability showed fathers were rarely assessed (Wiegerink, Hocutt, Posante-Loro, & Bristol, 1980; Blacher, 1984). Stoneman and Brody (1982) reported that fathers of children with special needs are half as likely as mothers to act in a teacher role for children; other research indicates that fathers of children with disabilities do not differ from other fathers in providing care and often assume more responsibility in other areas (Shannon, 1978; Turbiville, Turnbull, & Turnbull, 1995). Many fathers are highly committed to their special needs children and consistently provide physical care and emotional support (Brotherson, 1995). Turbiville et al.'s (1995) study showed that among 84 fathers of children with and without disabilities, the fathers with a disabled child spent slightly more time at home, performed slightly more child care, and were more likely to hold their children and practice nonverbal interactions. Despite recent advances, we still have much to learn about "how much time fathers spend with children who are developmentally disabled or how they spend that time" (Lamb & Meyer, 1991, p. 153).

Narrative Knowing and Generative Fathering

Narrative approaches to knowing recently have received a great deal of attention in the social sciences (Dollahite et al., 1996; Josselson & Lieblich, 1993; Kotre, 1984; McAdams, 1985; Palus, 1993; Polkinghorne, 1988; Reissman, 1993). Narrative approaches encourage the telling, hearing, and analysis of stories to capture experience and explore meaning making. Dollahite et al. (1996) suggest that the integration of *theory* and *story* is a powerful way both to understand lived and interpreted experience, and to help teach others how to change in positive directions. Dienhart and Dollahite touch on this theme in Chapter 12, this volume. (An excellent example of the power of a theory-story linkage of generative fathering with a special needs child is Snarey's (1993, chap. 5) insightful case study of Joseph and Patricia.)

The study presented here is focused on the caring activities of fathers who have a child with a disability or other special need. We examined narrative accounts told by fathers about how they connect with and care for their children. The themes and patterns of fatherwork we identified in these accounts demonstrate the generative ingenuity of fathers whose creative capacities for giving care have been evoked. The value of this project lies in our addressing both the content and meaning of fathers' caring experiences and using the conceptual ethic of fathering as generative work to provide insight into the narrative accounts.

With the rising emphasis on promoting better fathering in both public and academic forums (Blankenhorn, 1995; Snarey, 1993), the need for research to examine the generative experience and potential of fathers and encourage a positive approach to facilitating such potential has increased. The purposes of this research are (a) to obtain a better understanding of the caring behavior and experiences of fathers with special needs children, and (b) to use the conceptual ethic of fathering as generative work to frame patterns of care and generative ingenuity that may be useful for fathers in such circumstances.

Research Design, Sample, and Procedures

The research approach is qualitative, using father's narrative accounts obtained through carefully conducted, in-depth interviews. The research design was interpretive, aiming at description and interpretation of meaning in fathers' experiences, both by researchers and fathers themselves.

Sample. Participants in the study consisted of 16 married fathers chosen from among a population of families in central Utah with at least one special needs child (physical or developmental disability, terminal illness, etc.), most of whom were involved in a local support program for such families. Most of the special needs children were under age 3, but several families had older disabled children as well. It was assumed that the situation of being a parent to a special needs child would elicit more intensive needs for care in the father-child relationship, thereby making available many differing examples of paternal care. Participants were mainly Caucasian, middle-SES fathers in their late 20s to late 30s with two to four children. All were married. Included also were one African American father and one father from China. Nearly all of the participants were members of The Church of Jesus Christ of Latter-Day Saints (Mormon), which teaches that fathers should place their highest priority on caring for the next generation (Hawkins, Dollahite, et al., 1993).

Procedures. Participants were first contacted by phone, and interviews were set up. The qualitative interviews were conducted by two-person interviewer teams, usually a man and a woman, and each lasted approximately 1 ½ to 2 hours. The questions asked were meant to engage the participants in telling stories about their experiences caring for their special needs children. All of the interviews were tape-recorded and transcribed later to capture the language and experiences of the participants. The interviewers conducted themselves in the spirit of being students of the fathers participating in the study, consistent with Josselson's (1993) ideal of "listening to people talk in their own terms about what had been significant in their lives" (p. ix). The narrative accounts collected from these in-depth interviews were carefully read, coded, and analyzed within the framework of the four categories of generative work suggested in Chapter 2: ethical, stewardship, development, and relationship.

Stories of Fatherwork With Special Needs Children

The primary research question was, What themes and patterns specific to generative fathering are present in fathers' accounts of caring for their special needs children? Our interest was in identifying the most common themes and patterns described by these fathers. The main focus was *not* the amount of time spent between father and child; rather, the events occurring during that time together, and also apart from it, were explored (Bristol & Gallagher, 1986; Snarey, 1993). These findings are intended to represent models of generative ingenuity among fathers and common themes concerning generative work as discovered through a qualitative exploration of fathers' narrative accounts. The concepts are discussed in turn for ease of presentation, but the categories of generative work and their accompanying responsibilities and capabilities are in reality closely connected and generally occur in combination.

Generative Ingenuity in Ethical Work

Ethical work comprises two responsibilities of fathers in the conceptual ethic of generative fathering: to *commit* and to *choose* for the benefit of children. The central principle of ethical work involves acting as a moral agent for the benefit of others. Results of this study indicated that ethical work was demonstrated particularly under two circumstances: (a) during times of economic, emotional, or physical stress on the family or child; and (b) at times of personal importance or need to the child (such as conflict and achievement) (Brotherson, 1995). Fathers with a special needs child may feel an added sense of ethical concern for the child due to the additional stresses of parenting in such a situation (Wikler, 1981; Snarey, 1993). It is noteworthy that care for children in other areas of generative work often occurs in combination with these elements of commitment and choice.

Commitment in fatherwork involves binding oneself in a relationship of obligation to a child. In the fathers' narrative accounts, commitment often was manifest by both physical support and presence and mental awareness and involvement with a child. Important patterns of commitment reflecting generative ingenuity included positive responses to diagnosis of a child's particular need, restructuring work schedules to support the child, and engaging with the child according to his or her interests.

Learning of a child's disability or other special challenges is often a critical time for parents (Wikler, 1981). Fathers face the concern of being seen as "second-class parents" at such a time, but their response has potentially the most impact on how the entire family handles the situation (Bristol, 1984). A father who commits himself to the best welfare of a child with special needs can set the tone for an entire family. One father who adopted a young disabled girl of another race recounted:

We knew about [her disability] from the day that they called us with the possible adoption. We had contacted this agency in Mississippi and they said that they don't adopt to families who are Caucasian—they mainly put black children in black homes. But when they came up with this child, knowing they wouldn't have a place for her and we'd just talked to them, they called us back and said, "Are you still interested? We have this child and she has this special need." At first, we didn't even know what it was because it's a very rare condition. So, we tried to find out some information. As far as attitude is concerned, I think that we were kind of excited that here's another baby. You take the chance that any baby you adopt or have born might have problems, and that wasn't a factor. We were looking for a child with problems . . . you have to be aware of them, and you have to be able to deal with them.

This father expresses how making a commitment with energy and devotion to a child's welfare from the beginning might creatively shape the family's response to a challenge.

A common pattern of commitment in the narratives was taking action to cut or change work hours or change jobs to devote more time to a child. Creative adjustment of work patterns to give priority to a child's needs exemplifies one instance of generative ingenuity. One father illustrated this and what parental commitment means to him in describing an encounter with his sick child:

Last night I stayed up till about 4:00 a.m. because Lee[1] was having a high fever, etc. When a kid gets sick you really reach out to them. . . . The first thing I did this morning was to call the doctor and make an appointment for him. It wasn't an emergency but the high fever was very bad. I would use two towels, putting water on them and helping him to cool down. Then, today I went to work and called the doctor's office again. They told me that the doctor would be in by 9:00. So I took about two and a half hours off of work today and missed lunch at work. I took him to the doctor because I feel that this is what fathers are for—to stand up and take responsibility when your children need you.

This father suggests that commitment involves making family and children a first priority over other considerations, including work, and that fathers are "to stand up and take responsibility when your children need you." The narrative also shows that the context of medical need creates a situation in which commitment by the father is more critical.

Another common theme of commitment in the narrative accounts involved fathers spending significant time in activities meaningful to the child so as to foster learning and build the relationship. It seemed important that fathers be responsive to doing those activities the children were interested in—whether it be reading stories or playing dolls—and not simply doing what the father enjoyed doing. This facet of commitment calls for mental awareness of children's interests and personal involvement with them in such activities. One father noted the need for patience in responding to his son with special needs:

I went home to help [my father] put tile down on Mom's bathroom floor, and Luke [the son] came in and wanted to "ride the horse" because I was down on my knees. He wanted to jump on my back. So, I let him do it while I was doing that and my Dad was about going nuts. He said, "Gee, you're a lot more patient than I am." Maybe I am . . . but you've got to be that way because Luke likes to be in the middle of things with you. That's how he learns. So, it's being patient with him and letting him do things.

Fathers must commit themselves to interacting in creative ways that fit the child's need. This is consistent with research that suggests responsiveness to children is important in developing healthy relationships (Lamb, 1981b).

Choice in fatherwork involves making decisions in day-to-day life that meet the needs of children. Examples of generative ingenuity in fathers of special-needs children included choosing to relieve mothers' stresses and being individually responsive to a child's unique needs or desires.

Fathers may impact a child's welfare for good as much by their indirect influences as by direct interactions. Lamb and Meyer (1991) note that mothers' ability to cope with raising a special needs child and to experience more marital satisfaction depends, in part, on their husbands' involvement with their other children and with housework. One father expressed how he aided his child through strengthening his spouse:

> That first year of his life, even though he wouldn't let me have a lot to do with him one-on-one, we'd set the alarm clock to get up every two hours for Pam to breast-feed him. She was very uptight and tense, so she'd sit in the rocking chair to feed him and I'd stand behind her and rub her shoulders to help her calm down and relax. . . . I don't know what's typical or not typical, but my wife has breast-fed all of the kids and the deal from day one was that when it was time I would get up and get the baby, change the baby's diaper, and bring the baby in so she could feed him. It's worked out pretty well for the most part.

This father manifests generative ingenuity in choosing to care in ways that indirectly affect the child by providing support to his wife. This may be one of the most important ways that fathers can create a healthy atmosphere for a special needs child.

One common pattern of choosing on behalf of children was deciding to respond personally to meet a child's physical needs for care and support, or a child's desires for help and involvement. Two important trends were found here. One clear pattern was that a father's perception of the importance of responding personally increased significantly when the situation involved responding to a child who was ill or in pain (rather than just a child who desires to play). This suggests that the condition of a child's dependence on the father heightens a father's sense of ethical responsibility, a situation that may be more common with special needs children and represents an example of the positive consequences of generativity chill (Snarey, 1993). A second noticeable trend was that a father's perceptions of his child's sense of having a positive relationship tended to relate to the father's responses not only when it was critical (medical need, etc.), but particularly when the response was just wanted (a request to play, etc.). A father whose child was having language difficulties explained:

> He had something like a book and asked me to sit down with him. I didn't have the time. I don't know if it was something he was doing or something he said, but something let me know that was the moment he needed to practice his verbal skills or his interaction skills. I said to myself, "I'll never let a moment like that pass again," and I haven't. . . . I had a similar experience at the other place we lived. One of the [other] kids [not with special needs] was out trying to ride a bicycle and I came home. One of the kids asked me to come out and

help. . . . She learned to ride the bike that day. I just held her up for a second and ran along by her and next thing I knew she was riding the bike. . . . You do learn things almost instantaneously when they do happen, and if you miss that moment then you've missed the moment. There is nothing else you can say. . . . You have to do them or you miss them forever, and I mean forever. . . . I don't want those moments to pass with me and my children.

Generative Ingenuity in Stewardship Work

The stewardship work component of generative fathering is characterized by the following responsibilities: to *create* and to *consecrate* for the benefit of children. The basis of stewardship work is providing resources and opportunities for and dedicating personal talents and energies to the benefit of the child.

Creating for one's children involves meeting a child's material and emotional needs through work that provides resources and opportunities the child requires. The narratives showed a pattern of generative ingenuity in which fathers created the opportunity to have meaningful interaction with a child through activities to stimulate learning and enhance the relationship. Parenting a special needs child may hold greater challenges for such interaction (Gallagher et al., 1981). A father's creative ability to interact with his child may thus be particularly important, as developmental delays may exist and can create constraints on the relationship. One father expressed his creativity in this way:

I don't think [the child having spina bifida] changes anything for me personally. Obviously it's going to come into play later—I don't think that he's going to be a real hiker. But we'll find ways to deal with that. I don't think it's going to have a big effect. . . . He can still learn [to fish], too. You don't know me very well; I'd park in the stream if I have to. I've taken my dad out and he can't walk. I just say, "All right, you sit here in the truck." I drove up and parked in the stream so he could fish. That was fun!

This father asserts the idea that in fathering a special needs child creative effort and ingenuity can be critical to aiding the child's development. It also may better the father's sense of esteem in relating to the child, a potential concern for fathers of special needs children (Cummings, 1976).

To *consecrate* for one's children involves dedicating a major portion of one's time, talents, resources, and energies to their well-being. One primary theme that emerged in the narratives was sacrificing time and energies. An important element of this pattern was the sentiment expressed by fathers of their responsibility to protect and provide for their children. One father reflected such dedication in addressing the needs of his disabled son:

> His needs are very unique. . . . He's got a lot of big gaps in development and will slow down on us, so we have to adjust to having Jeff around with us probably for the rest of our lives. We will have to figure out a way to plan for Jeff beyond our deaths, so that he is cared for [over] the next forty years.

Preparing for the long-term welfare of a special needs child embodies generative ingenuity focused on consistency of care over a child's lifetime.

Generative Ingenuity in Development Work

The relationship between a father and child is always growing and changing, and the efforts to make this relationship a healthy and adaptive one constitute development work: to *care* and to *change* for the benefit of children. Development work emphasizes maintaining supportive conditions and adapting to varying situations as needed for children. In caring for a disabled or special needs child, this means a father must mature and adapt to the child's needs.

Care in fatherwork is concerned with providing for children what they need most. As was seen with commitment and choice, a central theme in the narratives concerned with care was fathers being present during times of illness or giving physical assistance and emotional support to a child. These physical and emotional elements were combined in most examples. Providing care for special needs children as a father means to do so with the whole self—reaching out to the child with one's heart and mind as well as one's hands. The narratives gave strong evidence that fathers generally can be and are involved in giving such care to their children. One father, whose 5-year-old daughter was suffering from leukemia, related this story:

> Maybe the hospital is the part we like to forget but can't. When her pain got to the point that she couldn't go to the bathroom, I was the one that got to do her bedpans for her. She would only let me do it; I was the one that did that. It wasn't a thing for Mom, and she didn't want anybody else in the room. She kicked everybody out of the room—nurses, Mom—Mom had to be outside the door, and I would get the bedpan as best as I could under her bottom without hurting her. Moving the sheets hurt her. It was not a good thing. But she let me do that for her, and I was able to take care of her needs, and it helped me that

I was the only one she'd let do it. That was kind of neat. You wouldn't expect bedpan shuffling to be a wonderful memory, but it was. She trusted me to do my best job not to hurt her, and that was special to me that she let me do that.

This example suggests that physically caring for a child's needs, however mundane, symbolizes the love a father can express through his fatherwork. Fatherwork involves making the effort to adapt the care given as children and fathers mature. The narratives showed that *change* as a fathering principle includes both adaptation to varying circumstances and personal maturation. The capacity to see the need for change and how to adjust to a child's special needs epitomizes generative ingenuity. One regular pattern of change identified might be called adaptational change. This reflects the idea of adapting one's parenting practices in a certain way to be most helpful according to the child's particular needs and temperament to meet the specialized needs and circumstances of each child for his or her greatest development (Brotherson, 1995). For example, with a disabled child, a parent must learn to adjust to the differing developmental concerns that may arise from spina bifida or Down syndrome (Lamb & Meyer, 1991). A father whose son had hearing problems expressed how he made this adjustment:

When he was a year old he was talking like any normal kid. He was starting to say words and then all of a sudden there was nothing. We tried and tried to get his ears cleared up with antibiotics, etc., and it didn't work. It was really kind of hard when you see other kids his age talking and communicating, and Matt would just sit there and do nothing. Physically he was fine. He could run and jump and throw. . . . I guess I'm kind of proud but I always wanted to be the best at what I did, and I thought, "Poor kid, he's got go to through school and he'll be behind." But then I decided he could catch up if we work with him, and so we've got to do it now and hold up our end of the deal. At first, it was kind of hard, but it doesn't bother me now. . . . I've seen him do [it] and how he can learn. He doesn't have a learning disability, he's just had a hard time hearing and now he's got to catch up. . . . Now, I've seen that it will work out.

It seems likely that those fathers who can creatively adapt to a special needs child, whether playing particular games or learning how to help the child grow, will foster more happy and healthy relationships.

Generative Ingenuity in Relationship Work

The primary responsibilities of a father that are outlined in the concept of relationship work are to *connect* and to *communicate* for the benefit of children. Relationship work is fundamentally concerned with building relationships and fostering love between parents and children. This is accomplished through relating to one another in ways that facilitate healthy attachments and promote mutual understanding.

Connecting with children in fatherwork involves forming healthy, lasting attachments with a child (and the child's mother). Fathers expressed a sense of connection with their children in a wide variety of situations, both at times of sadness or concern and at times of great happiness. It was expressed in gentle affection and playful bouts of wrestling. In the narratives, connecting with one's child was a critical criterion by which the quality of the father-child relationship was assessed. The most significant pattern of connecting to one's children was a father being personally involved in activities with a child, specifically in activities of recreation, play, learning, work, or attendance at important events. The prevalence of this pattern may suggest that these fathers connected well with their children in an informally structured environment that allowed for mutual participation and common interests, as well as playful interaction. A father shared this illustration of connecting during a learning moment with his infant son:

> When Stan was three months old, I laid him in the bottom of the tub and put in a washcloth so he wouldn't slide around. I put him in the bottom of the tub and slowly filled it with water until it was at his ear level, so that I knew if he turned one way or the other he could at least be safe. He didn't have very good motor movement at the time as a baby and was sort of jerky, but once he got into the water like that almost immediately his motor coordination began. I don't know how to explain it, but he started kicking and moving his arms, he brightened up and there was something almost transcendental about the moment of looking into his eyes while he was there in the water and he was making a moment of progression in his body. Somehow, he was on his own. It's very difficult to explain it, but you could see the water, his eyes, and the sky in all that one moment. It was just an important moment for me. . . . It may just be because you have moments when you look at people and there is a connection there which is inexplicable. I can't explain it. I looked into his eyes and said something. It was just a tie between father and child.

The multidimensional pattern suggested here provides insight into how fathers can engage in many different types of activities with their special needs children that will strengthen the relationship. A father expresses generative ingenuity in those connecting activities most suited for his child.

Fatherwork involves building sound relationships through *communication,* which in generative fathering means relating with children by sharing meaning both verbally and nonverbally. Two key factors in the fathers' communication patterns were what was communicated and how it was expressed to the child. How these aspects of communication occurred in combination seemed vital to whether the fathers felt the parent-child relationship was being furthered or injured. The primary theme in the narratives regarding communication was how a father communicates in expressing harsh or positive feelings and actions in dealing with discipline or other situations of concern. Potentially no situation is more sensitive with a special needs child than how a father communicates when encouraging compliance or meting out discipline (Stoneman & Brody, 1982). Not surprisingly, this pattern showed that harsh, punitive communication was associated with negative effects in the relationship, whereas firm but loving communication accompanied positive experiences in the relationship. One father expressed the challenge that can exist in handling a disabled child:

> Tim is having a very difficult time with toilet training. . . . We've been trying for a year and a half now to potty-train him and it's not working. I have a hard time understanding why it's taken so long and the emotions that a three-year-old is going through under this type of thing. So, a lot of times it gets very frustrating for me. When Tim has an accident in his pants, rather than consoling him and being patient with him and showing him what to do, I lose my temper. I might say, "Tim, I'm not going to take you to work with me if you can't learn to do it in the toilet!" or "Why are you doing it this way?" I try to rationalize with Tim and it doesn't work. Because it doesn't work, I get frustrated, Tim gets frustrated, the relationship gets a little strained. What Tim needs is the positive enforcement on that and not the negative, and I think that I've failed there because for the last six or eight months it's been negative.

This father's story illustrates a particular facet of generative ingenuity that lies in developing innovative modes of discipline that are kind but effective with special needs children. Healthy and positive communication acts as a foundation for ensuring a sound, growing relationship with such a child.

Conclusions

In caring for a special needs child, fathers face some differing dimensions of generativity chill but also experience many of the same joys, challenges, and opportunities that are faced by any parent. The fathering narratives shared in this study represent themes and patterns of generative ingenuity in fatherwork with special needs children and offer some insight and meaning into these fathers' individual caring experiences. They also illustrate the application of the conceptual ethic of fathering as generative work to a specific population and how those concepts can enrich our understanding of fatherwork in these challenging circumstances.

Good fathering, particularly for special needs children, requires generative ingenuity. The examples of generative ingenuity shared here range from rearranging a work schedule to changing bedpans for an ill child, but all reflect a similar underlying theme—the creative exercise of a father's abilities to love and respond to a child's needs and desires. Fatherwork with special needs children usually takes extra effort. The fathers whose stories are shared here are ordinary men doing both ordinary and extraordinary things. Fathers everywhere can learn from their example of accepting the ethical responsibility of fatherwork.

The farmer-author Wendell Berry (1986) finds an image of "the best and most responsible kind of agriculture" in "an old man caring for a young tree" (p. 129). We find one of the best images of generative fathering to be a committed father caring for a special needs child.

Note

1. All participants' names have been changed unless otherwise requested.

7

Teen Dads

A Generative Fathering Perspective
Versus the Deficit Myth

J. LYN RHODEN
BRYAN E. ROBINSON

When my girlfriend told me she was pregnant, I wasn't really surprised. We'd been dating for two years and had been having sex a lot for the past eight months. Yeah, we talked about protection and sometimes I used condoms, but mostly we just liked having sex without even thinking about a baby. The night she told me she'd missed her period, both of us got real scared. After talking about it for a couple of days, we went to a doctor in the next town over and found out if she was pregnant or not. (quoted in Robinson & Barret, 1986, p. 170)

Fifteen-year-old Robert, quoted above, had barely begun shaving when his girlfriend Lisa's pregnancy flung him unprepared, emotionally and financially, into parenthood. His friends talked mostly about soccer games and tests at school, but he could only think about what he was going to do about Lisa and their baby.

Even though things seemed to be closing in on me, I dreamed about how good things could be—how we'd get married and I'd be a father. I knew it wouldn't be easy, but I could get a job at the mill, and we could live on my family's farm. I just knew that somehow we'd make it. (quoted in Robinson & Barret, 1986, p. 170)

Lisa's mother and father, however, "wouldn't listen to anything we had to say and kept asking how she let this thing happen and telling [Lisa] what a no-good creep I was," Robert lamented. "Finally, after what seemed like hours, they told me to get out, so I left" (quoted in Robinson & Barret, 1986, p. 171). Robert was told to stay away from Lisa.

Introduction

Until the 1980s, teenage fathers were excluded from studies on adolescent parenting or given little positive attention in the social science literature. "All eyes are on the unwed mother and her baby, while the other partner stands awkwardly in the background, too often ignored or even forgotten completely" (Connolly, 1978, p. 40). This treatment reflects the overall neglect of fathers in the family or parenting literature. Societal stereotypes depict teenage fathers as psychologically maladjusted youths who act out their sexual experiences by sexually exploiting their girlfriends and then abandoning them and their children. This perception of teenage fathers is at odds with the cultural expectation that fathers accept the responsibilities of emotionally and financially supporting their children (Kiselica & Sturmer, 1993). Myths aimed at unmarried fathers in the 1940s continue to be applied to teen fathers of the 1990s. Imputed unconscious motives for unmarried fathering run the gamut from the need of latent homosexual fathers to prove their heterosexuality and the expression of hostility by sexually insecure men whose wives were infertile to the acting out of unresolved oedipal fantasies by unwed fathers who had a need to prove their virility (Robinson, 1988).

Findings from more recent research challenge the stereotypical images of teenage fathers. We are learning that the stereotype of teenage fathers as uncaring and uninvolved males is not always true and that given the chance, many of them report that the fathering experience is a central event in their young lives. Many teenage fathers are emerging as young men who want to be active fathers. Given the opportunity, teenage fathers are often involved in raising their children; they often have daily contact, contribute money, and participate in decisions regarding their children's welfare (Barret & Robinson, 1982, Robinson & Barret, 1986). In Erikson's terms, they are learning to care for "what has been generated by love, necessity, *or accident* [italics added]" (Erikson et al., 1986, p. 37).

Teen dads, like adolescent mothers, are faced with substantial obstacles, including interruption of education and job or career preparation as well as economic disadvantage. In spite of these many hurdles, some teenage fathers do succeed as parents. Many others, however, fail to receive the support that would help them in surmounting the obstacles.

The purpose of this chapter is to contrast the common perspective of teen dads based on stereotype and myth with a newer, generative perspective of teenage fathering. This perspective is based on a more optimistic and proactive stance for young fathers, and includes the recognition that societal support can cushion the harsh blow for teen dads with positive implications for father, mother, and child. We have included many comments from real teen dads generated from our clinical and empirical data (Robinson, 1988; Robinson & Barret, 1986) and other research on teen fathering.

The Deficit Perspective

Distinguished researchers and medical experts convened in 1982 at a conference of the Division of Mental Health of the Institute of Medicine. Among the many sessions on adolescent pregnancy and parenthood, the teenage father was barely mentioned. When he was discussed, he was portrayed as the stereotypical villainous stud.

> Although data are scanty, some boys view a girl's pregnancy as a sign of their sexual competence, and for those who are disadvantaged, this may be perceived as one of the few successful achievements in their lives. In addition, a boy's peer group may identify him as "being a stud," and the boy may feel a heightened motivation to impregnate the same or another girl again. A differing reaction, however, may take place . . . a small proportion of men have feelings of conflict when they become fathers, and their hostility may be directed outward. Although this type of study has not been done on teenage fathers, there may be a percentage of boys who act out their emotions in violent or quasi-violent ways." (Harrison, 1982, p. 49)

A deficit perspective generally involves comparing two groups, emphasizing the ways in which one group differs from the other and framing those differences as deficits. This perspective is pervasive in the literature on adolescent fathering. Our knowledge about teen dads has been clouded by studies in which they are subsumed within larger samples of older unmarried fathers so that a true profile of teen fathers cannot be discerned. In addition, common stereotypes generalized from these studies of older fathers support myths contributing to false notions about adolescent fathers and perpetuate a deficit perspective focusing on the ways in which adolescent fathers do not measure up to our culture's expectations of fathers.

This deficit perspective on young fathers excludes them from involvement in parenting from the start. Professionals who carry this mind-set are guided unwittingly in ways that exclude and demean young men from any involvement. Lisa Connolly (1978), a social worker for the Children's Home Society in California described her deficit attitude: "I discovered that I was counseling with the expectation that the fathers didn't want to contribute. I wasn't confronted with my own values until I saw some natural fathers who really wanted to get involved, [and who] wanted to see their babies" (p. 42).

Myths and Reality

Teen dads are frequently neglected in discussions about adolescent parenting, or when they are included, they are generally presented in a negative light based more on stereotypes than scientific corroboration (Barret & Robinson, 1990). A growing body of research refutes six commonly held myths about teen dads:

1. The Stud Myth. The myth: He is a worldly, wise, villainous "stud" who knows more about sex and sexuality than most teenage boys. The reality: Although adolescent fathers become sexually active earlier and have more varied sexual experience than adolescent mothers, most young fathers are as uninformed about sex and sexuality as young mothers (Barret & Robinson, 1982; Brown, 1983). Failing to use birth control and making comments such as, "I did not think she would get pregnant because we only had sex once a week," seem to indicate these young men were as uninformed about sexuality as their female partners (Barret & Robinson, 1982).

2. Don Juan Myth. The myth: He exploits unsuspecting and helpless adolescent females by taking advantage of them. The reality: Research and demographic trends have shown that it is rare for an adolescent male to take sexual advantage of a seemingly helpless adolescent female; usually, adolescent parents are within 3 or 4 years of each other's age, come from similar socioeconomic backgrounds, have equivalent schooling, and are involved in a meaningful relationship (Elster & Panzarine, 1983).

3. Macho Myth. The myth: He feels psychologically inadequate, has no inner control, and unlike other boys his age has a psychological need to prove his masculinity. The reality: Adolescent fathers are psychologically and intellectually more like than different from their nonfather contemporaries (Earls & Siegal, 1980; Pauker, 1971). Teenage fathers have been found to feel as much in control as adolescents who had never fathered a child (Hendricks, 1980; McCoy & Tyler, 1985; Robinson, Barret, & Skeen, 1983).

4. Mr. Cool Myth. The myth: He usually has a fleeting, casual relationship with the young mother and has few emotional feelings about the pregnancy. The reality: Contemporary research indicates that adolescent males do experience emotional feelings about their impending fatherhood. When we interviewed 17-year-old David, he said of his son:

> I didn't think I'd feel this way. He's so little and needy and I'm afraid I've screwed up his life forever. It's hard for me to let them just give him away to some stranger, but I guess I don't have much choice. He's got a better chance with them than he ever would with me.

Young fathers express care for the health and welfare of the mother and baby as well as concern about being able to support the mother and child financially (Panzarine & Elster, 1983; Hendricks, 1988). Young fathers also express concern about their relationship with their partners; strong ties often exist between couples. They often feel estranged from participation by understandable, yet unbridled hostility from their girlfriends' fathers, intimidation from the courts, and neglect by the social service agencies. Robert, in the opening case, eventually discovered that Lisa's parents had taken her to a nearby town for an abortion and then sent her to another state to live with relatives. "I couldn't believe it! Sometimes I get real angry that nobody asked me what I thought needed to be done. I don't think I'll ever get over it," he stammered as tears flowed down his cheeks (quoted in Robinson & Barret, 1986, p. 171).

The anguish of a 17-year-old boy waiting while his girlfriend had an abortion is typical of the turmoil experienced by teen dads: "I thought I was a much more liberated man. I'd be able to walk in here and sit down and say, 'Here's an abortion,' and that would be it. But now that I'm here, I'm a wreck. . . . How about me? Do they have something for me to lay on while I die?" (quoted in Rothstein, 1978, p. 208).

5. Phantom Father Myth. The myth: He is absent and rarely involved in the support and rearing of his children. The reality: Most studies on adolescent fatherhood reveal that young fathers want to become deeply involved with their children. Many of these fathers seek involvement in spite of their awareness of limited education, money, and physical resources. Teen dads tend to remain involved physically or psychologically throughout the pregnancy and childbirth experience (Kiselica et al., 1994). Research also suggests that teen fathers do contribute financially to their child's care in the postnatal period and maintain contact with the mother (Rivara, Sweeney, & Henderson, 1986; Vaz, Smollen, & Miller, 1983). Structured interviews with 289 adolescent welfare mothers revealed that teen father absence did not necessarily equal uninvolvement. In fact, the teen father's involvement was often expressed by his economic contribution more than his actual presence, which was determined by whether the mother permitted him to be involved (Danzinger & Radin, 1991). "I'll take care of them," said James, a 16-year-old we interviewed. "I'll give money to buy milk for our baby and I'll pay the doctor bills and for other things." Similarly, Jason, 18, said, "I plan to take care of my baby and my girlfriend and try to give them anything in the world they want."

6. Big Spender Myth. The myth: He completes school and enters a high-paying job, leaving his partner and offspring to fend for themselves. The reality: As adults, adolescent fathers have truncated education, remain in lower-paying jobs, and have lower incomes than men who become fathers in adulthood (Card & Wise, 1978; Rivara et al., 1986). Carl, another teen father we interviewed, said,

> If only I'd known how hard it was going to be, I'd never've let this happen. I thought only about the good times, teaching him to talk and walk, feeding him every now and then. But he cries all the time, and I have to come up with so much money for his things I can't even afford records anymore. I hate my job, and I feel like I'll never be able to finish high school.

Although some adolescent fathers fit the stereotype, most do not, according to a profile of the teen father compiled from research findings. Before childbirth, the adolescent father typically is uninformed about sex and sexuality, does not use contraception or uses it inconsistently, has difficulty coping with the knowledge of pregnancy, shows signs of stress or depression, and experiences role conflict over being both an adolescent and a parent, but plans to provide financial support and participate in child care. During childbirth, most adolescent fathers attend some of the mother's clinic visits or participate in preparation classes for labor and delivery and stay with the mother during labor. After childbirth, the teen father typically maintains contact with mother and baby; contributes financially to the care of their child; and worries about financial responsibilities, education, employment, his relationship with his partner, and parenting. When teen dads are distinguished from adult dads in research, a more positive profile of teen fathers emerges. For example, data from a national survey of 227 men who fathered their first child during adolescence indicated that these teen fathers had marital satisfaction levels and intimacy difficulties similar to those of men who had first fathered during their 20s (Heath & McKenry, 1993), but teen dads reported greater parental satisfaction than did older fathers. In another study distinguishing between adult and teen fathers, researchers reported that younger males, more than older ones, were judged by teen mothers to be more involved with their children (Danzinger & Radin, 1990).

Premature Developmental Transition

In contrast to the deficit perspective, the generative or generational perspective shifts the emphasis and focus from inadequacy to a perspective of teenage fathering as an early but potentially positive experience contributing to the well-being of the teen dads, their partners, and their children. The generative perspective is based, in large part, on Erikson's (1980) psychosocial concept of generativity. Erikson proposed that individuals have tasks to achieve at each developmental stage based partly on society's expectations of individuals at that age. In our society, during adulthood individuals are expected to contribute to the well-being of the next generation, typically through rearing biological or adoptive children, guiding other children, and making the world better for those who will soon inherit it. In contrast, the primary developmental task of adolescents in our society is the clarification of their own individual identity. Adolescents are generally so focused on the task of trying to figure out who they are that a generational connection is out of synch with their own developmental status. For the teenage father, the psychosocial crises of intimacy versus isolation and generativity versus stagnation are complexly and prematurely woven into the challenge of establishing an identity. An adolescent father is faced with the task of connecting the present to the future in a meaningful way before he has had the opportunity to establish the very meaning of the present.

An adolescent father experiences the conflict of being a teenager who is trying to cope with the adult work of fathering. Cliff illustrates how adolescent fathers are frightened by what Fry and Trifiletti (1983) called "the undefined social territory into which they are stepping" (p. 221):

> I've thought about it [fatherhood] a lot, and it scares me. Hell, I'll admit it—I'm not a full grown man and I never try to pretend to be. I'm still, well, a child in a sense. . . . I'll love it [the child], but I'm not sure I'll know how to teach and guide it" (Panzarine & Elster, 1983, p. 119).

Prospective young fathers must deal not only with the stressors of pregnancy and caring for young children, but also with the stresses of normal adolescent development and the unscheduled developmental tasks of adulthood (Russell, 1980; Sadler & Catrone, 1983). Thus, generative fathering is particularly difficult to achieve for teenage fathers.

The four areas of generative work discussed in Chapter 2 of this volume (development work, relationship work, ethical work, and stewardship work) present unique challenges to teen dads. Developmentally, the generative work of fathering conflicts with the identity work of the adolescent. Also, the teen dad's efforts to, in the terms used in Chapter 2, "maintain supportive conditions" for a child are complicated by his own need, as an adolescent, to be supported by others. In a related factor, teenage fathers may find the ethical work of fathering to be challenging because it is difficult for teen dads to "ensure a secure environment" and "respond to needs and wants" of a child when the adolescent fathers are in such an intense period of transition and surprise in response to an unanticipated pregnancy and the birth of a child. Teenage fathers and mothers who are not in a permanent relationship may find relationship work challenging because they often do not receive the sanction and support of others, who may in some cases even try to pull the couple apart and prevent the father from caring for his child. Finally, stewardship work challenges the teen father to "provide resources and opportunities" for a mother and child when likely he has not yet finished school or is in a low-paying job.

Despite these daunting challenges, adolescent fathers are capable of generative feelings and actions. In fact, research suggests that many teen males are interested in and feel responsible for their young children, but practices, policies, and programs based on the deficit perspective restrict their involvement. Indeed, it appears that most societal responses are based on the assumption that teen dads will fail in their developmental task of caring for the next generation and thus reject their offspring (Erikson, 1982).

Because the generative work of fathering is very difficult for teenagers, teen fathering is clearly not the ideal for father, mother, child, or society. Erikson (1964) himself wrote that it was essential "that the control of procreation be guided . . . by a universal sense of generative responsibility toward all human beings brought planfully into this world" (p. 132). When teen males do become fathers, however, our society responds as if these young males are responsible adult men with the emotional and financial resources to accomplish the generative work of fathering. As a culture or society, we send teenage fathers a mixed message: "We expect you to be a responsible parent, but we will not provide you with guidance on how to become one" (Kiselica & Sturmer, 1993, pp. 488-489). Here, again, is the deficit perspective: Teenage fathers are held accountable for not measuring up to the expectations set for adult fathers but are not provided the societal support to bridge the gap between their adolescent stage of development and the adult yardstick with which they are measured. Teen dads need emotional and social support and guidance rather than the downgrading perpetuated by these stereotypes. By denying emotional support and services to teen fathers, our society maintains a punitive mind-set toward these young males and consequently does not support their generativity with the means for them to resolve the developmental dilemma in which they find themselves: the stressors and tasks of generativity created by fatherhood imposed on normal developmental stressors and tasks of adolescent identity.

Interventions for Generativity: Proactive and Reactive

In the absence of valid information about teenage fathers, the professional community has relied on stereotypes that have been debunked by a growing body of research. Although males as well as females are at risk in teenage pregnancy, males and their families have been grossly overlooked in service delivery practices. Research suggests that the teen father population is underserved relative to teen mothers. A study of 103 social service agencies in one midwestern state showed that a significant number of agencies offered fewer services to teen fathers than to teen mothers (Kiselica & Sturmer, 1993). Programs that fail to reach out to young fathers not only ignore their emotional needs but also overlook a significant support system for the mother and baby. It is important that practitioners examine and, if necessary, overcome biases against teen dads and try to make sure that these adolescents are included in every aspect of service delivery. A generative mind-set is called for in which teen fathers are viewed as an at-risk group who have the same emotional vulnerabilities and fears as well as parenting potential as teen mothers and who require the same services known to be essential. Interviews with teen dads indicate that they are interested in receiving preparation for fatherhood, including training in the responsibilities of child care (Panzarine & Elster, 1983).

Aggressive outreach efforts have been called for that are supportive and nonjudgmental (Kiselica et al., 1994). Teen dads can be identified by tapping into existing services for pregnant teen moms or obstetric-gynecological clinics, Planned Parenthood, and pediatrician's offices. Information regarding services for teen dads can be distributed where teen males are likely to congregate (e.g., playgrounds and recreational facilities). More formalized, established networks such as churches, mental health service providers, and school counselors can lead to referrals. Public service announcements in the media that feature males talking realistically about their experiences as fathers and the help they have received from programs may attract other teen fathers in need of support (Robinson, 1988).

Professionals who work in the area of adolescent pregnancy can develop and promote a generative perspective of teenage fathering. Schools need proactive programs that provide information on relationships and ways to formulate and attain goals. A developmental process in schools can begin teaching males at an early age that parenting includes fathering as well as mothering. Boys need places where they can discuss their relationships with girls and become more aware of the consequences and responsibilities of parenthood at any age.

Teenage fathers need support and guidance in identifying the means and resources for generative fathering—not the denigration of past stereotypes inherent in the deficit perspective. Outreach programs to young fathers have demonstrated that, once involved, many males are eager to become more competent and caring parents. They need counseling to help them deal with the stresses surrounding childbirth, reconcile the competing developmental requirements of the teenage years and parenting, and integrate their adult role responsibilities with their normal adolescent needs. Vocational counseling can support teenage fathers in realizing their good intentions of providing financial support through education and occupational training. They need guidance in dealing with the stresses of financial responsibilities and problems in their relationship with the mother of their child. Clinicians can play a major role in involving teenagers in the lives of their infants and helping these adolescent males cope with the difficult situations in which they find themselves. When interviewing pregnant adolescents, professionals can routinely include questions about the teenage father. Simply asking about the father's involvement and whereabouts, however, is not sufficient. Encouraging the teen mother or mother-to-be to bring the father in for an interview or arranging activities for expectant teenage fathers during clinic hours underscores the potential value of the father. Reaching out to teenage fathers has potential advantages for the total family system.

Reaching out to the parents of expectant teen dads could be one way to activate a network that can be a strong source of support. Seeking out men as speakers who have succeeded in spite of their young fathering could be a powerful influence on subsequent fathering behavior. Training ministers and teachers to be helpful along with promoting models of father involvement may encourage teen fathers to come forward. Finally, merely preaching to teenagers is not going to work. Rather, listening to them talk about what is happening to them while providing support and guidance can help young fathers experience more control over their lives and the lives of their children at a time when many are prone to concede to a seemingly overwhelming situation by considering minimal or no involvement.

Two programs designed to be responsive to the unique needs of teen dads illustrate a positive, proactive approach to supporting and facilitating teen fathers' potential ability to provide generative parenting. Kiselica and colleagues (1994) propose a group psychoeducational model to support teen dads in becoming loving and effective parents. This course on fatherhood was designed to respond sensitively to the particular needs of teen fathers in the context of a group support process. Because teen dads may be made wary by judgmental reactions from their parents and other adults, special attention is given in creating a supportive and nonjudgmental environment in which teenage fathers can explore issues related to their ability to become committed and competent parents. Such issues include personal questions that the fathers are ready to face, such as their reactions to unplanned pregnancy and their attitudes about fathering, to child development and child care, and finally to more difficult subjects, such as sexually responsible behavior. In helping young fathers or fathers-to-be clarify their beliefs about fathering, acquire parenting skills, and assume sexually responsible behavior, teen dads can experience affirmation of their worth as individuals and their potential contributions as a parents, as well as acquire the necessary skills to realize this potential, thus setting the stage for generative parenting.

Boulder Valley Schools Teen Parenting Program illustrates the generative mind-set of teen fathering in action (Parmerlee-Greiner, 1993). This nationally recognized program is designed to meet the educational and vocational needs of all school-age parents and expectant parents, fathers as well as mothers, and their children. This program is unique in its particular sensitivity to the challenges of child rearing experienced by teen dads while achieving their own personal and economic self-sufficiency. After young fathers are identified, contacted, and encouraged to return to school, they are offered social and career counseling and linked with appropriate agencies for job training and placement. These young dads also participate in support groups, parenting classes, natural childbirth councils, and serve on advisory councils for the program. This degree of responsiveness to the needs of teenage fathers demonstrates the value of these young men and offers the support and guidance that can result in generative fathering on their part.

Teen Dads: Principles for Generative Fathering

Several of the myths about teenage fathers cited earlier, when turned upside-down, yield important and fundamental principles fostering generative fathering:

1. Responsible sexual behavior includes understanding that sex carries with it a responsibility, so that males become parents at the appropriate developmental time and under the appropriate developmental circumstances.
2. Generative fathering needs to be grounded in fathers' positive feelings about their own identity and masculinity and an internal locus of control.
3. Responsible relationship behavior includes emotional and physical availability as well as active decision making with regard to fathering.
4. The realities and implications of fathering include a knowledge of child development and child rearing and the responsibilities inherent in fathering.

Proactively, these principles fostering generative fathering need to be introduced early in the lives of young males through our educational system. Counselors and teachers in public schools can work together to develop programs for males and females in family life education, sociology, psychology, and home economics that provide information on human reproduction, contraceptive responsibility, parenting, and family planning. These programs should be comprehensive enough to help young children and teenagers build positive self-concepts, feelings of self-worth, and an understanding of the consequences of teenage parenting. Programs at the junior and senior high school levels can teach youth about how the family functions as a system and how each member influences and is influenced by the system. Young males who understand and internalize a generative perspective of fathering early on are more likely to make responsible parenting decisions, including postponing fatherhood until the developmental time and circumstances under which generative fathering is more likely possible. When teen males do become fathers or fathers-to-be, however, social systems need to be in place to provide the support and resources necessary for teen dads to develop and realize these principles in their parenting.

8

Generative Fathering After Divorce and Remarriage

Beyond the "Disappearing Dad"

KAY PASLEY
CARMELLE MINTON

Current estimates suggest that 56% to 62% of all first marriages end in divorce (Martin & Bumpass, 1989; U.S. Bureau of the Census, 1990), and most divorces include children under the age of 18 years (U.S. Bureau of the Census, 1990). Most men and women eventually remarry (U.S. Bureau of the Census, 1990, 1992), and remarriage occurs fairly quickly after divorce, usually within about 2 years (DeWitt, 1994; U.S. Bureau of the Census, 1992). Because dating is the common pathway to marriage, adults choose a new spouse during the often brief period between marriages. What this means for both adults and children is that there is little time to adjust to the many transitions inherent in terminating one marriage and beginning another. In addition, parenting after divorce and remarriage is complicated.

Unlike most divorced fathers, men who have physical custody of their children often are viewed positively, as noted by DeMaris and Greif in Chapter 9, this volume. These fathers are touted as uncommon, often heroic, men who love their children so much that they are willing to assume responsibility for their care. Divorced, nonresident fathers, however, typically are described in pejorative ways that reflect absence, abandonment, or incompetent parenting—they are called disappearing fathers, deadbeat dads, and Disneyland daddies. The negative images of divorced, nonresident fathers as disengaged, uninvolved, and uninterested are pervasive in both the professional and popular literatures. Here, we focus on the experience of nonresident fathers after divorce from the man's perspective. We address obstacles in marital transitions to a father's continued involvement with his children and offer suggestions for decreasing these obstacles following divorce and remarriage. Several assumptions underlie our thinking. First, we concur with other scholars that fathers are important to children's lives in general (Biller, 1993). Second, we assume that continued contact with one's father after divorce enhances children's adjustment, and some evidence supports this belief (Brody & Forehand, 1990; Emery, Hetherington, & DiLalla, 1984; Hetherington, Cox, & Cox, 1976; Wallerstein & Kelly, 1980). Third, we believe that continued involvement with one's children is beneficial also to fathers, and some research supports this (Guttman, 1989; Jacobs, 1982). Fourth, we assume that most fathers want to be involved with their children and to fulfill their responsibilities as a father, consistent with a theme of this volume first sounded in Chapter 1, this volume; evidence also supports this assumption (e.g., Arditti, 1992; Haskins, Richey, & Wicker, 1987). Finally, we assume that good fathering after divorce is hard work that requires especially creative efforts, an important part of fathering highlighted in Chapter 2. With these assumptions in mind, we turn our attention to fathering and the complications that make it difficult in the face of marital transitions.

Good Fathering as Good Providing

Thompson and Walker (1989) suggest that the pervasive societal definition of a good father emphasizes first and foremost being a good provider. Through assuming responsibility for providing, men maintain status in their families (Jones, 1991). Loss of job means loss of self, self-respect, and sense of competence to men. Rubin (1994) shows that not having a job prompts working-class men to question their value to the family.

It is this latter finding by Rubin (1994) that has intrigued us, because it suggests that providing and fathering may not be distinct aspects of a man's self-definition. Much of the literature examining social roles implicitly suggests that roles are unique and distinct from one another. For example, Ameatea, Cross, Clark, and Bobby (1986) assess the salience of four social roles (spouse, parent, worker, and home care) as separate entities. They assume that these roles may be associated, but that being a parent is not the same as being a spouse. Our preliminary findings from several focus groups of fathers suggest that men in intact, first marriages may have an integrative view of self. For these men, providing was included in their self-definitions of fathering; being a good father incorporated being a good provider. This is evident in the comments offered by two of our fathers:

If I am doing my job well, I'm providing a good role model for my children regardless of what I do. . . . My job has taken on a whole new dimension for me as a father.

If you're good in your job and you can make those green stamps, then you can provide more for your son.

Furthermore, our findings show that the inclusiveness of men's self-definitions of fathering incorporated the marital relationship. Several fathers wrote that being a good father meant being responsive to their wife's needs and that this provided their children with a model for their relationships:

My wife works, too, so I do things my own father would never do, like changing diapers, cooking dinner, or washing clothes. This shows my children (18 months and 3 years old) that it's important to share the work in the family.

We suspect that such overlap in self-definitions may not be the case for women. A woman's self-definitions as a wife and mother are less likely to include providing or spousal behaviors with two exceptions: women in dual-earner families and women in single-parent families, whose self-definitions may reflect overlap in mother and worker. Unlike men, we believe women in general are less likely to evaluate good mothering according to how well they provide for their children financially or what they do in their marital relationship. If the overlap of identities associated with roles that is evident in our work is common, our failure to recognize the inclusive or integrative nature of fathers' self-definitions may cloud our understanding and interpretation of how self-definitions translate into fathering behaviors and how behaviors, in turn, affect self-definitions. Thus, we suggest that men may define themselves as fathers in complex and inclusive ways that reflect overlap of several identities. How this complexity of men's self-definitions is redefined after divorce is unknown, although some scholars (Ihinger-Tallman, Pasley, & Buehler, 1993) have suggested that redefinition occurs.

Because self-definition occurs in a broader context, fathering behavior is culturally influenced. Today, there is more emphasis placed on men's increased involvement in daily family life than in earlier times (Garbarino, 1993; Gerson, 1993; Griswold, Chapter 5, this volume; LaRossa, 1988; Ritner, 1992). Men are being called on to do more with their children as a means of participating in family work. Yet, for many men and women, and for society in general, men's primary responsibility and commitment to the family continues to be judged by their ability and willingness to provide financially. This is evident after divorce as well. Many men are required by the legal system to continue providing for their children by paying child support or maintenance in the full amount and on time. These behaviors become an important criteria by which fathers are evaluated. "Deadbeat dads" are those fathers who fail to fulfill these expectations; such men are seen as poor or bad fathers rather than simply poor or bad workers or providers. Thus, although there is increasing social pressure for men to be involved in child care and household work, fathers are judged on behavior that is more narrowly defined (i.e., providing). As a result, men receive mixed messages about what fathering means and what behaviors constitute good fathering.

If men's self-definitions as fathers are broad and inclusive, but men's performance as fathers is judged primarily on the basis of providing, confusion and ambiguity are likely outcomes. Even among social scientists, there is disagreement about what constitutes fathering. Garbarino (1993) suggests that fatherhood is essentially a social invention based on motherhood. Pruett (1993) presents an opposing view to fatherhood, stating, "Fathering is not mothering any more than mothering is ever fathering" (p. 46). He suggests that fathers do not need to be mothers to be good parents, but they do need to behave in ways that feel comfortable to them. Men today are being asked to become more involved in the care of their children, but they are also being told to care for them in ways that mothers do. Therefore, they are evaluated on competing criteria (time in child care means time away from providing and vice versa).

The confusion that results from ambiguous and often competing self-definitions is exacerbated following divorce. Fathering behaviors common before divorce that reinforced fathering identity (e.g., getting the child ready for school in the morning) become limited or eliminated altogether. Thus, redefinition of self as father is probable (Ihinger-Tallman et al., 1993). It is to this ambiguity and the need for redefinition of identity that we now turn our attention as we examine how fathering changes after divorce and remarriage.

A Closer Look At Nonresidential Fathering After Divorce

Scholars suggest that men are connected to their children through their relationships with their wives (Doherty, Chapter 14, this volume; Frustenberg & Cherlin, 1991), and that mothers mediate men's relationships with their children by monitoring, supervising, and delegating certain tasks to fathers (Backett, 1987). If this is so, then father involvement after divorce should diminish when a man's connection to his wife is severed or dramatically altered. It is too simplistic to assume that the reason fathers disengage from children is because the spousal relationship ends, however; the process of marital dissolution is more complicated.

It is true that many fathers decrease or discontinue their contact with their children after divorce (e.g., Dudley, 1991; Furstenberg & Harris, 1993; Furstenberg, Nord, Peterson, & Zill, 1983; Hoffman, 1995), although recent studies show less disengagement than reported earlier (Braver, Wolchik, Sandler, Fogas, & Zvetina, 1991; Maccoby & Mnookin, 1992; Seltzer, 1991). Contact is not the only indicator of father involvement. Payment of child support is another way of assessing father involvement, and surveys show low rates of both child support awards and payments (Seltzer & Bianchi, 1988; U.S. Bureau of the Census, 1991, Table C). Many fathers are not court ordered to provide for their children. Of those who are, many fail to do so. The reasons fathers disengage from their children physically and economically and the obstacles that discourage engagement are insufficiently studied (Ihinger-Tallman et al., 1993), but for at least partial answers, we direct our attention to this literature and the results of our own research.

What Prompts Fathers to Disengage From Their Children?

Furstenberg (1990) summarizes much of the literature on father disengagement in suggesting, "Some fathers are pushed out of the family. . . . Geographic mobility, increased economic demands, and new family responsibilities, which often accompany remarriage, may erode the tenuous bonds between noncustodial fathers and their children" (pp. 387-388). What is clear from the literature is that the decision to limit contact with one's children is neither straightforward nor easy for men to make, although some men experience relief after divorce and welcome freedom from parenting responsibility. If the assumptions we made earlier are accurate (that most fathers want to maintain contact with children and fulfill their paternal responsibility), then most men will experience emotional pain, frustration, anger, and confusion about how to maintain meaningful relationships with their children after divorce. We offer the comments of some of the 92 divorced, nonresident fathers that were part of our earlier study (see Minton & Pasley, 1996). These two comments emphasize the difficulty of fathering after the end of a marriage:

> The most painful thing was not being able to be with my sons, to tuck them in bed, to say good night to them.

> It has not been easy! I have much to learn. I've made many mistakes, but I am praying and trusting God for wisdom. . . . I desperately want to be a faithful father to my children.

Other comments reflect the obstacles to fathering after divorce identified in the literature. We discuss several key obstacles here to demonstrate the increased complexity of fathering following divorce.

The Effects of Legal Decisions. Some obstacles to continued father involvement result from court decisions regarding custody, visitation, and child support and the way men perceive these decisions. In most cases (almost 90%), mothers have custody of children after divorce (Emery, 1994). Although some states give preference to joint legal custody (providing fathers input into decisions affecting their children), how the custody arrangement influences daily life varies (Emery, 1994; Maccoby & Mnookin, 1992). For some, joint legal custody means fathers are equally involved in decisions affecting children's lives (e.g., medical care, education), and children reside part of the week with each parent. For others, joint legal custody does not mean fathers have input into decisions or much access to their children.

We know that decisions about custody and visitation affect the contact between fathers and children, fathers' self-definitions, and the emotional experience of fathers after divorce. For example, joint legal custody is associated with more contact between father and child and the father's feeling closer to the child and more influential in the child's life (Arditti, 1992; Greif, 1979). Some scholars suggest that joint legal custody implicitly validates fathers' influences in their children's lives, as men adjust better to divorce when they have joint custody (Bertoia & Drakich, 1993; Coltrane & Hickman, 1992). We concur with other scholars (Arendell, 1995; Bertoia & Drakich, 1993) that joint legal custody gives fathers the impression that society recognizes their importance to their children.

Court orders that fail to recognize the value of fathers, granting only limited access or sole maternal custody, serve as obstacles to father involvement.

The meaning attached to the "visiting status" can be an obstacle to father involvement. Being labeled a visitor results in extensive intrapersonal conflict and emotional turmoil for fathers (Arendell, 1995; Bertoia & Drakich, 1993; Furstenberg, 1988b), and maintaining close bonds with children is more difficult because of the arrangements. This means that some men struggle to keep seeing their children, whereas other men do not and then they struggle to feel okay about disengaging from them. Both types of struggles can result in emotional pain; the greater the pain, the less likely the father is to continue visitation. Thus, disengagement may be a coping strategy for managing emotional pain. Many of the divorced fathers in our study expressed their pain and frustration with the legal system and outcomes, as evident in this father's comment:

> I believe that the system [judges, attorneys, etc.] have [sic] little or no consideration for the father. At some point the system creates an environment where the father loses any natural desire to see his children because it becomes so difficult, both financially and emotionally. At that point, he convinces himself that the best thing to do is wait until they are older.

Furthermore, the actual patterns of access and visitation serve as another obstacle to father involvement after divorce. The typical visitation pattern assigned by courts is two weekends a month, or every other weekend. The fathers in our research and those in other studies (e.g., Arendell, 1995; Bertoia & Drakich, 1993) believed that decisions around visitation relegated them to an insignificant role by denying them liberal access to their children. This was particularly true in situations where fathers saw themselves as highly involved prior to divorce, a finding supported by other scholars (Arditti, 1992; Kruk, 1991). In our research, many divorced fathers wrote about their resentment of visitation limits and the legal system:

> I have been rendered almost impotent/powerless as a father by the legal system.

> I don't get to spend as much time as I would like raising my son. I feel like I got a raw deal in my divorce and would love to have my son with me all the time.

> The legal system has essentially invalidated and undermined all of the moral teaching I had spent years to develop and nurture in my children and have made a mockery out of being an upright, involved, and loving father. They have

instead showed that their mother's deceitful, immoral lifestyle is rewarded by the state while the honest, etc., father is stripped of everything he holds dear.

The Coparental Relationship. Beyond obstacles to father involvement resulting from court decisions around custody and visitation, the way in which former spouses interact may create additional obstacles. Some evidence shows that mothers can and do block and sabotage contact between nonresident fathers and children (Ahrons & Rodgers, 1987; Arditti & Keith, 1993; Arendell, 1995; Dudley, 1991; Johnston, 1992; Kelly, 1991; Wallerstein & Kelly, 1980). "Gatekeeping" by mothers that limits access to children can become a means of getting back at a former spouse (Arendell, 1992, 1995). Fathers express anger about such behavior by their former spouses:

I had problems for the first two years of our divorce with visitations. Going up to three months without being allowed to see my sons. I finally had court-ordered visitation worked out which helped for awhile. In the past three years, I've had an average of 20-25 times when my visitation has been denied for no reason. My last two attorneys have given no help in resolving this problem.

She refuses to compromise and it has always been her way or no way. Every situation for which she justified [her behavior] is for the good of the boys, but it will ultimately be for the good of herself.

The level and nature of conflict between former spouses are common obstacles to fathering after divorce, although studies show a decrease in conflict over time (e.g., Ahrons & Miller, 1993; Ahrons & Rodgers, 1987; Johnston, Gonzales, & Campbell, 1987; Maccoby, Depner, & Mnookin, 1990). Disagreements over discipline and treatment of children often pervade interaction between former spouses and reduce the frequency of visitation (Dudley, 1991; Greif, 1979; Kruk, 1992). A primary way former spouses attempt to exercise control over one another is through visitation and the payment of child support, and conflict over these issues is common. Arendell (1992, 1995) and others (e.g., Bertoia & Drakich, 1993) show that payment, nonpayment, and delayed or reduced payment are strategies men use to influence former spouses in gaining access to or influence over children. Because society is most concerned over men's failure to meet their financial obligations to children, courts are readier to deal with child support noncompliance than visitation or access issues. In fact, judges often appear to ignore or evade "collateral issues" such as visitation. Evidence suggests that judges feel less comfortable resolving access issues (Emery, 1994). Men, thus, see themselves as punished by the legal system in this common power struggle, whereas their former wives remain unpunished (Arendell, 1995).

Power struggles evident in the payment of child support may serve as obstacles to father involvement over time. For example, when men perceive the former spouse is squandering the money meant for their children on herself or nonessentials, they are less likely to pay child support in full and on time. They often complain, as this father did, that the system fails to monitor the mother to assure child support is used on the child's behalf:

> It seems as though child support becomes a guise for alimony without any checks and balances. The government places a strangle-hold on those willing to be responsible for child support by an inequitable tax structure, thus placing some negative fault for divorce decree. Trying to comply with judgments on financial matters makes father a dirty and muddled word because of the emphasis placed on an unmonitored amount paid in child support.

Another scenario is that men believe the former spouse obtains more child support than is needed or that a father is not compensated either financially or by simple recognition for the "voluntary" support he provides when the children visit (e.g., they need new shoes for school and he buys them). Under these types of circumstances, he is less likely to pay, especially when he sees the former spouse as making decisions not in the child's best interests.

> My ex-wife often complains about her own finances, but with a $20,000 year job of her own plus about $10,000 a year from me in tax-free money, I have a hard time feeling too sorry for her, especially since she only had a car payment when she left. I resent her for taking my daughter so far away. She did not stop to consider my daughter's needs for two parents who live close.

Yet another scenario is the man who is delinquent in payment, perhaps for good reasons, such as unemployment. Evidence shows unemployment is the best predictor of nonpayment (Braver, Fitzpatrick, & Bay, 1991).

In all of these scenarios, the bottom line is that the mother may deny visitation, thinking or saying, "When he pays, he can see the kids." The father may think or say, "When she lets me see the kids, I'll pay." These kinds of impasses place children at risk. Child support and visitation become control strategies for former spouses who fail to consider the effects of nonpayment and lack of contact on the well-being of children. Because the payment of child support and contact or visitation are associated (Seltzer, 1991), behaviors of former spouses that reduce either the payment of child support or visitation are obstacles to father involvement.

Social Support. Being in a social context that is unsupportive of involvement after divorce is another obstacle to fathering. Ihinger-Tallman and her associates (1993) argue that, according to identity theory, commitment to an identity increases the chances that the identity is salient to the individual and, thus, reflected in their behavior. Commitment to an identity stems, in part, from a father's social network (e.g., friends, former in-laws, parents). Some evidence shows that support for continued involvement is associated with frequency of visitation, even when the coparental relationship is conflictual (Arditti, 1992; Hetherington, Arnett, & Hollier, 1988; Kruk, 1992; Tepp, 1983).

Preliminary findings from our study also support the relationship between social support and father involvement. We found that among our divorced, nonresident fathers, those who reported receiving more encouragement also reported more involvement in child-related activities ($r = .22, p < .05$). Thus, when social support is lacking, as would be more common for divorced fathers, they are less involved.

Other Obstacles. Other obstacles that affect the engagement patterns of nonresident fathers after divorce are noted in the literature. Greif and Kritall (1993) found that a child may reject the father or that extended kin may interfere and make involvement more difficult. We found these to be themes for our divorced fathers as well:

> The divorce caused my wife to turn my daughter against me, though it took two years to do this after the divorce. Now we [my daughter and I] are trying to turn it around. It is a long, uphill fight, but it is being done, however, slowly.

> Her and her family have gone out of their way to keep my son from me. They are using him as a tool to hurt me.

In addition to rejection by one's child or interference by extended kin and former in-laws, geographic distance can impede fathers' connections with their nonresident children, especially visitation. This is often frustrating and emotionally difficult for fathers:

My daughter and I were extremely close. It was devastating when my ex-wife moved 350 miles away. For several months it was very emotional when I would visit and have to leave. Adjustments have come slowly. I think of her often.

If it were not for the unique opportunities the job I found after divorce affords me, I would be economically deprived of any meaningful involvement and influence with my children. [He resides 800 miles away.]

Fathering After Remarriage

When a remarriage occurs, fathering becomes even more complicated. Men often must redefine themselves to incorporate a new identity as a stepfather or accommodate themselves to their children having a stepfather. In remarriage, relationships between biological parents and children have the longest history and strongest emotional bond. New stepparents are outsiders, lacking knowledge and understanding of preexisting patterns of interaction. As a further complication, the competing developmental tasks of adjusting to life as a newly remarried couple occur simultaneously with the parenting of children.

Under these circumstances, we see at least two factors that make the process of identity redefinition complex. First, scholars (Cherlin, 1978; Giles-Sims, 1984; Pasley, 1985) have argued that the norms and sanctions around stepfathering are not clear, so stepfathers experience even more confusion about how to parent than do biological fathers. In addition, previous biological parenting experience does not translate well to stepparenting (see Pasley, Dollahite, & Ihinger-Tallman, 1993, for a brief review). In other words, parenting behaviors that work in first-marriage families are less effective and sometimes ineffective in stepfamilies (Hetherington & Clingempeel, 1992). In addition, the acceptable behaviors of supervision and monitoring common among biological fathers are less desirable in stepfathers, especially early on in the remarriage (Bray & Berger, 1993).

Second, for many men remarriage following divorce occurs quickly, with 50% of men and 33% of women remarrying within 1 year (DeWitt, 1994; U.S. Bureau of the Census, 1990); adjustment to divorce, however, takes about 3 years (Hetherington, Cox & Cox, 1982; Wallerstein & Blakeslee, 1989). Within this adjustment period, two important changes occur: Fathering is redefined initially, and much of the conflict around coparenting diminishes. When remarriage occurs too quickly, redefinition and coparenting issues are not adequately addressed, so confusion about appropriate behavior as a father or stepfather is likely. Such confusion can undermine the development of cooperation between former spouses, and coparental conflict can exacerbate the confusion around how best to father children and stepchildren. Such role confusion is a reminder that the developmental task of establishing an identity, primarily associated with adolescence, is woven throughout the life cycle (Erikson, 1988) and may be especially visible at times when dramatic shifts occur in adult life circumstances.

The legal system provides additional obstacles to fathering after remarriage. In cases where a man becomes a stepfather, the laws governing stepparents fail to clarify his rights and responsibilities (Ramsey, 1994). Stepfathering probably is more poorly defined than fathering after divorce, which is already ambiguous. The ambiguity shows up when stepparents attempt to gain access to stepchildren following a divorce or when they attempt to make decisions on behalf of stepchildren in medical emergencies.

It is apparent that the remarriage of either former spouse affects fathering after divorce. The typical pattern is one of decline in contact that may represent a reevaluation of arrangements of residence and custody of children (Maccoby & Mnookin, 1992). The least contact is common when only one parent remarries, especially the mother, and more contact when both parents remarry (Furstenberg et al., 1983; Hetherington et al., 1988; Maccoby & Mnookin, 1992; Seltzer, Schaeffer, & Charng, 1989). When one parent remarries, this decline may reflect the need of the new stepfamily to form stronger boundaries so a sense of cohesion develops. If the mother remarries, she may think that one way to do this is to limit contact between the child and his or her father, as evident in the following comment:

> For a period of about three years after my ex-wife remarried, I had very limited visitation privileges with my son. The ex-wife said that she wanted to establish a sense of family with her new husband and I would confuse my son's feelings about this.

Fathers who remarry and become stepfathers often assume some responsibility, financial and emotional, for their stepchildren. Less father involvement with the biological child shows in a decline in payment of child support and a decrease in his availability (Buehler & Ryan, 1994; Seltzer, 1991).

Research also shows that remarriage creates stress in the relationship between the former spouses (Ahrons & Wallisch, 1987; Wallerstein &

Blakeslee, 1989), which can become an obstacle to fathering. Remarried former spouses report more hostile feelings and negative opinions toward one another than do divorced, nonremarried former spouses (Masheter, 1991; Schuldberg & Guisinger, 1991). These emotions are associated with fewer child-related discussions between former spouses after remarriage (Seltzer, 1991) and reduced contact between fathers and children.

Few researchers have examined the effects of the relationship with a former spouse on a father's involvement after remarriage. Buehler and Ryan's (1994) findings from 109 divorced fathers are worth noting. First, they found that the relationship with the former spouse was more difficult in stepfamilies when only the father had remarried, but that father involvement was more likely to discontinue when only the mother remarried. In other words, the wife's remarriage but not the husband's served as a barrier to continued father involvement. Buehler and Ryan suggested, "The addition of a new husband (and, possibly, a new father figure) increased the complexity of the binuclear family system in such a way that former husbands found it either unnecessary or too difficult to maintain pre-remarriage levels of involvement with their children" (p. 146). Fathers also may see the stepfather as needing to assume additional responsibility (e.g., financial) for his children, and then they lower their levels of child support (Tropf, 1984). Second, when the mother remarried, higher levels of conflict between the former spouses were associated with *more* father involvement (more frequent and longer visits). This suggests that a nonresident father may react to the remarriage by firmly enacting his commitment to his children and to fathering behaviors. Such an interpretation would be consistent with Snarey's (1993) concept of *generativity chill,* that is, feeling a threat to the developmental achievement of learning to care for the next generation (Erikson, 1950). A nonresident father who increases his involvement with his children in the face of his former spouse's remarriage may do so in response to a sensed danger to his generativity. Last, cooperation was strongly associated with child support compliance for remarrieds but was unrelated when neither of the former spouses were remarried. Taken together, these findings show that both remarriage and the coparenting relationship after marriage can serve as obstacles to fathering.

Easing the Transitions

In the face of the multiple changes inherent in divorce and remarriage, maintaining a connection to one's children is difficult. We return to the assumptions we outlined earlier that fathers are important to children's lives, children do best when fathers remain engaged following marital transitions, and fathers want to continue fulfilling their responsibilities. Doing this requires new ways of thinking about self as a father, changes in fathering behaviors, and changes in the broader context to support involvement. In this final section, we discuss some ways to decrease the obstacles and ease the transition to fathering after divorce and remarriage.

We acknowledge that change is difficult for most people, and fathers in marital transition are no exception. All participants in divorce experience discomfort and stress as daily life is altered. Because divorce affects so many aspects of life (e.g., residence, jobs, chores, interaction patterns), distress is common. Recognizing and anticipating changes in the ways nonresident fathers can and are able to function as fathers is essential for them to feel competent and satisfied over time. Fathers who think more flexibly and creatively about how to father best after divorce and remarriage likely experience greater ease in these transitions. This means that one's self-definition must become more individualized to accommodate the ambiguity associated with societal expectations about fathering after divorce. If a nonresident father defines himself and his behaviors by norms that reflect resident fathers (e.g., tucking children in bed nightly), he will evaluate himself negatively after divorce because circumstances may not allow these common behaviors. We believe that divorced, non-resident fathers do best when they define themselves and their behavior in ways that are unique to their situations. And they must reconstruct their relationship with their children on an ethical commitment to the children's well-being (Dollahite et al., Chapter 2, this volume). Several examples written by the fathers in our study show such redefinition and reconstruction:

> Basically I talk to my children daily for 15 minutes–1 hour over the phone [bill is $150 a month]. It is surprising how they will open up to you and tell you about their difficulties. I am 300 miles away from my kids and I know more about them than their mother. I also know more about my kids than my father knew about me.

> I only see the girls for 10 days at Christmas and 3 months during the summer. I write them weekly, discuss scripture in the letters and how to apply it to their lives. My determination is for them to feel close to me and supported by me even though they live on the other side of the country.

> One therapeutic activity for me has been keeping a daily journal of all my thoughts, anger, love, prayers, feelings, etc., that I will give my daughter at a

time when she is mature. My ex-wife, I'm sure, is telling her things that are only half true, if true at all. I want her to know my thoughts and that she was loved and thought of daily by me.

Flexibility also means working out a pattern of contact with children that is predictable and stable, yet responsive to changes in the children and life circumstances in general. Research shows that this is good for children and for parents (Issacs, 1988; Johnston, 1995; Pearson, Thoennes, & Anhalt, 1993; Maccoby & Mnookin, 1992). To do so, former spouses must be able to focus first and foremost on the needs of the children. When this occurs, the quality of the parent-child relationship is enhanced and both children and parents do better (Johnston, 1992; Kline, Tschann, Johnston, & Wallerstein, 1989; Buchannan, Maccoby, & Dornbusch, 1991, in press). This means that former spouses must overcome the conflict common in the coparenting relationship because conflict serves as a barrier to ongoing engagement.

The trend toward parent education programs and short-term interventions for divorcing parents is encouraging. These programs may help lessen conflict between former spouses and inform participants about support services in their communities, reducing some of the barriers associated with the coparental relationship and social support discussed earlier. A common goal in these programs is conflict management and refocusing parents' attention and commitment to meeting the children's needs (see McIssac, 1996, for a special issue of *Family and Conciliation Courts Review,* "Parent Education in Divorce and Separation"). Such programs and the additional social support parents access as a result of their participation (Kramer & Washo, 1993) can help reduce the stress associated with divorce and create less volatile coparenting relationships (S. L. Braver, personal communication, January 27, 1996). These programs will likely be ineffective for the estimated 10% of couples who remain engaged in high conflict after divorce, however (Maccoby & Mnookin, 1992; Johnston, 1992). High-conflict couples and those with a history of domestic violence need more intensive and extensive interventions to resolve the issues and promote father involvement (Führmann & McGill, 1996; Johnston & Campell, 1993; McBride, Robertson, & Lane, 1996).

Last, scholars (e.g., Fine & Fine, 1992; Ramsey, 1994; Pearson et al., 1993) have called for legal and social reform to reduce some of the obstacles around custody, visitation, child support, and the rights of stepparents. We support their suggestions that the legal system has not gone far enough in validating fathers; rather, for complex reasons it has implicitly and explicitly devalued fathers' and stepfathers contributions to their children and stepchildren. Courts recognize the financial contributions divorced, nonremarried fathers make to their children, but such contributions are often ignored when they are made by stepfathers. Furthermore, because unemployment and money problems predict child support noncompliance, services that enhance fathers' money management (e.g., debt counseling) and provide job training are warranted (Pearson et al., 1993). These additional services can help fathers meet their financial responsibilities. Also, because typical child support awards do not adequately meet the actual costs of child rearing (Pearson et al., 1993), educating fathers about the true costs can diminish their perceptions that mothers squander resources meant for the child.

From the perspective of the divorced, nonresident father, legal reform must do more to enforce access (custody and visitation) agreements (Pearson & Anhalt, 1992). For stepfathers, reform must recognize their contribution to stepchildren, so that if a second divorce occurs, their desire for continued access is not ignored because of their nonbiological status and the law's preference for blood relatives. Men in both cases can feel shut out of children's lives by former spouses and helpless in their attempts to see (step)children. When men have such experiences or feel this way, disengagement increases and children lose. Courts would do well to give equal consideration to issues of access as they do to child support compliance. In this way, the message men receive is that their generative work as fathers extends beyond providing.

Beyond these recommendations, we find it hopeful that many of the fathers in our study wrote sentiments similar to this:

> In the last 4 ½ years, I have developed an incredibly strong and loving bond with my two sons. I am actively involved in all aspects of their lives. I have even coached their soccer and basketball teams for the last three years. The time I spend with them is very quality time—if anything, the divorce has made me a better and more caring father . . . not to say this would not have happened if my marriage had worked out.

Fathers can and do redefine themselves in ways that allow them to stay engaged and feel good about fathering even in the face of what may seen to be overwhelming obstacles brought about by marital transitions.

9

Single Custodial Fathers
and Their Children

When Things Go Well

ALFRED DeMARIS
GEOFFREY L. GREIF

Erikson (1974) suggested that in adulthood, successful development involves learning "what and whom you can take care of" (p. 124). For a growing number of single custodial fathers, the developmental task of learning to take care of the next generation takes on added meaning. Parenting, a challenging endeavor even under the best of circumstances, is especially difficult for single parents. Proportionately far fewer fathers than mothers are awarded custody of their children upon divorce. Although courts have accepted the fact that fathers are fully capable of caring for their children, in many courtrooms the presumption is still in favor of awarding custody of children—particularly young ones—to mothers. Hence, fathers must prove themselves especially competent at parenting to become custodial parents. Once he has custody, however, it is not clear that a father will be supported in this endeavor, especially at work. Employers still see a commitment to parenting as interfering with a commitment to the job. And at home, fathers may find themselves faced with many new tasks, such as cooking and housework, with which they have had little prior experience. Despite these challenges, most single custodial fathers become competent and nurturant single parents. The deficit paradigm of fathering discussed in Chapter 1 clearly does not account well for the experiences of these men.

In this chapter, we provide a profile of the types of single fathers who appear to have more successful experiences as custodial parents. The discussion is grounded in several years' work with a large national data set on single custodial fathers collected by the authors. Additionally, we report some new results from a heretofore unpublished study of these data, in which we discriminate more from less successful fathering experiences based on a number of variables. To begin, we briefly describe how we collected the data and what measures we used to tap different aspects of fathering.

Data and Methods

The Sample

The information presented in this chapter comes from a four-page, 104-item questionnaire distributed in the October 1987 issue of *The Single Parent,* the membership magazine of Parents Without Partners (PWP). PWP had more than 160,000 members at the time the survey was published. Fathers raising children 18 or younger a majority of the time were asked to complete the instrument and fold it into a postage-guaranteed envelope for mailing. Although exact return rates are difficult to calculate, we estimate that the rate was approximately 20%. Additionally, questionnaires were mailed to fathers whose names were obtained from court records in three metropolitan areas: Washington, D.C.; Baltimore; and Philadelphia. To ensure that the sample consisted exclusively of fathers with sole custody of their children, we included in our analyses only those fathers whose children resided with them at least 5 nights per week. This resulted in a final sample of 1,132 men, 18% of whom came from court records.

One weakness of this approach was that it only surveyed members of a self-help group or those who chose to respond when mailed a questionnaire. Moreover, all information on fathering was obtained from the fathers themselves, rather than their ex-spouses, the children, or others who could provide independent reports. The sample is larger than many others used in previous research on fathers, however, and despite its limitations permitted a number of sophisticated statistical analyses that would have been precluded by smaller sample sizes.

Characteristics of Sample Fathers

The average age of sample fathers was 40.8 ($SD = 6.7$). Their marriages had lasted an average of 11.8 years ($SD = 5.8$), and they had had sole custody for about 4 years ($SD = 3.4$). At the time of the survey, almost all of the fathers were divorced, as opposed to maritally separated. They were raising an average of 1.7 children 18 or younger ($SD = .8$), with the oldest child being about 13 years old ($SD = 4.6$). They were most likely to be raising sons exclusively (42%), with a smaller proportion raising children of both sexes (31%), and the remainder raising only daughters (27%). Occupations ranged from professional work (physician, lawyer) to unskilled labor, with nearly half of the sample describing themselves as professional or business people. Fathers had completed an average of 2.4 years of college ($SD = 2.7$ years of schooling) and had a mean income of $33,500, ($SD = 15,700$), with half the sample earning above $30,000. By comparison, the mean income for white male householders (96% of these fathers were white) with no wife present, in 1986, was $26,247 (U.S. Bureau of the Census, 1987). Thus, our sample evinced somewhat higher income than single white males in the United States in general.

Measures of Successful Parenting Experiences

To distinguish more from less successful fathering experiences, one must define what constitutes success. Because we only surveyed the fathers themselves, we were necessarily limited to what fathers felt about their experience and performance as parents; henceforth, we use quotation marks around "success" to indicate that such impressions are purely subjective and do not necessarily convey a professional judgment about parenting quality. Questionnaire items were designed to elicit fathers' feelings.

The primary measure of parenting performance was the Index of Parental Attitudes (IPA). This scale was designed to measure the severity of problems in parent-child relationships, as reported by the parent. It consists of 25 statements, such as "My child gets on my nerves," "I get along well with my child," and "I feel that I can really trust my child." Respondents indicate how frequently they experience these feelings toward a referent child or children, with responses ranging from "rarely or none of the time" to "most or all of the time." In our survey, fathers were asked to complete this scale in reference to "the children living with you." Scores of relationship problems on this scale range from 0 to 100, with higher scores signifying more problematic relationships with children.[1]

In our sample, the mean score was 13.3 (SD = 9.9). Scores of 30 or higher indicate a clinically significant problem in parent-child relations; only 6.4% of the fathers in our sample had scores in that range. Other measures of parenting quality consisted of four single items. Fathers were asked to rate themselves as parents and to rate the quality of their relationships with their children, both on 4-point scales ranging from "poor" (1) to "excellent" (4). They were asked how satisfied they were with their children's progress in most areas, on a scale from "very unsatisfied" (1) to "very satisfied" (5), and how comfortable they were as single parents, also on a 5-point scale, from "very uncomfortable" (1) to "very comfortable" (5). Finally, they were asked to tell how difficult the combination of working and raising children had been for them, with possible responses "very," "somewhat," or "not at all."

Findings

We begin by summarizing the findings of several analyses of this sample of fathers conducted in the past 5 years or so. These studies have, for the most part, focused on only one or another of the indexes of parenting success enumerated above. We extend this work by drawing a profile of the most "successful" fathers in our sample, based on a consideration of all measures simultaneously.

Attitudes Toward the Children

One elemental feature of the single father's household that appears to affect his parenting outcomes is the age and sex distribution of his children. Fathers seem especially to perceive young daughters as the least troublesome children to raise. We found that relationship problem scores were lower on average for fathers raising children under 13, and that this was especially true for men having custody only of daughters (DeMaris & Greif, 1992). Younger children, and especially girls, are probably easier for fathers to control. Girls are known to cooperate more with each other and therefore probably play better together and have fewer altercations. They are also more likely to help out in the kitchen and pitch in on household chores than boys. Another possibility, of course, is that fathers are less likely to get custody of young girls. Hence, those who do are probably a select group of fathers who have already established high-quality relationships with their children. In other studies, we have indeed shown that fathers who have custody only of daughters are more likely than others to have had to fight for custody in court (Greif & DeMaris, 1989), and that fighting for custody is associated with more positive attitudes toward one's children (DeMaris & Greif, 1992; Greif, DeMaris, & Hood, 1993).

Assuming a given age and sex distribution of the children, several other factors affect whether fathers' attitudes toward their children will be more or less positive. The extent to which a man receives support for being a single father is perhaps the most important of these. The more support received, the lower the relationship problem score (DeMaris & Greif, 1992). More important, the key individuals in a support network seem to be employers, coworkers, and friends. Support from these people proved to be more important than support from family members (such as parents or adult siblings) in affecting fathers' relationship problem scores. In fact, controlling for support from friends, bosses, and coworkers, support from family members had no significant effect on relationship problems with children (Greif et al., 1993). This finding highlights the importance to fathers of being able to manage the simultaneous demands of work and parenting in a satisfactory manner. When work schedules or bosses' demands become inflexible, or when coworkers (who are also often friends) fail to understand the difficulties faced by the single father, his relationships with his children tend to suffer as a consequence. This is underscored by our finding that the more difficulty encountered by fathers in satisfying the demands of both work and child care, the higher their relationship problem scores (Greif et al., 1993).

Fathers with more positive attitudes toward their children were also those who had been involved in their care while married, rather than relegating this task to their wives (DeMaris & Greif, 1992). Parenting is work, as suggested by Dollahite et al. in Chapter 2; and like all work, the quality of its performance depends upon experience. Fathers who take an active part in their children's upbringing during a marriage develop skills needed for parenting when they go it alone. Men who have been less involved in parenting tasks necessarily have a more difficult transition upon receipt of custody. We found that fathers who had been involved in child care prior to the marital breakup were more likely than others to say that combining work with child care had "not been difficult" for them (Greif et al., 1993). We also found that such fathers were more likely than others to be awarded child support from their ex-wives by the courts (Greif & DeMaris, 1991). No doubt, fathers' participation in child care communicates a dedication to being a primary parent, and this pays dividends to fathers in a variety of ways.

The final key predictor of problems in father-child relationships is conflict with an ex-wife. Surprisingly, we found that conflict at the time of the breakup was more important than current conflict in elevating relationship problem scores (DeMaris & Greif, 1992). In all likelihood, this reflects the deleterious effect on children of living in a home characterized by continuous martial conflict. Once the child is residing with one or the other parent, conflict between the ex-spouses can often be compartmentalized so that the children are more easily sheltered from it.

Change Over Time. We resurveyed 117 of the fathers 2 years after the initial survey to examine whether any significant changes had occurred in their relationships with their children (Greif & DeMaris, 1995). Overall, there was a slight, but significant increase in average relationship problem scores between the two surveys (12.79 vs. 13.3). In other words, fathers' attitudes toward their children became slightly more unfavorable over 2 years' time. In that children were aging over this period, this result was probably due to the increase in the proportion of fathers raising teenagers. We found that, controlling for other factors, older children created more problems for fathers than younger ones (Greif et al., 1993).

An interesting pattern also appeared with respect to the method by which fathers had gained custody. Men who had to fight in court to obtain custody had lower relationship problem scores than others in the initial survey. Yet, upon follow-up, this group ended up having higher IPA scores than others. In particular, the scores of the court-contest group increased over time, whereas those of others decreased. One reason this pattern emerges is most likely due to a "halo effect" associated with fighting for custody. Fathers who contest custody are probably so preoccupied with obtaining it in the first place that they tend to minimize parenting difficulties in the short run. Therefore, their attitudes are especially positive at first, but experience more erosion over time as the difficulties of parenting manifest themselves.

Discomfort as a Single Parent

Of the 1,132 fathers in the initial survey, fully 72% said that they were comfortable as single parents. On the other hand, 28% were not. In an analysis of this latter group, we found that several factors accounted for discomfort in this area (Greif & DeMaris, 1990). Fathers with sole custody for a longer time were less likely to express discomfort. As has been noted previously, parenting skills typically become stronger with experience. But there is also a period of adjustment that fathers and children must work through, in which they learn their limits with each other. The longer fathers have had custody, the more likely these limits have been explored and resolved. Fathers with less positive attitudes toward their children were also more likely to feel discomfort, as one might expect.

Part of the difficulty of having custody of children is certainly the potential for conflict with ex-wives over visitation and the potential for conflict with children over a father's need to maintain a social life. It comes as no surprise that fathers who were able to handle visitation decisions amicably with their ex-wives were less likely than others to be uncomfortable as single parents, as were fathers who were satisfied with their social lives.

Balancing Work and Parenthood

Of the sample fathers, 1,102 responded to the item asking how difficult it had been to manage the demands of both work and child care. Among these, only 17% said that it had "not been difficult." What characterizes fathers for whom these tasks were unproblematic? We explored this issue using multivariate statistical techniques to identify the characteristics that distinguished these fathers from others (Greif et al., 1993). The results reinforced many of the findings from our analyses of fathers' attitudes toward their children. Fathers who were involved in child care before the marital breakup, those who fought to obtain custody, and those with strong social support networks were all more likely to say that work and child care were not difficult to combine. In line with the contention that experience is beneficial in the parenting endeavor, older fathers were more likely to see work and child care as unproblematic. Fathers who had had to make more changes in their work schedules to accommodate the demands of custody were less likely to see this process as trouble free. As outlined above, the ease of negotiating the demands of both work and parenting was strongly linked to parental attitudes. Fathers who found these tasks difficult to balance had substantially higher relationship problem scores than others (Greif et al., 1993).

Predictors of "Successful" Parenting Experiences

So far we have examined various indexes of parenting outcomes on an individual basis and tried to discern the factors most associated with each. In this section, we attempt to identify fathers in our sample having had the most "successful" fathering experiences, based on a consideration of several outcome criteria simultaneously (again, it should be kept in mind that our judgments are limited to fathers' impressions of their progress as custodial parents).

To identify a subset of fathers for whom the parenting experience appears to be going especially well, we coded as "successful" only those fathers who gave positive responses on each of five variables reflecting their parenting experience; fathers were considered to have a "successful" parenting experience if they rated the quality of their relationships with their children as "good" or "excellent," rated themselves as "good" or "excellent" parents, were "satisfied" or "very satisfied" with the children's progress in most areas, were "comfortable" or "very comfortable" as single parents, *and* scored in the lowest quartile (scores under 7) on the relationship problems scale. Of the 1,104 fathers in the current analysis, 220, or about 20% had "successful" parenting experiences by this criterion.

To discern the characteristics that discriminated this group from all other fathers we used a multivariate technique called logistic discriminant analysis (LDA) or logistic regression (see DeMaris, 1992, 1995; Hosmer & Lemeshow, 1989; Press & Wilson, 1978, for an explanation of this technique). LDA is similar to linear regression in that a dependent variable is regressed on a set of explanatory variables to discover which predictors have significant impact on it while the other effects in the equation are controlled for. LDA is superior to regression when the dependent variable has only two categories, as in this instance. The set of explanatory variables used in our analysis and the resulting coefficient estimates are shown in Table 9.1. To clarify our presentation, the significant explanatory variables and their effects are shown in Figure 9.1.

Overall, 10 variables were significant discriminators of the "successful" from the "less successful" parenting experiences of fathers in our sample. The figure identifies these variables by number. In the legend (on the right-hand side in Figure 9.1), the numbers are linked to short labels that identify the variables (refer to Table 9.1 for more complete variable labels). In this type of analysis, it is convenient to phrase effects as odds. For example, if the odds of having a "successful" fathering experience are two, that means that a father is twice as likely to enjoy "success" as not. The effects shown in the figure are called odds ratios. These represent the estimated *change* in the odds of having a "successful" fathering experience for a one-unit increment in the predictor, holding all other effects constant. For categorical predictors (e.g., involvement in parenting, contested custody), the odds ratio is the ratio of the odds of "success" for those in the category of interest versus those in the contrast category (see Table 9.1 for contrast categories of categorical predictors). To take the

Table 9.1 Logistic Discriminant Analysis of "Successful" Parenting
Experiences Among Single Custodial Fathers

Explanatory Variable	b	Exp(b)
Intercept	−5.838	.003
Father Involved in Child Care While Married	.920***	2.509
Number of Work Changes to Accommodate Child Care	−.065	.937
Degree of Current Conflict With Ex-Wife	−.150*	.861
Father Obtained Custody Through Court Contest	.684***	1.981
Children Are of Mixed Ages	.007	1.007
Children Are All 13 or Over[a]	−.179	.837
Children Are All Boys	−.615*	.540
Children Are All Girls[b]	−.615*	.540
Father's Annual Income	.017**	1.017
Father's Years of Schooling	.020	1.020
Father's Age	.014	1.014
Father's Social Support	.841***	2.319
Father Has Two Children	−.405	.667
Father Has Three or More Children[c]	−.713*	.490
Frequency Ex-Wife Telephones Children	−.015	.985
Nights Per Month Children Spend With Ex-Wife	.029	1.029
Father's Satisfaction With Social Life	.425***	1.530
Frequency of Father's Dating	−.384**	.681
Frequency Father Has Sex	.104	1.110
Father is Currently Cohabiting	−.346	.708
Pseudo-R-Squared[d]	.203	

NOTE: $N = 1,104$. Shown are the additive (multiplicative) impacts on the log odds (odds) of having a "successful" parenting experience, for unit increases in predictors.
a. Contrast category is: All children are under 13 years of age.
b. Contrast category is: Children are of both sexes.
c. Contrast category is: Father has only one child.
d. Estimate of the proportion of variation in "successful" parenting that would be accounted for if it were measured on a continuous scale. See McKelvey and Zavoina (1975) or DeMaris (1995) for details.
*$p < .05$; **$p < .01$; ***$p < .001$.

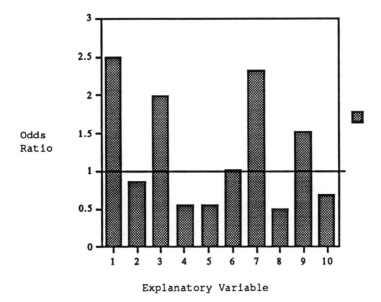

Explanatory Variable

Figure 9.1: Predicted Changes in the Odds of Having a "Successful" Parenting Experience for Fathers Who Are a Unit Apart on Selected Explanatory Variables, Based on a Logistic Discriminant Analysis

Explanatory Variables
  1 = Involvement in Parenting
  2 = Conflict With Ex-Wife
  3 = Contested Custody
  4 = All Boys
  5 = All Girls
  6 = Annual Income
  7 = Social Support
  8 = 3+ Children
  9 = Satisf. With Social Life
10 = Frequency of Dating

first predictor as an example, fathers involved in parenting during marriage have about two-and-a-half times the odds of having a "successful" fathering experience as those who were one unit less involved in parenting. The horizontal line in Figure 9.1 located at "1" on the vertical scale shows the reference point for predictors that raise, as opposed to lower, the odds. All odds ratios above this line indicate predictors that enhance the odds of "success"; all odds ratios below this line represent variables that reduce the odds of "success."

Continuing with the analysis, we see that contesting custody, having a higher income, having more social support, and being more satisfied with one's social life also enhance the odds of a "successful" parenting experience. On the other hand, having more conflict with one's ex-wife, raising either girls or boys exclusively (as opposed to raising children of both sexes), having three or more children (as opposed to only one child), and dating more frequently all reduce the odds of a "successful" experience. These results tend to be consistent with what has been found in our previous analyses, although some new findings emerge when we consider several indexes of parenting quality simultaneously.

It is now apparent that having children of only one gender tends to reduce the odds of "success." Also, fathers' income has a slight but beneficial impact on the odds of "success." Clearly, fathers making more money are more in a position to hire others to do some of the work of the household, thereby easing some of the burdens of child care. Having too many children (e.g., three or more) is also detrimental to fathers' parenting experience. This makes sense, in that the more children, the more effort is required to manage all of their needs competently. The opposite effects of satisfaction with one's social life and frequency of dating seem at first to be somewhat counterintuitive. At a given level of satisfaction with one's social life, however, the more one dates, the more conflict one is likely to encounter with children over the time spent away from them or over other issues raised by dating. On the other hand, holding dating frequency constant, the more satisfactory one's social life, the more positive one feels about being able to raise children alone without it interfering with one's adult activities.

Implications for Practitioners

How can a mental health or family practitioner make use of this information to help a single custodial father seeking assistance? Some of the findings about who is "successful" are descriptive in nature. They suggest characteristics a father may "walk in with," and, as such, cannot be changed. Other findings can be tied to behavior, lending themselves to suggestions for interventions.

If we assume for a moment that an "unsuccessful" father may be more likely to seek help than a "successful" one, then the father-as-client may be a man with little prior involvement in parenting, a slightly lower income than his counterparts, a past history of conflict with his ex-wife, a substantial number of children at home, and children of only one gender. These are not variables a therapist can change. Yet, the perception a father holds of one of these variables, prior involvement, is key in its potential relation to the notion of generative fathering (Snarey, 1993).

A father's history of involvement in parenting prior to the marital breakup may be directly related to the way he perceives his role as a father. Pruett (1995) states that men battle a feeling of inadequacy when they start life as a parent. In the face of feelings of incompetence, it is easy for a father to be convinced that his role is to be the financial provider in the family. When faced with a father who adhered to this belief while married, the practitioner needs to help the father place his behavior in context. A father who worked an extra shift and was not available—or chose not—to participate in child care because of this, should not engage in self-recrimination when he does not know how to handle his children. He was fulfilling a role that he believed was correct at the time and that many other fathers continue to fill. By placing the father's behavior and attitude toward work and child care in a context that is cognizant of gender, the stage can be set for discussion of future critical topics. Other topics might include dealing with loneliness, feelings of emasculation, or conflicts related to the family of origin (Greif, 1995). Family of origin issues may arise when the messages the father received when growing up about the value of two parents in the home or the appropriate behavior for a father stand in sharp contrast to what the father is currently experiencing.

The finding related to conflict with the ex-wife suggests the potential importance of mediation during the breakup. It also suggests that the coparental relationship *after* parents are divorced is fertile ground for discussion. Many divorced people remain emotionally tied to each other after the breakup. Their ability to make rational decisions about child rearing and to work with an ex-spouse in the best interests of a child is negatively affected by the anger or hurt they feel in relation to the ex-spouse. When conflict boils over, it is often because of such unresolved issues. Three common approaches can work with a father in conflict with his ex-spouse: (a) educating the father about the normal ups and downs after a breakup and what can be anticipated will help him to feel that his experiences and reactions are not out of the ordinary, (b) coaching him about what to say before and during a fight with his ex-wife can assist in deescalating some of the conflict, (c) helping him achieve insight into his own feelings may lead to an understanding about why there is conflict.

The importance of helping the father gain social support from others, another key variable related to "success," should also be addressed. A father, his coworkers, and his boss all can play crucial roles in easing the father's adjustment to what traditionally have been the conflicting roles of parent and full-time worker. This potential conflict should be acknowledged if, for example, the father feels he is not able to give as much to the workplace or the coworkers feel they are covering for the father or not receiving the same level of output from him they once were. A discussion of the shift in performance can help all parties achieve greater sensitivity. Support groups for single parents do exist in most communities. These groups can focus on, for example, educational issues, social support, or legal problems and can be helpful stepping-stones in the father's adaptation. Helping a father reconnect with family and friends, if there has been emotional distancing following a breakup, can also prove fruitful to his long-term adjustment.

Finally, a father's achieving a comfortable dating life could also enhance "success." Fathers are frequently unsure what type of dating situation they are interested in when they become single again (Greif, 1985). Are they looking for a mother for their children, a friend, or a sexual partner where there are no commitments for long-term intimacy? If the father is ambivalent about his needs, the person he is dating is placed in a precarious position, which can lead to miscommunication and unhappiness. When he was last single, perhaps as long as 10 or 20 years prior to his divorce, role expectations for men and women were different. Exploration of expectations and pressures on a newly single father (e.g., finding a mother for the children, dating a lot to "make up for lost time," etc.) can help the father adjust to a changing social scene.

With more than 1.3 million fathers raising their children alone in 1994, an increase of 15% over the previous 4 years (U.S. Bureau of the Census, 1995b), the unusual may soon appear quite common. The fathers in our study are at the forefront of what "successful" fathering can be in a society with high divorce rates. Their struggles and successes provide a blueprint and can pave the way for the growing numbers of fathers who are exercising their legal options and increasing their involvement in their children's lives.

Note

1. Reliability of the IPA in the current sample was .91, suggesting strong internal consistency. The IPA has also been found by others to possess good convergent, discriminant, and construct validity (Hudson, 1982).

10

Men and Women Cocreating Father Involvement in a Nongenerative Culture

ANNA DIENHART
KERRY DALY

North Americans live in a culture where there is a paradox between the ideological exaltation of the family and an intensifying work ethos that leaves families with less time for each other than ever before. In this chapter, we argue that couples committed to shared parenthood must be very deliberate in their efforts to surmount the countervailing forces of the larger culture that place increasing temporal demands on family members. Specifically, we are concerned with the manner in which a select group of men have created, with their partners, an experience of parenthood that is, by their own definitions, based on the principles of sharing, partnership, and balanced responsibility. We are also concerned in this chapter with the cultural environment in which these couples set out to create an experience of shared parenthood. We refer to this environment as a nongenerative culture for both women and men because it is a culture wherein accomplishment, status, and material acquisition are hegemonic and care for children and family, the primary developmental tasks of adulthood (Erikson, 1950), are subordinate. Men, especially, do not live in a generative culture; they continue to live in a performance culture where their parenting commitments are undervalued and their touted rewards are still concentrated in the money economy. The men that we report on in this chapter are men who in spite of the vapid environment of which they are a part have managed, with their partners, to create and sustain an experience of fathering that is generative in nature. In short, we reverse LaRossa's (1988) often-cited "culture/conduct" distinction and look at the conduct of generative fathers in a nongenerative culture. Becoming a generative father is not fully amenable to private control, as Gerson also argues in Chapter 3 of this volume. To talk about involved fatherhood as a private dimension of experience, one must include in that discussion "the unbalanced mixture of everything" including work, inequality, politics, and economics (Beck, 1992). In this regard, the private relationship conflict between men and women is part of a much larger social structural contest in which the values of family and home life are pitted against the values of productivity and performance. Thus, to understand what it means to become a generative father, it is necessary to explore generative fathering as a private challenge amid a larger set of public issues associated with fatherhood. It is the private trouble/public issue dialectic (Mills, 1959) that serves as the conceptual foundation for our analysis.

In this chapter, we first discuss the research project from which our ideas have emerged. Second, we provide an overview of the nongenerative culture in which men operate. Finally, we examine the relationship between specific manifestations of the nongenerative culture and the private efforts of men and women to contend with these cultural influences. In each of these cultural contexts, we focus on the stories of success that provide insight into the way that a group of men have met the challenge of the "ethic of generative fathering," discussed in Chapter 2.

The Research Data

In this qualitative study, we explored the resourcefulness of men and women in 18 couples, selected specifically for their self-reported commitment to share parenting responsibilities and activities. The men and women were interviewed, both individually and as couples, to explore the ways they coconstruct "fatherhood"—their beliefs, expectations, behaviors, and reflective experiences. A purposive sample drawn from convenience referrals met three criteria: (a) both partners agreed that the man was an active and fully participating father in everyday family life; (b) the couple had at least one child between the ages of 2 and 6, to enable us to capture experiences in those early years of high-demand parenting; and (c) the respondents had to be a first family with biological children. The average age of the couples in this study was 38 and 36 for men and women, respectively. There was a range of educational and occupational experiences. The 18 couples represented several different configurations of family structure: 3 families had dual earners; 3 families job-shared; in 4 families the woman worked part-time; in 2 families the man worked part-time; and there were 3 stay-at-home fathers and 3 stay-at-home mothers. Thematic and constant comparative analysis of the 36 narrative accounts revealed a diversity of interactive possibilities for men and women to cocreate generative fathering.

Nongenerative Culture

To suggest that men live in a nongenerative culture is to dichotomize the world into two dominant conditions: one that is positive in its appreciation and attentiveness to the ethical challenges associated with the care by men of the next generation, the other negative and oblivious to or discouraging of the care that men might bring to their fathering responsibilities. Recognizing that any such dichotomy is artificially polarized, we argue in this chapter that the parenting culture for men has an epicenter most closely aligned with the negative pole of this dichotomy. Although one of the explicit purposes of this volume is to be prescriptive and transformative with respect to the way that fathers parent (see Chapter 1), that transformation involves taking first steps within a culture that has not been supportive of men in their parenting work. In this chapter, we define nongenerative culture to mean informal and formal mechanisms that usurp the primacy of fathering in men's lives.

There are numerous expressions of nongenerativity for fathers in our culture. In all domains in which fathers carry out their daily activity, there are cultural forces they encounter that divert their attention from their commitment to fathering or directly discourage commitment to fathering work. Although the overriding culture of fatherhood is nongenerative, it is useful to think of the many domains within which this nongenerativity is encountered. Men encounter the forces of nongenerativity in their work, their relationships with other men, their recreation, and even in the intimate sphere of their family relationships. In light of this, it is more realistic and manageable to think of multiple nongenerative cultures. These include the culture of maternalism rooted in women's traditional claim to the activity of the domestic sphere; the historical culture of fatherhood that has been rejected as inadequate and largely irrelevant for the demands placed on parents today; the culture of quietude about fathering that characterizes men's relationships with each other; the culture of men's work, which is still heavily performance oriented; and finally, the culture of recreation, which gives men a greater entitlement to leisure. The men and women in our research spoke passionately about their generative lifestyle and what that required of them. Their commitment to cocreate a *generative family culture* called them to believe in and do many things differently from how they were raised and differently from what they know is endorsed for men and women in the larger culture.

The Culture of Maternalism

Feminist writers have made reference to the "cult of maternalism" (Duffy, 1988) or the "fantasy of the perfect mother" (Chodorow & Contratto, 1982), which emphasize the ideological exaltation of mothers as indispensable, natural, and necessary. There are two corollaries of this perspective. First, mothers are the target of blame when trouble arises in the family. Second, fathers are seen as dispensable, unnatural, and unnecessary. Underlying these perceptions is the cultural expectation that mothers should be fully committed and devoted to their children whereas fathers are incapable or even dangerous if given too much responsibility for carrying out these tasks, for which they are ill equipped. Overall, the domination of mothers in the domestic sphere is well embedded in our ideology of families.

In practice, too, most mothers continue to carry out primary responsibility for parenting. Pleck (1985) and others (e.g., Baruch & Barnett, 1986; Gilbert, Holahan, & Manning, 1981; Yogev, 1981) speculate about women's adjustment to sharing "power" in a sphere that they have traditionally dominated and the challenge of fending off internal guilt from perceived neglect of their maternal role. The possibility of women remaining the family "expert" on the quality of men's caregiving and performance of household tasks impacts the father's satisfaction with his parenting role (Lamb et al., 1987, citing Defrain, 1979; Russell, 1982). This leads some authors to hint at the difficulty of "making room for Daddy" (Benokraitis, 1985; Lamb et al., 1987). Backett (1982), in a qualitative study, explored these ideas and concluded that men and women experienced a "taken-for-granted" role for mothers but that the role for fathers was more problematic. The absence of open spaces for fathers in the parenting relationship is part of the nongenerative culture of fatherhood. The culture of maternalism constrains both men and women. The couples in our study found their ability to cocreate greater father involvement in their families meant both the man and the woman had to approach parenting differently. They challenged the cult of maternalism embedded in the larger culture in several ways.

Value Difference and Specialization. Men and women saw a potential benefit in being different from their partner, with each having particular specializations. Accepting that they might do things differently from their partner seemed to allow men more freedom to claim greater father involvement. Knowing their partner also tolerated difference seemed to make doing things their own way less threatening to the partnership and encouraged more paternal involvement. Acceptance of difference and specialization is a key to facilitating men's desire to claim their place in the family as a generative father. One stay-at-home mother, Janice, told us:

I do the Monday-to-Friday type dinners and my approach is, "You kids go do something else, mommy's getting dinner ready." Charles, on the other hand, spends Saturdays or Sundays cooking up big batches of things to freeze and gets them involved. So they have fun doing things, learning things.

Men Taking Responsibility for Their Parenting Skills. Countering the culture of maternalism requires men to take responsibility to learn parenting skills for themselves. Men describe a sense of tension between succumbing to the "cult of motherhood" by relying on women to teach them and finding other ways to learn parenting routines. Although they feel they have learned a great deal about parenting from their partners, they also go to some length not to rely solely on their partners to teach them everything. Men's willingness to enter the unknown, to experiment and adjust their approach as they go along, is an important element in developing a comfort to claim a broad repertoire of parenting involvement. Although not noted in the following excerpt, several men talked about taking parenting classes and reading child care and child development books and magazines. Tom, a man in his early 40s, had decided to leave his management job a few years earlier to become the designated stay-at-home parent when the couple's second child was born. He refers here to the tension between men learning from women and finding other ways of taking responsibility for acquiring the skills to parent effectively:

I've heard of men who sit while the kid cries, they sort of look at their wife, I've seen it! I've seen them say why is she crying? Oh! [I say] Why would she know? [laughs] Why would she know why the baby's crying or why don't you get up and go look? [I do it] by experimentation. . . . Sometimes, the baby is a reluctant burper and I've noticed when I get up and kind of bounce gently he burps. What works works. And it's never 100%. I think that's why I'm clumsy at it, it's never 100%.

Men's Willingness to Challenge Their Partner's Expertise. Countering a culture of maternalism may mean men also encounter situations where they need to challenge their partner's stance on a particular issue. This is a tricky area, where men seek to balance their respect for their partner's experience, ideas, and knowledge about child care with their own views about how to handle the situation. Men were willing to challenge their partners when they had strong ideas about the situation at hand. For example, Jason suggests below how he was firmly committed to stopping his son's thumb sucking. Jason is in his early 40s with two children and works full-time in his own business. To support his challenge to his wife, who had decided to let the matter of thumb sucking go, he sought a doctor's opinion and persevered in his efforts:

At our five-year-old checkup with the doctor, I brought up thumb sucking as an issue and the doctor said there are a lot of opinions, here's what I recommend. Hillary was on the bandwagon with me for a while, trying to convince him not to suck his thumb, then she quit the program and I've stayed on. I'm still working with Mike [the son] to get him to stop his thumb sucking.

Women's Experience of "Letting Go." Women often mentioned their sense of feeling the need to let go of their culturally sanctioned "maternal entitlement" to set the parameters and standards of parenting. Letting go means relinquishing parts of a practiced or cherished repertoire of mothering. It means changing involvement in certain interactions or responsibilities to create space for the partner to be involved.

Women's descriptions of relinquishing a claim on particular aspects of maternal involvement highlighted *both* their intentionality *and* their hesitation. Intentionally letting go reflected an awareness about how a woman's willingness "to do" or "to take the lead" in parenting could be experienced as curtailing her partner's opportunities to be involved in the parenting dance. Women's hesitation to let go reflected a complex struggle regarding their commitment to shared parenting *and* their effort to trust that anyone else (even their partner) could provide the care they themselves wished to provide. Two issues were of particular importance for these women as they sought to reconcile the tension between letting go and holding on to their "maternal entitlements": "feeling displaced" and "primary parent acculturation holdover."

Women spoke at times about their dual awareness of how sharing parenthood *both* relieved them of feeling all the responsibility *and* also left them feeling displaced. Even when a woman wanted her partner to get more involved, when her partner actually got involved in aspects she had enjoyed as her domain, she felt somewhat displaced. A woman's feelings of being displaced might interact *both* to limit *and* to create space for both her and her partner's involvement. Women often noted how feeling displaced perhaps had more potential to keep her involved in some spheres of parenting—even when she had a desire for her partner do more of that work. Hillary, a woman in her early 40s with two children who is just finishing her graduate degree, spoke to this tension:

> I realize that one thing I've worked through to this point is the jealousy and that's painful for a mother always, no matter what the issue is. I rarely feel left out anymore, but I've gone through plenty of times and years where I felt like I had to do everything, or be in the middle of everything. That takes a lot of effort to get past [feeling that] I do everything better or—of course, I still think I do [laughing] but it doesn't mean that things have to be done [my] way. . . . Mostly, now I'm both relieved and happy when I see him doing those things, being sometimes emotionally supportive, but there certainly have been times [when] I've felt less positive. I do think women are also . . . playing a big role in keeping things standard and the status quo despite the fact that it's against their desires and interests. I try to tackle that, but it takes perseverance.

Many women said they noticed they felt "mother guilt" about not being the "primary parent," but had difficulty explaining why that was. With our further probing, it became clear that these mothers were experiencing a kind of acculturation holdover from their own parents in feeling a strain between thinking they should be the first line of contact for their children and an awareness that their partner could also handle the situation at hand. These women *both* wanted to be called on first *and* resented being called on first. Kate, a woman in her early 30s who has two children and works full-time, commented on this tension:

> I felt guilty because they couldn't reach me and second, . . . why are they calling me first anyway? They know he's always in one spot and they know that I'm all over the place, 'cause I've said that to the [school] secretary before. So, . . . I should have been where they could get me! I think I should carry the burden . . . that probably goes back to well . . . maybe that's what I heard. Or society. . . . Like I should be doing it!

Kate spoke about her sense of wanting to do things differently but caught herself feeling pulled into a whirl of "shoulds" about being the parent of first contact. She returned to an awareness that if she shares parenting responsibilities then there are times when she is not going to be there for her children. Her story highlights the potential for women to feel the holdover of their acculturation in their everyday lives and how this might serve at times to keep them involved to the exclusion of their partners.

The Dismissed Historical Culture of Fatherhood

When men look to the horizons of the past, there are few clear images that tell them who a father should be. One of the key themes in the fatherhood literature is the absence of any significant role models for how to be a contemporary father (Daly, 1993a). As Daly reported in that study, the most obvious candidate for modeling fatherhood roles is a man's own father. Although men frequently talk about their own fathers in response to questions about models, the fathers often primarily served as negative role models or reference points for what the men wanted to change in their lives. In this regard, men typically seek to "rework" or compensate for deficiencies that they perceived in their own fathers.

Although some men talked about their own fathers being good role models to them, for most the conditions of parenting had changed so dramatically that the style of parenting their own fathers used bore little resemblance to the options open to them and therefore had little relevance to the task of fathering that lay before them. Most men talked about a complete departure from the kind of father model that was presented to them. The emphasis that their own fathers placed on work, at the cost of their family experiences, was something that concerned these men. Thus, when they look within the culture of fatherhood, the models of the past are insufficient.

Nevertheless, as men created their own version of generative fathering, they often came face-to-face with several cultural holdovers from their historical models, particularly on issues of providing for the family and feeling challenged to find a place on the parenting team.

Men as Providers. As Cohen (1994) found, men place a higher priority on family than on their work lives. The men in our study felt a tension between providing for the family and being with the family as an involved member of the shared-parenting team. Men noted how they feel their perspective on providing has changed to a long-term view since they have had children. Even when their partners work, they often feel the pressure of being the major financial support for the family and that worries them. Although these men have usually chosen to work in situations where they do not have to put in long hours, they find themselves, at times, missing family time to handle the demands at work. Several men suggested there were times when they would relinquish their daily involvement at home to secure long-term financial stability. At the same time, these men stressed the importance of "providing" for their families and how they saw it as one way of being involved. They share the results of their paid labors with their families. Charles, in his mid-30s, has two preschool children and is co-owner of a service industry business. He said,

> I guess the responsibility that goes with [providing for my kids] is, if anything happened, all the eggs are in one basket in this situation. You're always worried that you can keep things going, you're not really in total control of the situation. Everybody's affected by the economy and the last few years have not been that positive in terms of the economy generally . . . that brings worries, late nights lying in bed thinking of things—responsibility as opposed to remember when you didn't have to worry about supporting a wife and kids, so it's just "Please God, let's make money." So, it's more I guess long-term kind of thinking now as opposed to what's happening tonight. . . . If it gets busy, really busy, I'll have to stay and work, but I prefer not to do that and most of the time I don't have to. It's really been a decision on my part not to miss it [miss out on family time].

Men Finding a Place in the Family. An important aspect of the acculturation holdover for men was the awkward, and at times hurtful, realization that they could not find their place with the child. In as much as these men wished to transcend their inherited tradition of fatherhood, their difficulty in finding their place resulted in the temptation to say, "Forget it, I won't claim any more involvement." At the same time, men learned to persevere for the long term, to claim their involvement as father, even if that involvement was overshadowed temporarily by the mother's importance in the child's life. Sam, a 40-year-old with two children who works as a management trainee, noted how it would have been all too easy to miss out in the long run because the current situation was difficult. He and his wife went through a tough period with their older daughter, Keltie:

> Meg [his wife] kept waiting and waiting and waiting for four or five months for Keltie to develop some sort of crush on me. I'll give an example: She always wanted her mom to be with her and we were taking groceries out of the car and she refused to let me take her into the house. My gut reaction was, it pissed me off. My other reaction was I was determined not to run away. You know I kept trying. . . . It's fun now with Keltie; she tells me she loves me and I think she really means it.

The men in our study did not expect themselves to give up the various traditional ways of being "father" learned through acculturation but to develop them within a broader repertoire of actively fathering and sharing parenthood's responsibilities with their partners. These men spoke of expanding their parenting repertoire by taking responsibility for learning and practicing new ways to be a father, as well as cooperating with their partner to choreograph a new parenting dance.

Deliberate Departure From the Past: Commitment to Partnership. These men typically lamented the absence of a flourishing role model for their own creation of ways to express generative fathering. They seemed to find their path to involved fatherhood through their commitment to a family partnership model. Family partnership requires them to be involved, actively and fully. Yet, becoming involved fully and actively was *both* an individual effort *and* part of a dance between the man and his partner. Rodney said:

> If you were in a partnership with somebody, there's no way that you'd get away with doing 20% of the work and somebody else doing 80%, so [we have] a partnership. When somebody's not feeling well, or somebody's down about things, you pick up the slack and you're a little stronger than what you were, or what your partner has to be. In a partnership everything is shared.

The men and women in this research spoke passionately about their commitment to their family partnership. The men especially stressed their partnership commitment and how that model cast them as just one part of a larger whole. Their partnership model was undergirded with goodwill and beliefs about "we are all in this together" and "to keep us together it is imperative to work it out to everyone's best interest." They did not see themselves as operating in their family along the lines of a "male privilege" or the "zero-sum" or "individualistic" proposition so prevalent in the larger culture. Men spoke at length about cooperating and negotiating in their families. This usually meant a man was aware he needed to suspend the culturally sanctioned entitlement to use "male privilege and power" in the family and instead interact as a part of a collaborative team. Dan, a man in his mid-30s with three children, highlighted the intentionality of such decisions:

> It became quite clear to me that I had quite a powerful hand to enable or disable Liz's chances in her career. Enabling Liz meant my life changed. That was the point where I realized that I could lay aside power and control for my self-protection and instead use it creatively.

As Dan hints, a family partnership model requires men to place equal value on their partner's life as on their own. Valuing their partner's opportunity to develop the full spectrum of her life interests, whether in a job or career outside the home or other interests, is critical for men as they create generative father involvement. Men often noted that having a partner engaged in interests outside the home gave them an opportunity to be with the kids on their own. Although it was an opportunity, the partner's absence was a compelling reason to serve as an involved parent. Involvement was important for these men not only for their own sakes but out of respect for their partner beyond her being the mother of their children. This underscores the link between caring for children and caring for the children's mother, a point also noted by Dollahite et al. in Chapter 2 of this volume.

The Culture of Quietude

Although the everyday discourse about fatherhood in our culture is not silent, it is but a murmur in relation to the powerful and dominant discourse of motherhood. As one expression of this, men talk to each other relatively infrequently about their day-to-day experiences as fathers, whereas women often talk among themselves about parenting matters (Daly, 1994). The implication is that the "looking glass" of fatherhood is rarely found in other men. When men have little opportunity to see themselves as fathers in the eyes of other men, there are few catalysts to reshape or transform the fathering identity on the basis of masculine cues. Furthermore, because fathering is often not seen as the most salient identity for men, other people are less likely to elicit conversations from men about their experience as fathers. Nevertheless, our study suggests men quietly monitor how others perceive them in their role as father.

Suspending the Impact of the External Gaze. Men's perception of how others see and judge their involvement in family life is often thought to influence their willingness to parent actively. External judgments, especially stereotypical criticism of "men doing women's work," still permeate our culture and contribute to the culture of quietude. Yet, the men in this study readily dismissed the idea that the "external gaze" makes much of a difference to them. Though their strategies to deal with potential judgments suggest they have developed creative ways to protect themselves from criticism, they often succumb to the culture of quietude.

These men adopted a few strategies to counter a critical "external gaze." Men said that although they might take notice of supportive reactions they typically dismissed unsupportive responses. A second strategy seemed to be one of selective sharing; that is, they shared their experiences of their family life and generative fathering only with those people who they believed would be supportive and withheld that kind of sharing from others. When they engage with supportive persons and share their experiences of generative fathering, they break the silence. They also seemed caught at times by the culture of quietude and retreated into an "individualist" stance, however. As "individualists" they saw their involvement as their personal choice, negotiated within the privacy of family with their partner. Their stance on the "external gaze" was one that allowed them to bracket the influence of critical opinion (and mixed messages found in the larger culture about men's involvement in family life), locating the basis of their involvement in the personal or private arena rather than in some larger political arena. Like Rodney, a man in his early 30s with two children and a partner who works full-time, these men did not much care what others aside from their partner thought about how, what, when, and where they were involved.

> My priorities are my family comes first and if you don't like the fact that I can't be there [at work], then do what you have to do. . . . It's always been something with me, and no matter what profession or career I could be in, that would still be my attitude. If the people I'm working for can't understand that because there's some strong, bald-headed ego male there, then that's their problem, not mine. Maybe, I shouldn't be working there if that's their attitude; maybe, I'm in the wrong place.

Culture of Work

For many men, one of the key obstacles to a generative pattern of fathering is "work fixation." For men, there are many contradictions that arise within this fixation on work: sacrificing oneself for something one has neither the leisure, the needs, or the abilities to enjoy; aggressive competition for nothing; exhaustion for professional and organizational goals with which one cannot identify but must pursue anyway (Beck, 1992, p. 112).

At the corporate level, there continue to be tremendous gender disparities in the practices that affect the participation of men and women in child care. Although some work organizations have developed family-friendly work policies, these are clearly the minority. Many of these programs are designed for and directed toward women on the continued assumption that they carry primary responsibility for the care of children in the home. As Pleck (1993) has suggested, there is wide spread skepticism that family-supportive policies are even relevant to men. The gendered nature of corporate culture also appears to discourage men from taking full advantage of available leaves, with informal sanctions among male peers operating to curtail what might have been a well-intentioned effort to take advantage of the leave policy (Haas & Hwang, 1995). Despite the introduction of the Family and Medical Leave Act (1993) in the United States, few analysts believe that men will take advantage of the new law because most families cannot afford for the father to stay at home without pay (Haas & Hwang, 1995). Furthermore, and perhaps most important, most men do not see leave as part of their conception of their father role (Pleck, 1993). As this would suggest, the work culture for men is one that is still based on principles of company loyalty, performance, and commitment. Although work performance is viewed by many men as an expression of their commitment to their children and families, direct child care generativity is less a priority and is poorly supported in this environment.

Work-Family Balance: Flexible Time Management. The men in this study felt constrained by the dominant work culture. Their jobs or careers and the general expectations of employers constrained their freedom to be as involved as they wished in their children's lives. At the same time, these men described some things they have done to rearrange their employment to accommodate more time with the children.

A few men had considerable flexibility afforded by being their own boss or working in a field that gave them primary control over which hours they worked. Other men, like Rick, who is quoted below, have limited job flexibility and resort to creative time management strategies to rebalance work and family life. Men often arranged their workday to start and end early or late or trade extra hours on certain days for days off. A couple of men got up early and did a few hours of work at home before the children got out of bed; then they would go to their workplace after they had covered children's morning routine. They did this shifting of hours to get more time with the family when the children were most likely to be home. All these men mentioned how important it is for them to have weekends and evenings, at the very least, to participate in family life. They also make their family priority apparent to colleagues at work. Rick's description of his situation hints at both the constraints and the degrees of freedom he has in being part of a management team. Not all employees find similar freedom, and as he implies, that makes it very difficult to be actively involved:

I'm working straight days [now], that helps a great deal. I can't imagine working shift work [again]. [With shift work] you are either at work or sleeping, and I can't imagine being like that. So in that way, the work is facilitative. Hindering in that my responsibilities are to be there. If it wasn't such a responsible position, I could opt out more. [When I quit working Saturdays] I was more or less directing the work to people who are working for me as supervisors. I was pretty honest. I [presented it] more on a personal level. This is me wanting to give up some of the hours. I didn't feel I was inconveniencing their lives because I still go in first thing in the morning to open and leave last at night.

The Culture of Recreation

The focus in the literature on work-family balance has been on the way that mothers and fathers balance the responsibilities of their paid work and their family duties. Leisure and recreation do not figure prominently in that literature, and when they do, they are usually treated in a residual fashion. Yet, recreation, leisure, and free time play an important role in people's everyday lives. In some ways, leisure represents a contradiction in our culture, for it is highly valued insofar as it is held out as the reward for hard work, but scorned when there is insufficient time to meet all the responsibilities of work, family, and household chores.

The normative uncertainty associated with leisure is manifested in conflicts about men and women's entitlement to leisure. Entitlements are culturally embedded practices (Restrepo, 1995), and there is a considerable literature suggesting that in our culture men and women have a different entitlement to leisure time (Cyba, 1992; Henderson & Dialeschki, 1991; Hochschild, 1989; Shaw, 1992). Men, because of the traditional separation between their work lives and home lives, have had greater access to "time off" from work. Women, by contrast, have greater difficulty separating or compartmentalizing their paid and unpaid work and leisure experience. For housewives, the demands of the day tend to be fluid, seamless, and inclusive, which makes compartmentalizing free time or leisure time difficult (Firestone & Shelton, 1994). Even among wives who work in the labor force, there is a tendency to feel that they never "earn" leisure because the duties of domestic work are never done (Henderson & Dialeschki, 1991) due to greater responsibility for the "second shift" (Hochschild, 1989). The conclusion in this literature is that men see leisure as a right and are more likely to feel entitled to take time away from their spouses, whereas for women responsibilities to paid and unpaid work results in a diminished sense of entitlement to "free time" (Henderson & Dialeschki, 1991).

Men's entitlement to leisure combines with women's disentitlement to leisure to contribute in an important way to the nongenerative culture of fatherhood. Although work time continues to have primacy for men, leisure time is more likely to compete with family time for men. The implication is that men operate in the face of greater distractibility where commitments to family time have a higher probability of being derailed by their own personal leisure. As an extension of this, men have been criticized in the feminist literature for taking on the more fun aspects of family work and child care rather than the repetitive or mundane parts. Although these "fun" activities are important generative activities for many fathers, they are more likely to be cast as leisure than parental responsibility. The net result is that within the cultural domain of leisure, fathers are construed in a nongenerative manner.

Men as Playmates. One of the most frequently stated differences between men and women—by both women and men—was how much more men engage in active play with their children. Within the differential culture of recreation for men and women, men's play with children is often depicted as less important than the interactions women have with children. If women engage in play activities, they are seen as contributing to the child's development. If men engage in play activities, they are seen as "just having fun." Men stressed how "play" was one important part of their generative repertoire as a father. As Phil put it,

> [There's] a song about parenthood—"Moms Are for Maintenance and Dads Are for Fun"—and I think that's true to some extent, although I do my share of maintenance. Anita [child] and I play games that Kelly [wife] and Anita don't. Like we have, as somebody said this word at day care, roughneck [play]. You know, when you're roughhousing around. It's something that she and I play; she has had me try and teach her mommy how to do that.

Phil obviously enjoys "roughhousing," but he seems to think it is important that we understand he does his share of the maintenance required in daily family life, too. He introduces "fun" or play into routine maintenance tasks. He noted how in his morning routine with Anita, they have created a ritual, a game, around getting breakfast together. Like Phil, many men introduced play in a routine, daily maintenance task, whereas many of the women approached similar tasks simply as a parenting task. A mother's approach could be seen as parenting work, a father's as play. For these men, a parenting task was often *both* work *and* an opportunity to be creative in their parenting.

These examples from everyday family life challenge us to think about how seeing men as playmates for their children could make us miss valuing the variety of involvement these men have in their families. Men noted how active play can help children develop an appreciation for their physical capabilities and the potential learning from fantasy play and learning about limits in situations. There is also the obvious connection children make with their parent who plays with them. Later in the conversation, Phil went on to note how he also engages in quiet time, serious time with Anita, seemingly acknowledging the importance of a broad repertoire of ways to be involved.

Conclusion

These men have managed, with varying degrees of success, to construct, with their partners, a private solution to the public issue of greater father involvement. Their ability to do this seemed to rest on several key strategies. First, the partners had an underlying commitment, or guiding light, that made the challenge of becoming shared parents one that was deliberate and intentional. Second, they valued each other's different approaches to parenting and were able to allow the other partner room to specialize in those parenting tasks for which he or she was best suited or had the greatest interest. Third, men had to take responsibility for developing their own parenting skills and assert their entitlement to parent in their own way. This includes, for example, awareness and acceptance of play as an important and creative aspect of generative involvement. It also meant that their partner, the children's mother, appreciated a man's play for the delight their children experienced, as well as for the complex contribution their husband was making to accomplishing daily routines and the general rearing of the child. For women, it meant letting go of some of their exclusive claim on caregiving to make a place for the father. Fourth, for these fathers, it meant closing themselves off from some of the mixed messages found in the larger culture about men's involvement in family life. Although this cast their efforts to become generative fathers as a highly private and individualized process, it seemed like a necessary component to maintain their commitment to shared parenting in a nongenerative culture. Finally, the men in this study appeared to be diligent in their efforts to control the way they allocated their time to the demands of their paid work.

In spite of their best efforts to be involved fathers, however, there are a number of cultural influences with which they contend to make generative fathering a reality on a day-to-day basis. Central among these is the long tradition of idealizing motherhood and dismissing fatherhood. Although the ideology of motherhood has emphasized the generative involvement of women in the care of their children, it has been by the exclusion of men. As a result, men who seek to be involved fathers for their children must do so without the benefit of hindsight. As the data from this study have indicated, both women and men experience tension and ambivalence as they move away from the idealization of the all-powerful and fully involved mother of the past toward a model of parenting based on an expectation of shared responsibility. For women, this has meant a feeling of being displaced from the fulcrum of family experience and reconciling their guilt at not living up to the historically rooted expectations of what mothers should be. For men, this ambivalence was expressed in terms of the strain between their continued responsibility for providing and their heightened responsibility for caring as they sought to establish themselves as equally contributing members of the parenting team.

The private efforts of these couples to become a shared-parenting team are certainly illustrative of successful strategies men and women can adopt to create generative fathering experiences in their families, even in a nongenerative culture. Unfortunately, it is unlikely that their quiet efforts will revolutionize the kind of patterns that are entrenched in labels like "women working the second shift" or dads "helping out at home" or "babysitting the kids." Like all changes in the politics of gender, these changes are more evolutionary than revolutionary. Nevertheless, the vision of diverse possibilities is clear and some possible paths have been laid out. For these personal efforts to become public concerns, there needs to be a heightened public discourse about and celebration of the merits of shared parenting, not only for the well-being of men and women as parents, but for the well-being of the children they serve, as Gerson argued in Chapter 3.

Researchers will contribute to creating aspects of this public discourse. It will require taking different lenses to our studies of fatherhood. In this study, seeing the generative aspects of men's experiences in these shared-parenthood families required a fresh research lens. It required a willingness to take the critical pinpoint focus off dominant cultural discourses about men's deficiencies as fathers compared to women as mothers. It meant a willingness to refocus on men's generative potential in mundane everyday experiences. In taking this perspective, it may be tempting to discount the public importance of this small, select group of men. Yet, in their mundane everyday experiences, these men shared how they viewed themselves as adopting a generative stance toward their family. Although their parenting activities are not revolutionary, they do demonstrate a kind of generativity that may have been lost on researchers focused on categorizing differences between men and women and then seeing women's ways as "better."

PART III

Encouraging the Application of Generative Fathering in Practice and Scholarship

The five chapters in this section provide practitioners and scholars with more specific ways to understand and encourage generative fathering by applying concepts of generative fathering to parent education, therapy, conceptualization of paternal involvement, academic discourse, and university courses.

In Chapter 11, "Promoting Generative Fathering Through Parent and Family Education," Glen Palm summarizes the state of the art in working with fathers in family life education settings. The chapter contributes to the overall volume by summarizing the main ideas developed thus far on working with fathers in educational settings and by integrating the ideas on generative fathering into an educational context.

In Chapter 12, "A Generative Narrative Approach to Clinical Work With Fathers," Anna Dienhart and David Dollahite suggest ways to integrate the ideas of generative fathering into narrative therapeutic strategies and use the power of personal story to encourage ethical reflection and cognitive, affective, and behavioral change. The chapter authors argue that because effective fatherwork demands sustained commitment and the development of broad skill repertoires and potentials, clinicians should work with fathers to help them embrace generative fathering.

In Chapter 13, "Reconstructing 'Involvement': Expanding Conceptualizations of Men's Caring in Contemporary Families," Rob Palkovitz shows how taking a nondeficit, generative fathering approach can alter scholarship on fathering in significant ways. Palkovitz undertakes a reconstruction of the construct of *involvement,* arguing that much of the thinking that fosters deficit models of fathering stems from limited, narrow, and short-sighted conceptualizations of this construct. This chapter contributes to this volume by broadening the construct of involvement to capture more effectively men's experiences of their fathering work. The ability of scholars and practitioners to understand and encourage good fathering rests on this more phenomenological foundation.

In Chapter 14, "The Best of Times and the Worst of Times: Fathering as a Contested Arena of Academic Discourse," William Doherty makes a case for reasoned scholarly dialogue on the contributions that fathers make to children. He sketches various debates in the fathering literature, such as between those who favor a "family structure" approach and those who favor a "family process" approach, and calls scholars to move beyond the existing polarization between those who champion the "irreplaceable dad" and those who bemoan the "deadbeat dad." The chapter contributes to the objectives of the volume by opening space for reasoned, constructive discourse about fathering that avoids further polarized debate.

In the concluding chapter, "Questions and Activities for Teaching About Generative Fathering in University Courses," David Dollahite, Stephanie Morris, and Alan Hawkins summarize the main contributions of this edited volume on generative fathering and provide questions and activities for use in university courses on such topics as fathering, parenting, adult development, work and family issues, and gender relations. The chapter authors suggest a number of chapter-specific discussion questions designed to encourage productive and nonpolemical classroom discussion about generative fathering and provide chapter-specific activities intended to reinforce student learning about the issues raised in this volume. The authors conclude with a few broad, integrative discussion questions and activities for linking, theory, research, and practice on generative fathering.

11

Promoting Generative
Fathering Through Parent
and Family Education

GLEN F. PALM

During a recent visit with my father-in-law, I asked him about a couple of photographs my wife had hung on our living room wall. The photos, taken in the late 1950s by a photographer for *Life* magazine, depict a day on which fathers of first graders were invited to Frances Parker School in Chicago to learn about first grade. Two photos depict a father and daughter painting a picture together and a group of fathers and children dancing. I was struck by the similarity of the father and daughter painting together with scenes of dads and kids in our family education program. The gentle, involved, protective stance; the immersion of the father and child together into a joint activity—their picture. The continuity of the image of a caring, involved father from the 1950s through the 1990s was indeed striking. As I examined the second photo, I chided my father-in-law about the stiffness of the dancer fathers, all dressed in suits and ties (with the exception of himself and one other dad who appeared to be very suave). My insight here was about the comfort level of this activity—the men in general did not look very comfortable and definitely not as comfortable as they were in a third photo of fathers and children together on the monkey bars on the playground. Some of the suit coats were now off and they all looked more at ease. The point is that these fathers of the late 1950s, who are so often painted as distant and uncaring, appeared to enjoy being with their children and seemed genuinely to care about their children, a point supported by Snarey's (1993) research.

In this chapter, I do not focus on the history of fatherhood, but some perspective about fathering from the past can remind us that men do care about their children, as Griswold documented in Chapter 5, although they often struggle with expressing this care in a way that children readily understand. Awareness of the importance of fathers and efforts to increase father involvement (Anderson, 1933, to Blankenhorn, 1995) have been ongoing themes from the 1920s through the 1990s (Griswold, 1993). Here, recent efforts to support fatherhood through family education (Johnson & Palm, 1992a; Kliman & Kohl, 1984; Levant, 1988) will be examined and integrated with the concept of generative fathering. Although there are many similarities between fathers in the 1950s and the 1990s, fathers in the 1990s face some new challenges. Men in the 1990s are struggling with the redefinition of masculinity and trying to reintegrate the fragmented image of fatherhood (Blankenhorn, 1995). Generative fathering, as described by Snarey (1993) and in Chapter 2, this volume, provides a useful framework for fathers to patch together important ideas from the past (Pleck, 1987) in a new image of good fathering. The challenge to parent and family educators is to guide men toward good fathering in diverse circumstances with a sense of hope, optimism, and even excitement.

There are five main areas that this chapter will cover: (a) a description of parent and family education, (b) an overview of the current educational services that focus on supporting "good fathering," (c) adapting parent and family education to include fathers and a male perspective, (d) emerging principles of best practices for fathers in parent and family education, and (e) future issues and challenges for family educators working with fathers. In this chapter, "fathering" is used in an inclusive manner to refer to any man who is committed for the long term to support and nurture a child or children. This definition reflects the current reality that education and support programs for fathers include men who find themselves in a variety of family situations, such as single custodial fathers, noncustodial fathers, stepfathers, and traditional breadwinners.

Parent and Family Education: An Evolving Field of Practice

Parent and family education (PFE) has a long history, which has been described in a variety of sources (e.g., Brim, 1965; Lewis-Rowley, Brasher, Moss, Duncan, & Stiles, 1993). The many attempts to define family life education have not yet led to consensus (Arcus, Schvaneveldt, & Moss, 1993), which reflects the complexity of the field as well as the diversity of approaches to providing education about parenting and family life. The task of educating parents has been undertaken in a variety of settings, from social service agencies to health care, educational, and religious institutions (Cooke & Thomas, 1985). There are also a variety of disciplines that provide some training for this task, including social work, child psychology, early childhood education, health care education, religious education and ministry, family and consumer sciences, and family social sciences (Roberts, 1983). It is interesting to note that during the 1920s and 1930s PFE began to define a separate professional field (see Anderson, 1930) and that a similar attempt has reemerged in Minnesota in the 1970s and 1980s with the creation of teaching licenses in Parent Education and Early Childhood Family Education (Council on Quality Education, 1981). The diversity of practitioners in this field continues to be the reality in the 1990s with new approaches and programs such as the Family Resource and Support movement (Weissbourd, 1987) and the Family Literacy Programs (McIvor, 1990) adding new branches to a large, growing tree. The strength of a diverse set of family education practitioners is the requisite diversity it creates to match the increasing diversity of families. The limitation is a lack of clear boundaries and professional ethics to guide parent and family educators. The term parent and family education is used in this chapter as an umbrella description to cover a broad array of professionals who deliver education and support services to fathers in a variety of settings and formats (from individual counseling sessions and small groups to massive gatherings organized by religious leaders). These services stretch across the life span but focus on the goal of supporting and educating fathers.

The PFE field has a number of important characteristics that help define both the nature and scope of practice. These are presented here as the broad context for understanding the current picture of services for fathers; they also suggest that this diverse field does have some integrity.

1. PFE by its nature is *multidisciplinary* (Roberts, 1983).

2. PFE is concerned with the *ethical issue of defining "good parenting"* and supporting this work through appropriate communication and discipline techniques.

3. PFE is focused on *improving relationships* between parents and children.

4. PFE is focused on *typical developmental* issues in child development and family life and some of the *common stresses* that families face (Johnson & Palm, 1992c).

5. PFE stresses *respect for differences,* including individual differences, family system differences, and cultural differences.

6. PFE is focused on *individual parent and family strengths* as the place to begin any intervention into family life (Doherty, 1991; Hawkins & Dollahite, Chapter 1, this volume).

Parent and family education as a field is congruent with the concept of generative fathering, as discussed by Snarey (1993) and by Dollahite and his colleagues in Chapter 2. The term *generative fathering,* of course, derives from the pioneering theoretical work of Erikson (1980, 1982), who defined generativity as the developmental task of learning to care for the next generation. Men need both education and support, especially as expectations change and the focus moves from prescribed roles to relationships. Even though initially men may be more comfortable with an individual approach to support generative fathering, the importance of group support for fathering will become apparent to men. In a study of parent education needs (Palm, 1988), men rated support as the least important goal in parent education, yet fathers in groups quickly experience and appreciate the support they feel. A strengths approach is also a comfortable fit for men who tend to value both the independence and the uniqueness that are stressed by this focus on strengths and capabilities. The developmental emphasis in PFE emphasizes the importance of growing into good fathers and outlines some typical and predictable patterns of change (Palm, 1993). This helps to minimize the concern that men may have with expecting instant parental competence from themselves. Finally, the focus on relationships and relationship skills connects with the men's motivation for a close, emotional bond with their children. This seems to be a primary goal for many fathers in the 1990s as they strive for a closer relationship than they had with their own father (Osherson, 1994; Snarey, 1993). The underlying principles of PFE are supportive to educators who promote generative fathering and to fathers who are concerned with the work of generative fathering.

Current Parent and Family Education
Services for Fathers: A Focus on Goals

PFE services for fathers have evolved over the past 50 years. The emphasis in parent education during the 1940s and 1950s was on mothers. Fathers were seen as breadwinners and perhaps assistant parents (Palm &

Palkovitz, 1988). Mothers became the primary audience and fathers were perceived to benefit from a trickle down of knowledge and skills through mothers. This perspective continues to be part of some parent education curriculums through the 1980s (e.g., Parentmaking; see Rothenberg, 1981). Practices in the 1980s often included a session for fathers in which involving fathers was the topic for the evening. I have frequently been invited to parent education sessions to talk about father involvement to a group of mothers. Changes began in the late 1970s when a number of different programs for fathers in special circumstances were created to help support and educate fathers. Fatherhood USA (1984) provides a record of the diversity of programs that were being designed for teen fathers, fathers of children with special needs, divorced and single fathers, stepfathers, gay fathers, and incarcerated fathers. The periodical *Nurturing News,* from 1984–1989, depicted fathers in a variety of different circumstances, each with unique needs and issues. The 1980s became a time to include fathers in programs by adopting an androgynous or generic concept of parenthood (Rotundo, 1985). This approach included fathers not by stressing their unique needs based on family structure but by accepting fathers as copartners (e.g., Bigner, 1994; Ehrensaft, 1990; Pogrebin, 1987). More recent programs developed for fathers have become more sensitive to gender differences (e.g., Hawkins, Roberts, Christiansen, & Marshall, 1994; Johnson & Palm, 1992b; Levant, 1988; McBride, 1990, 1991) and address the merits of separate programs for fathers. PFE programs for fathers in the 1990s still include a diverse group of fathers with special needs (e.g., MELD for Young Fathers; SEFAM Family Support Programs for fathers of children with special needs; see May, 1991; and programs for Incarcerated Fathers; see Giveans, 1988). The information about family education programs for fathers is still limited (McBride & Palm, 1992) because of the grassroots nature of so many programs and the lack of published information.

The recent organization of groups, conferences, and gatherings focused on fathers reflects a revival of interest in fathers and potential new resources and educational services for them. The thrust of programs during the 1980s was the support of more involved and nurturant fathers. The themes in the 1990s are creating responsible fathers and raising the standards for fatherhood (Palm, 1995, pp. 64-66), probably in response to the perceived erosion of fatherhood (Blankenhorn, 1995). The next 5 to 10 years will be an exciting time in PFE as the new influx of energy and resources creates new programs for fathers. (See Levine & Pitt, 1995, for examples of recent community initiatives to support responsible fathering.)

The array of services provided by educational, religious, and health care institutions and social service organizations in the 1990s reflects a diverse set of foci for fathers including (a) knowledge of child development, (b) the male role and the changing role of the father, (c) the development of effective communication skills, (d) increasing father involvement, (e) responsible fatherhood, (f) support for fathers in difficult situations, (g) fathers of children with special needs, (h) fathers as teachers and socializing agents, and (i) fathers as moral leaders. Many programs address a number of different goals, but their approaches reflect a bias toward different social or political goals and different educational strategies. Johnson and Palm (1992a) outline some of the differences in approaches. Services for fathers are typically grassroots in nature and have had few rigorous evaluations to be able to distinguish which programs or approaches are most effective (McBride & Palm, 1992). The diversity is a strength in reaching out to many different fathers in many different circumstances. The weakness of this strategy may be that services have been developed in isolation and cross-fertilization between programs has been limited. The conceptual ethic of generative fathering presented in Chapter 2 by Dollahite and his colleagues has the potential to provide a global approach for PFE for fathers and helps to define some important goals that may have been omitted in earlier programs. It is clear that PFE efforts for fathers have multiple goals and diverse audiences.

Table 11.1 offers a beginning description of parent and family education goals that emerge from applying the conceptual ethic of fathering as generative work to define and support good fathering in our culture. The table includes important goals for fathers that can be addressed through PFE and can assist family educators in defining educational objectives and important topics. The list is not complete, but I offer it here to stimulate thinking about potential goals and future directions for PFE with fathers.

Adapting Parent and Family Education to Include Fathers: Beyond Androgyny

Although practitioners in the parent and family education field support the basic concept of generative fathering, there appears to be another step required for them to become "father friendly" (Johnson & Palm, 1995). The ideology of androgyny has created the notion of the *generic parent*. This generic, or androgynous, parent is represented by a predominately

Table 11.1 Generative Fathering: Goals for Parent and Family Education

1. Ethical Work
   a. Fathers will become critically aware of and explore the cultural standards of good fathering.
   b. Fathers will reexamine their values before passing them on to their children.
   c. Fathers will identify the virtues necessary to do good fathering in the 1990s.
   d. Fathers will explore their work as models of masculinity.
   e. Fathers will explore the meaning of healthy male sexuality and gender equality.
   f. Fathers will examine their work as moral guides.

2. Stewardship Work
   a. Fathers will learn how to develop a healthy balance between work and family life.
   b. Fathers will explore their responsibility to maintain and nurture a healthy family.
   c. Fathers will gain skills in creating safe communities free of violence and prejudice.
   d. Fathers will understand the power of families as social change agents.

3. Development Work
   a. Fathers will understand child and adult development as a normative context for supporting their children's psychosocial, academic-intellectual, and physical-athletic growth.
   b. Fathers will understand and appreciate individual and unique characteristics of their children.
   c. Fathers will be sensitive and responsive to a child's changing needs.
   d. Fathers will understand their own development as adults.
   e. Fathers will understand and appreciate the development of family life over time.

4. Relationship Work
   a. Fathers will develop relationship skills to initiate and maintain a close, nurturing bond with their children.
   b. Fathers will develop support systems with other parents.
   c. Fathers will develop a coparenting relationship with their children's mother.
   d. Fathers will understand gender as it influences communication and relationships.
   e. Fathers will be able to express a range of emotions in appropriate ways within the family.

female model for "good parenting." Although fathers have many things to learn from mothers about parenting, men may also bring positive characteristics based on male socialization to the work of parenting. Although the content and the goals for PFE may seem to be the same for mothers and fathers, parents of both genders come to parenting from different backgrounds and may have different needs and goals. The following list of differences has been useful in identifying some important distinctions between men and women as they come into PFE programs. Of course, individual differences between same-gender parents is often greater than between-gender differences, yet recognition of some typical gender differences is essential to making programs sensitive to fathers' needs. Addressing solely the "generic parent" may lead to discounting of male strengths and needs.

Some of the differences (Palm & Palkovitz, 1988) identified here provide a male perspective that has been missing in parent education programs that have been marketed for the generic parent (e.g., STEP, Sibling Rivalry, Active Parenting). One of the false assumptions of generic parenting is that both men and women come to programs with similar goals, styles, skills, and knowledge bases. The differences described below are provided not to stereotype mothers and fathers but as important information about gender differences to help program implementers adapt to the needs of men, making programs more father friendly.

The first area of difference relates to the *goals* of PFE for mothers and fathers. Parents come to programs with a variety of needs and goals. One of the patterns of differences I've noted in my work with parents has been that the primary focus of most fathers is to create a close relationship with the child. Often, the model for this relationship is the father's own experience of his relationship with his mother, for he sees his father as having been relatively distant and uninvolved (Palm & Joyce, 1994). Mothers, on the other hand, often come to PFE seeking support from and connection with other parents. They do not view the closeness of their relationship with their child as their top priority for the program. Mothers value and understand the importance of maintaining a close relationship but may feel relatively confident about their level of emotional intimacy with their child and may even be concerned about being "too close." This difference is important because the focus, content, and methods of the program should support both mothers and fathers as they develop their images of good parenting.

A second area of difference relates to the *typical socialization processes* for boys and girls and the development of different skills and areas of knowledge. Many little girls play with dolls or practice the role of mothers and spend a great deal of time practicing the skills and learning the script for involved parenting. As they get older, they tend to have more experiential opportunities to practice some of these nurturing skills with real children through baby-sitting. In addition to the experiential learning about children and child management skills, many girls develop a knowledge base about child development and family life through courses in high school and college (Palm & Palkovitz, 1988). Individual boys may gain some of the knowledge and skills that girls learn about children and family life, but male socialization tends to discount this area of knowledge and skills. Consequently, as PFE services engage fathers and mothers, they are often building on different knowledge bases and levels of skills. A third difference noted in the research literature (e.g., Lamb, 1981c) is the different *interactional styles of mothers and fathers* with children. This research has tended to focus on interaction with infants and describes the differences as fathers being more physical, tactile, and arousing. Snarey (1993, p. 35) summarizes numerous studies showing that "fathers' preferences for physically stimulating and exciting activities are not restricted to young infants"; that "fathers of school children often participate in activities beyond the family sphere, such as scouting, Little League, and similar physically oriented organized activities"; and that "they use more verbal joking and rough physical play in their interactions with their older children. Likewise, fathers of adolescents spend a greater proportion of the time they are together with their children in . . . activities [that] tend to promote assertiveness rather than politeness." In other words, "from birth through adolescence," Snarey concludes, "a working-hard-at-playing quality distinguishes paternal from maternal childrearing participation." There is some evidence that more androgynous fathers (Palkovitz, 1984) continue to engage in rough-and-tumble play but also are more expressive of affection. Mothers and fathers also seem to have different expectations for independent and risk-taking behaviors in children. This difference is especially relevant when PFE programs include a parent-child interaction component (Kristensen, 1984). The male style of interaction must be understood as a distinct style that has some real benefits for the child. Parent and family educators must provide parent-child activities that are comfortable for both styles.

A fourth difference between mothers and fathers that has been noted by recent authors (e.g., Tannen, 1990) is *communication styles.* Tannen describes the differences between the report talk of men and the rapport talk of women. Men tend to focus on their status in their styles of communication whereas women tend to focus on connections and relationships. The implication of this for PFE is the tendency for most parent education to occur in the context of a small group. In this context, most women would be very comfortable making connections and giving each other support. VonNostrand (1993) describes some of the strategies that men may use in small groups of mixed genders to maintain status and avoid looking bad. For example, fathers fold their arms and sit back from the group as a way of withdrawing or they distract the focus of the session with a joke that discounts the importance of the topic. Mothers, on the other hand, tend to share problems and offer affirmation, support, and empathy to other parents. Parent groups can be structured to encourage fathers to share stories (e.g., begin with birth stories) and to discuss differences in a respectful manner (see Bowman, 1994). These gender communication differences can serve both as content for family education and as potential barriers for fathers.

A fifth area of difference relevant to parent educators is the *different styles of discipline* that mothers and fathers may practice. Fathers tend to be more distant, controlling, and consistent. This is often similar to the advice that male experts give to mothers about discipline (Thevenin, 1993). Mothers tend to be more emotional, ambivalent about control and concerned about the outcome of their actions on their relationship with their child. In problem solving (Holden, 1988), fathers may exhibit a more logical style whereas mothers may use a more complex system that involves more attention to relationships and individual differences. These two distinct styles of discipline can lead to family conflict with the mother concerned about the fathers' lack of connection to the child and the father concerned about the mother's inconsistency and lack of control over the child. The parent and family educator should see the merit of both styles as well as the tendencies for problems in each style.

The point of identifying differences here is that PFE services have primarily served mothers and tend to be focused on issues that mothers encounter. As the field evolves to be more inclusive of men, these differences must be addressed so that educators can adapt content, methods, and goals to include male needs and parenting strengths. Adaptations should be made with recognition of gender differences, acknowledgment of these differences when they lead to greater cross-gender understanding, and care not to reinforce rigid gender stereotypes.

Developing Best Practices for Working With Fathers

The development of some descriptors of best practices in working with fathers in parent and family education appears to be an important next step for the field. The Family Resource Coalition (1993) began a study of best practices in family resource programs to define characteristics of effective programs. The concept of best practices offers a compilation of the current wisdom about practices for the educator and some specific program characteristics for the researcher to study and evaluate. The best practices described here focus on fathers in various PFE settings. They build on the work of the Minnesota Fathering Alliance (Johnson & Palm,

1992c) and the Father Re-Engagement Roundtable in 1994 to articulate some best practices for working with fathers. The purpose of these statements is to begin a dialogue among practitioners and researchers aimed toward building consensus about our current understandings and insights into working with fathers.

1. *Parent and family educators working with fathers build on the male motivation to develop a close relationship with his child.* Educators believe that *all* fathers care deeply about their children. The reality is that many fathers may not know how to express this care because male socialization may not have prepared them for the fathering work they are being asked to do today (Bergman, 1991). All men can begin to work on good fathering by focusing on how to develop this relationship. This relationship-building experience for fathers gives them a "second chance" to develop relationship skills that may have gone underdeveloped during their youth (Palm, 1993).

2. *Parent and family educators working with fathers practice active outreach on an individual level.* Inviting fathers as generic parents reaches only a small proportion of men, what is often referred to as the "cream of the crop." The value of parent and family education for fathers may be best conveyed by individual invitation. Palm (1995a) identifies a number of strategies, such as working through mothers in programs, making home visits, asking young children to "invite" dads to parent-child events, asking men to invite a friend, and making individual telephone calls to fathers. An affirmative approach is necessary to reach and invite fathers as individuals to participate in PFE programs.

3. *Parent and family educators working with fathers listen carefully to the unique stories, needs, and strengths of fathers.* Fathers may not be able to describe their needs for services that they don't understand. Family educators can help men to identify their needs and interests by asking questions and observing father-child interactions. The author used an individual interview process with a group of incarcerated fathers as a preliminary step toward beginning a parent education program in a correctional facility. The interview process provided fathers with a chance to describe their situations, their relationships with children, and their personal beliefs about fatherhood. This process also helped to begin a relationship between the educator and each father.

4. *Parent and family educators working with fathers begin by identifying comfort zones—activities, settings, and topics—that feel safe for fathers.* Many fathers may be unfamiliar with PFE, and educators need to meet them in their "comfort zones." *Comfort zone* is used here as a

metaphor for space, activities, and topics that may be part of a family education setting. These comfort zones may be related to familiar activities, such as playing active games with children in a gym setting or taking children fishing. There may be wide variation in what individual comfort zones are; often, it is easier to identify areas in which men may not be comfortable (e.g., circle games where men dance around and hold hands; see Palm & Johnson, 1992).

5. *Parent and family educators working with fathers acknowledge some of the positive characteristics (strengths) that men bring to parenting from their socialization as males.* The practice of building on strengths is a basic principle of family education programs. The application to fathers can be confusing. First, it is often easier to identify male needs to be more sensitive or more emotionally articulate—in short, to behave more like "good mothers." Family educators may find it easy to identify strengths in men who behave like "good mothers." Men also have developed some strengths from growing up male that should be acknowledged as potential tools for building a relationship with their children. These may include such characteristics as playfulness, promoting risk taking, encouraging problem solving, providing a sense of security, and being less emotional (Palm & Johnson, 1992b). For example, a father teaching a child how to ride a bike may use a number of these characteristics to support his child in learning this new skill and enhancing their relationship. The purpose of acknowledging male strengths is not to reinforce male/female stereotypes but to avoid the tendency to see characteristics of female socialization as the only model for good parenting.

6. *Parent and family educators working with fathers recognize and appreciate the diversity of family forms, culture, and circumstance that influence parenting.* As a young parent and parent educator, I felt very secure about my behavior and beliefs as a nonspanking parent. I had learned as a preschool teacher and child care worker with children with special needs that there are many alternatives to spanking. I found that I had a hard time understanding and accepting spanking as a legitimate form of discipline. This belief (backed by research, of course) sometimes got in the way of my effectiveness, for it created a barrier in my relationship with some parents in different subcultures from mine who held alternative beliefs about disciplinary practices. I have learned to step back from the debate about spanking to understand how spanking fits into a particular family setting. I still provide alternatives to parents who spank and ask them to consider the potential negative consequences of spanking. As ethical educators, we must know our biases, temper them when

they get in the way of relationships, and learn to listen to and learn from other perspectives. Fathers may be in dual-earner families, in a joint-custody situation, or in prison and not married to the child's mother. Each family setting creates different challenges in developing a healthy co-parenting relationship.

7. *Parent and family educators working with fathers must pay attention to the needs and unresolved issues of women.* The tendency to become profather and be perceived as antimother can create new tensions and problems, a subject addressed further by Doherty in Chapter 14. When educators pay too much attention to fathers, mothers can become resentful. The father who receives praise for having the courage to change a diaper is resented by the mother who changes countless diapers with no praise or recognition. The gender tensions between men and women remain high, and educators working with fathers should acknowledge these and help both mothers and fathers to address them in a caring and constructive manner. (See Toffel, 1994, for an example of addressing gender tensions.)

8. *Parent and family educators working with fathers recognize the ethical nature of their work.* The call for higher or wiser standards (Blankenhorn, 1995; Dollahite et al., Chapter 2, this volume; Snarey, 1993) has brought back a focus on the importance of creating ethical guidelines for fathering work. The family educator must balance the potential absolutist tendencies of higher standards (e.g., Blankenhorn's, 1995, "good family man") with the reality of the young incarcerated father. An 18-year-old father in prison may care deeply about his 6-month-old daughter but is in no position to be a good provider or daily caretaker. High standards are essential at the cultural script level, yet all men can be encouraged to work toward good fathering by recognizing that it is a process, not merely role fulfillment. Educators have the difficult task of guiding fathers to consider both personal decisions about good parenting and cultural standards for good fathering. Family educators must have the courage to raise ethical questions and the skills to guide fathers through a thoughtful process toward the work of good fathering.

The best practices listed here begin to examine the principles of working with fathers that are critical to program development. This effort to define and describe best practices is an important beginning, but many questions remain. Do these practices apply to all populations of fathers? How do we adjust best practices not only for men but for men in difficult circumstances? How can best practices be used to guide program development and professional training? What research questions emerge from this list of best practices?

Challenges and Issues for Parent and Family Educators Working With Fathers

Looking to the future of parent and family education, there are a number of important issues that must be faced to help advance good fathering through education and support services. I have identified the following issues as most important for the next 5 to 10 years.

1. *Continue to expand services to larger circles of fathers.* It will be important to continue to build on the diversity of programs that currently serve men. It appears that many of the programs that focus on specific groups of men address needs only after they have become problems (e.g., divorced fathers, teen fathers, incarcerated fathers). Fathers in difficult circumstances need support and education services, but there also needs to be a more concerted effort to provide education and support to men just because they are fathers, not only when they have problems being fathers. The notion of all services as intervention needs to be reconsidered. One major barrier for men is their attitude that they don't need help with fathering unless things are really falling apart. More services are needed that can be seen as normative, educational experiences (i.e., parent education classes for fathers with children who are 0–2 years). This would help create a norm that men who participate in family education are responsible and forward thinking, countering the norm whereby men only ask for help when they are really lost or in pain. The circle should also expand to include men who are in greatest need of services. Instead of labeling fathers as deadbeat dads and punishing them, we should develop support and education services to help this group of men move toward generative fathering.

2. *Train and recruit male family educators.* An issue that has continued to be raised in Minnesota is whether men or women should work with fathers in PFE (see Konen, 1992). It has become clear that male educators who are specifically trained in PFE are at a real premium. The importance of male staff members has become clearer as we listen to men talk about their experiences with PFE. There were a number of men in a family literacy program who walked by a PFE class every day. They often peeked into the room and noticed immediately that there were no men in the room. They began to label the program as a "mother-and-child program." A male teaching assistant began to work in the program and soon these fathers felt more comfortable about attending some of the family functions. There may be many ways to recruit males to the field. Sometimes men in related fields, such as therapists, ministers, or social workers,

are asked to facilitate parent groups for fathers. This serves well as a short-term solution but also brings in some of the baggage of these other areas of training and other roles that these individuals may have. In PFE as a field, there needs to be a better job done of defining appropriate preparation for the educator role and to create training programs that will attract men to this field as a career versus a part-time job.

3. *Broaden an individual growth focus to include a family and community responsibility focus.* The focus of many parenting programs in our culture tends to be on the individual growth (e.g., self-esteem, skills development) of the parent. Comprehensive programs move beyond this base to develop job skills and couple communication skills. The work of fathering does involve self-improvement, but it also goes beyond this to include creating a healthy family climate and a safe community environment for families. It was too easy for fathers in the 1980s to concentrate on building their own family cocoons as the best way to insulate their family from increasing societal violence. Education for fathers must help men to look beyond their own family to the larger community. The interdependence of self, family, and community is a critical connection to make to support childrearing in the future.

4. *Evaluate effective practices for different groups.* In parent education in general, we need more useful evaluations of programs that could lead us beyond "Are parents satisfied with the program?" or "Does the program change specific target behaviors?" There has been a lack of systematic research on programs for fathers (McBride & Palm, 1992) because with the exception of a few programs for teen dads most of the programs have been part of grassroots movements. The programs that have been offered are often described as effective based on fathers' satisfaction or the assumed "goodness" of such important programs. As the field matures, it becomes important to evaluate more rigorously long- and short-term program effects. A research agenda for the future could include some of the following questions: Do programs have important impacts on father-child relationships? What types of methods work best with different groups of fathers? Are there certain program formats that are more effective? What are the goals that are most important to pursue with fathers? What is the interaction of various goals in PFE for fathers? This type of research would help to design effective, father-friendly programs.

5. *Raise the issue of good fathering to an ethical responsibility.* Responsibility will be an important area for parent and family educators to exhibit leadership and creativity in the coming years. In this chapter, I have already addressed the issue by defining it as an area of best practice.

The major point to be made here is that this is a very sensitive issue, where courage and prudence will be necessary as virtues of parent and family educators who address this issue. Educators must seek a creative balance between ethical principles and relativist or adaptable practices, between broad cultural scripts and individual translations. Parent and family educators are in a critical position to shed some light on these questions and to engage men in the process of ethical thinking and behavior. (The need for clinicians to approach their work with fathers from an ethical position is discussed by Dienhart & Dollahite in Chapter 12.)

6. *Broaden the focus from father-child relationships to include father-mother relationships.* The initial focus on the father-child relationship sometimes obscures the coparent relationship. There are some emerging services in this area, such as court mediation, to help couples to reestablish healthy coparenting relationships after a divorce. PFE can address and normalize some of the family transition situations. Educators can also assist fathers and mothers in building relationship skills and understanding of the other gender.

Summary and Conclusions

Parent and family education is a diverse field that holds great promise for supporting men in the work of generative fathering. The basic premises of parent and family education are consistent with the ethic of fathering as generative work (Dollahite et al., Chapter 2, this volume). This chapter begins to integrate the goals of generative fathering into a family education curriculum for fathers. As new programs grow out of the influx of new energy and resources directed toward responsible fathering, the development of best practices should be articulated to guide practitioners and generate research questions for researchers. The real challenge for parent and family educators is to guide the ethical discussion about good fathering and include fathers from diverse backgrounds in this discussion. Educators working with fathers will need persistence, hope, prudence, and creativity to guide them through these exciting times.

12

A Generative Narrative
Approach to Clinical Work
With Fathers

ANNA DIENHART
DAVID C. DOLLAHITE

This chapter applies ideas about generative fathering to clinical work using a narrative approach. We begin by discussing our foundational assumptions linking narrative therapy with the ideas of generative fathering, or fatherwork, discussed in Chapter 2 of this volume. We advocate a clinical approach committed to encouraging fathers' involvement in the best interest of their developing children. Then, we discuss our ideas of how a generative narrative approach can facilitate ethical, cognitive, affective, and behavioral change with fathers. Finally, we provide some clinical suggestions, mainly in the form of questions to ask in the clinical conversation, designed explicitly to encourage generative fathering.

Clinical Backdrop: Creating a Generative Ethic

Clinical work with couples, families, or individuals is always a blend of theory, judgment, technique, and creativity. It begins with the persons of the clients and the clinician. Clients come to therapy with their own beliefs, values, and sense of obligations. The counselor or therapist also enters the clinical relationship with what she or he believes and how she or he thinks and feels about the purpose and process of therapy. Clinicians bring with them thoughts, feelings, and beliefs about human nature, relationship dynamics, change processes, gender, culture, and family forms. Any stance a therapist takes in a clinical setting has implicit value foundations—even saying or doing nothing carries implied values (Taggart, 1985). Thus, clinicians operate in a morally laden context and have a privileged position for their ideas and values.

We propose a generative ethic for clinical work with fathers. Our conceptualization of a generative ethic embraces two interpretations of the word *generative*: (a) the interpretation from Eriksonian theory which values the transgenerational contribution of individuals living in our inherently relational world, and (b) the notion of clinical work with individuals and families as "having the power or function of generating, originating, producing or reproducing" (*Webster's Ninth New Collegiate Dictionary*, 1983, p. 510) adopted by some family therapists (Fine & Turner, 1991; Goolishian & Anderson, 1988; Hoffman, 1990). Thus, a generative ethic means we advocate that therapists take an explicit ethical stance to honor the intricate relational web of individual lives (Doherty, 1995) while helping clients generate unique ways to embrace and live out their relational commitments in everyday life. We see clinicians as guided by ethical obligations to try to help clients resolve their personal dilemmas and live with integrity in their relationships, particularly, in this instance, their relationships with their children.

Therapists as Relational Consultants: Ethical Dimensions

It is a tremendous challenge to engage in meaningful, helpful, and ethically responsible clinical conversations while not unduly imposing ideas and values on clients. From a postmodern cultural and professional perspective where diversity and local meanings are highly valued, this challenge is paramount. However, appreciating and celebrating diversity does not require that postmodern therapies be morally relativistic. A generative ethic based approach to therapy can flow from an integration of (a) the "ethical postmodernism" of the continental philosopher Emmanuel Levinas (1985, 1987), (b) Snarey's (1993) ideas on ethical fathering, (c) Doherty's (1995) call for the promotion of moral responsibility in therapy, (d) Parry and Doan's (1994) call for ethical narrative therapy, and (e) Dollahite et al.'s conceptual ethic of generative fathering (Chapter 2, this volume) and their ideas about the value of narrative in the change process for fathers. (Dollahite, Hawkins, & Brotherson, 1996).

Levinas (1985, 1987) presents a philosophy that begins with each human being's ethical obligation to respond to the needs of "the other," even at personal sacrifice. Snarey (1993) takes a similar position and applies it explicitly to men's relationship with their children. He states that the relationship between fathers and children has "moral significance" in that "fathers directly experience the moral claims of their children and are personally obligated to their children" (p. 357). Building on Erikson (1982, 1963), Snarey argues that parenting is perhaps the highest, and certainly the most constant, source of ethical reflection.

Extending Snarey's (1993) argument to the clinical setting, we see it as important that therapists be willing to explore working within a moral framework with fathers. Often, in our clinical work, fathers are making significant decisions with embedded moral dimensions impacting "others" in their relational network. Such issues as whether and how to divorce; how to maintain meaningful relationships with children and continue to provide economic support for children after a divorce (see Pasley & Minton, Chapter 8, this volume); how to care for children with special needs (see Brotherson & Dollahite, Chapter 6, this volume); and taking responsibility to end physical, sexual, or emotional abuse are not simply personal issues; they carry embedded moral dilemmas in a relational context as well. Whether and how a therapist addresses these dimensions of relational living is, indeed, in itself a moral decision.

Doherty (1995) argues that it is possible, desirable, and necessary for clinicians to promote moral responsibility in their clinical work—particularly in their work with fathers. He calls on therapists to move beyond the old paradigm of supposed value-neutrality where, in fact, therapists may have actively promoted what Bellah et al. (1985) called "expressive individualism" as the fundamental value that determined the processes and desired outcomes for psychotherapy. He argues that "psychotherapy has the resources to contribute to the formation of a new cultural ideal in which personal fulfillment will be seen as part of a seamless web of interpersonal and community bonds that nurture us and create obligations we cannot ignore and still be human" (p. 20). He suggests that therapists need to learn how to be better "moral consultants" in the clinical conversation.

In Chapter 2 of this volume, Dollahite et al. present a conceptual ethic of fathering as *generative work*. This framework is explicit about its ethical position. It calls for fathers to meet the needs of the next generation through conscious, continuous, and caring work—fatherwork. Their ethical frame of fatherwork assumes (a) that fathers have contextual and relational agency, that is, they can and must make important choices on behalf of the next generation; (b) that generational ethics take priority over adult preferences; and (c) that children and communities call fathers to perform *ethical work* (ensure a secure environment and respond to children's needs), *stewardship work* (provide resources and opportunities), *development work* (maintain supportive conditions and adapt to varying needs), and *relationship work* (facilitate attachments and encourage understanding). This conceptual ethic of fatherwork points fathers toward the intended consequences of good fathering: moral, productive, mature, and loving fathers and children.

Thus, our frame for "generative narrative" with clients proposes clinicians make apparent their generative ethic. As clinicians, we can be open about our commitment to honor the relational web of individual lives, while working with fathers to create meaningful shifts in their ethical, cognitive, affective, and behavioral choices and experiences. This means that we recognize our influential position within the therapeutic conversation (Goolishian & Anderson, 1988; Hoffman, 1990) while collaborating with our clients in an original and creative process to generate alternatives in their current view of possibilities. A *generative ethic* invites clinicians to work with the unique meaning structures of clients' lives and to engage respectfully clients in dialogue about their fatherwork.

Clinical Assumptions of a Generative Ethic

Clinical work promoting generative fathering begins from a position appreciating that most fathers want to be good parents and that parenting is a highly complex and challenging experience with conditions and constraints (Hawkins and Dollahite, Chapter 1, this volume). Fathering has the potential to draw out both the best and worst aspects of human potential. It is an everyday endeavor in which fathers face constantly changing interactions between parent and child and often between parent and parent (even when the parents are no longer in a couple partnership). Fatherwork is negotiated against a moving landscape of behaviors, feelings, and capabilities as the child develops. At base, the challenges of parenting, for men as with women, are about maintaining intricate relationships, facilitating complex development, managing resource scarcity, and resolving moral dilemmas. This stance includes the idea that men have the willingness and capabilities to embrace a *generative ethic* in their fatherwork and strive to develop deeply meaningful relationships with their children (Dollahite et al., see Chapter 2). Thus, clinical work with fathers should begin with a sincerely held respect for the people engaged in this sacred and most challenging endeavor.

We adopt another closely aligned foundational position, that of honoring the unique experience each client brings to the clinical setting and highly regarding their interpretive perspective. We see a "generative narrative" approach to clinical work flowing from an interpretive paradigm which emphasizes the human desire to understand self and others (Braybrooke, 1987), and as an opportunity to find meaning and hope through the stories people tell about their lives.

Finally, we view the clinical encounter as fertile ground for exploring and extending our appreciation for the myriad ways men contribute to the lives of their children. Modern cultural history is replete with notions of men's place in families centering on their being good providers and strong family leaders. Traditionally, many clinicians and family scientists have easily appreciated the complexity of instrumental and affective skills and intentions women typically bring to their parenting, yet have tended to see men as narrowly engaged in limited and specialized role tasks and activities (Doherty, 1991). Clinical theories and techniques may still have remnants based on keeping mothers central in the lives of children while relegating men to a peripheral place in the work of parenting. The "culture of maternalism" (Dienhart, 1995; Dienhart & Daly, Chapter 10, this volume) supports and perpetuates this limiting view. However, the authors in this volume and elsewhere suggest that, in complexity, richness, and difficulty, men's parenting experiences may be more similar to than different from women's (Biller, 1993; Cohen, 1987, 1994; Dienhart, 1995; Gerson, 1993, Chapter 3, this volume; Hawkins & Dollahite, Chapter 1, this volume; Lamb, 1995; Palkovitz, Chapter 13, this volume).

We believe clinicians must remain open to the overt and subtle demonstrations of fatherwork—staying alert to the mundane and the exceptional ways men participate in shaping their children's lives and in turn find their own lives reshaped. Recently, Dienhart (1995) found that many men mentioned that people do not typically ask them to share their stories of becoming and being a father and then listen with interest. Thus, we advocate a clinical stance of listening attentively to the voices of men about what they want and need as parents (Heesacker & Prichard, 1992; Johnson & Palm, 1992; Palm, Chapter 11, this volume). We advise clinicians to listen with interest and respect to fathers' stories and to their interpretations.

Taking a generative ethic to our clinical work, then, means allowing and encouraging men to claim and give meaning to their fathering experiences. It also means working with both men and women to enhance their claim on the importance of fatherwork in the lives of their children, in the man's own life, and in the life of the child's mother (whether or not the parents are still together).

A Generative Narrative Perspective: Promoting Change

In this section, we review our current ideas about the potential of a "generative narrative" approach to influence change in the lives of men (in general) and fathers (in particular). The purpose of this section is to summarize our ideas about how the clinical use of personal narratives can affect change in men's lives. These thoughts flow, in general, from the recent work in the behavioral and applied sciences and self-help literature focusing on change and the use of narrative to understand and assist people (Atkinson, 1995; Braybrook, 1987; Chinen, 1992; Day, 1991; Dollahite, et al., 1996; Josselson & Lieblich, 1993; Keen & Valley-Fox, 1989; Kotre, 1985; Mair, 1988; McAdams, 1985; Meade, 1993; Palus, 1993; Parry & Doan, 1994; Pittman, 1993; White & Epston, 1990) and in particular, from the work of Dollahite et al. (1996) on narrative, change, and generative fathering.

Along with McAdams (1985), we appreciate that identity is formed and changed through the personal accounts people create to make sense of their lives, in short, a "life story." Because narratives are usually collapsed and interpreted versions of the lived experience, they lend themselves to further exploration of detail and reinterpretation of events and meanings. As people explore and incorporate new meanings into their "life story" (Palus, 1993), they gain perspectives from which to embrace change. Thus, we see narrative as a powerful clinical vehicle to invite change in important areas of life (Parry & Doan, 1994; White & Epston, 1990).

As introduced earlier, when we use the term "generative narrative" approach to clinical work with fathers, we have in mind a kind of narrative approach that incorporates the ethical stance of a generative ethic. Parry and Doan (1994) explicitly call for an emphasis on ethics in helping people find meaning in their stories, which centers on meeting the needs of others in the family. Thus, rather than simply hearing client's stories and helping them find personal meaning, we believe clinicians can choose to consciously promote the value and the healing power for parents and children associated with fatherwork—with men committing to sustained and meaningful active involvement in the lives of their children.

All efforts to encourage change toward more generative fathering must recognize the tremendous variety of factors that influence men in their parenting. As this volume demonstrates, there is a wide variety of fathering that is related to the father's cultural, ethnic, socioeconomic, and religious backgrounds (see Allen & Connor, Chapter 4; DeMaris & Greif, Chapter 9; Rhoden & Robinson, Chapter 7). In this regard, an advantage in narrative approaches is that narrative is responsive to tremendous varieties of individual experiences. Thus, a clinician using narrative can remain open to diverse experiences, circumstances, and interpretations while working to re-vision future potentials (Parry & Doan, 1994). We believe that any clinical efforts to encourage deep, meaningful, and lasting change in human experience will involve *cognitive, affective, ethical,* and *behavioral* dimensions (Dollahite et al., 1996; Mahoney, 1991). Stories of one's life and associated meanings can be powerful clinical tools; they can be used to prompt thoughtful reflection (cognitive), encourage emotional exploration (affective), provoke moral examination of choices (ethical), and provide compelling images and concrete models for action (behavioral). We briefly discuss each of these dimensions here in relation to fatherwork.

Cognitive Dimension of Generative Change. In order for clinicians to prompt positive change, it is often useful for them to appeal to and engage fathers' creative processes; drawing them into the opportunity for problem solve. Eliciting and focusing on fathers' narratives has rich potential to draw them into meaningful interpretation of their own experiences and may create renewed interest in their generative engagement as parents. By highlighting many subtle aspects of father's stories, therapists can take them from their comfort zone and place them at the edge of different possibilities—facilitating the opening of space (Fine & Turner, 1991) for them to see things from different perspectives.

Affective Dimension of Generative Change. By inviting fathers to focus on the emotional connection and response implicit (perhaps) in their narratives, we may reach them in important ways. Their own stories, when explored for emotional nuance, may act as the necessary flint to spark personal transformation. If a clinician can use narrative to touch a man's heart, the man may move toward behavioral change; exploring the affective tones in a father's narrative may invite him to bypass cognitive defenses.

Ethical Dimension of Generative Change. One way for clinicians to become better moral consultants (Doherty, 1995) is to attend to the ethical and moral dilemmas in the stories fathers tell. Drawing on their own narrative accounts and using clinical mirroring can be a way to reflect back to them the positive images in their own life that indeed express their ethical desire to be a generative father. Then their narrative accounts can be explored further for the choices clients make in their everyday lives that concretely express or deflect attention away from their underlying desire.

Behavioral Dimension of Generative Change. Change in a man's fatherwork usually occurs as a process of revising and reformulating behaviors in the acts of negotiating daily activities. A man may tell parts of his own story, then reflect on it and its implications for possible directions of behavioral change. Many fathers like to refer to a pattern or model of action. Their own stories can be used as an initial blueprint for exploring those aspects of effective interaction in their lives that they can maintain as they redesign or retrofit others that they see are less generative. Because fathers may want specific behavioral examples when considering change in their lives, it can be useful to introduce narratives from other men to augment the clinical work. If men understand what can be done through hearing or reading about the experiences of other men, it may be easier for them to take action to do similar things.

Calling Forth Generative Narratives in Clinical Work With Fathers

In this section, we explore ways to elicit personal narratives and engage in clinical conversation about ethical fatherwork in four areas: (a) fathers' competency repertoire, (b) fatherwork models, (c) generative parenting examples, and (d) fathers' experiences with children. In each area, we provide some examples of specific, illustrative questions that clinicians might use to work with the narratives and to develop meanings with a potential to facilitate change toward generative fathering.[1] We also utilize a solution-focused orientation of building on existing strengths in clinical conversation (Furman & Ahola, 1992; Walter & Peller, 1992). The suggested questions flow from a perspective of inviting moral reflection about meeting the needs of children, rather than enshrining adult expressive individualism (Doherty, 1995). In reviewing the following sections, we suggest readers keep in mind that exploring these areas with men, women, and couples may evolve over the course of several sessions. Because in this section we speak directly to clinicians, we use first- and second-person pronouns.

Working With Fathers

Father's Competency Repertoire. We believe that it is crucial to work from a capabilities and responsibilities based model that respects fathers' parenting resources and obligations (Dollahite et al., see Chapter 2). Accordingly, it is important to create clinical opportunities for a father to tell you about the things he believes he does well in his fatherwork and to look for ways to take his resourcefulness to more challenging aspects of his fatherwork.

1. You may want to ask him to tell you about times and/or aspects of parenting he most enjoys and feels most competent or most comfortable to handle. You can use these examples to build an appreciation of his parenting behaviors, his affective connection, and the kinds of choices he makes in juggling his parenting with his other responsibilities and commitments in life.

For example, start with a question like, *"I'd like to hear about times you most enjoy being with your child(ren)."* Then, *"What is it about those times that you most enjoy?"* Then, *"I notice . . . , and I am wondering how your feelings about being competent in that area of being a parent might get overlooked by you when . . . (problematic situation)?"* Follow up with, *"I notice even in this (problematic situation) you have been able to . . . (list other competencies noticed)."* Or, *"What aspects of your competency that are so apparent in (enjoyable situation) might also work for you in (problematic situation)?"*

2. It may seem a paradox when focusing on his competency repertoire to include inquiry into areas of discomfort about being a father and how discomfort may shape what he is willing to do or to try to do with and for his child. However, you will also want to understand aspects of his experience as a parent that may restrict his ideas about what and how he can contribute to his children's lives, however. You can look for unnoticed competencies embedded in his stories and highlight them as a starting point for enhancing his sense of potential in these areas.

For example, you might explore this area with questions like, *"I am wondering about times when you may have noticed a certain sense of being personally challenged in interactions with your child."* Then, *"I am curious to hear what that challenge might be about for you."* Follow up with, *"I notice even in that kind of situation you are able to . . . (note some competency related to the cognitive, affective, ethical, or behavioral dimensions of parent-child interaction). How might remembering and highlighting that aspect of your competency impact your experiences of the challenges you face as you parent your child?"*

3. A closely aligned approach is to explore aspects of parenting in which the father expresses some desire to become more involved. You may ask him to tell you about a time he found himself holding back in his fatherwork. When listening to his story, you may hear about perceived obstacles which could be worthwhile exploring further.

For example, you might ask, *"I'd like to hear about times when you might have felt you were holding yourself back from being the kind of father you would like to be."* Then, *"I honor your desire to be involved . . . (in the way described) and I wonder what it is about . . . (that situation) that left you feeling like you should hold back?"* Follow up with, *"I'd like to hear about any situation that is sort of similar to (that situation) when you did not hold back."* Then, *"What aspects of . . . (similar situation) could you take to . . . (the more difficult holding-back situation) that could allow it to be more satisfying for you and your child?"*

Fatherwork Models. All of us have been fathered, and we remember and create stories of experiences with our father. Even in the absence of a primary father figure in our childhood, we formulate ideas about what a father can and should do for and with children. Often, these ideas shape how we want our children to be fathered, and we emulate, compensate for, or reject aspects of our early models.

Asking a father to relate a personal life story about remembered experiences of being fathered (or not fathered) may open a clinical conversation about what expectations he brings to his own fatherwork. You may elicit several types of fatherwork narratives and explore each from several angles.

1. Fatherwork narratives may include specific stories about (a) what kinds of memories clients have of their fathers at specific ages (using the ages of their own children currently could be very useful), (b) times they associate fondly with their father, (c) times when they associate disappointment or resentment with their father, (d) aspects of their father's life they value and what they have gained through their own father's parenting, and (e) aspects of life they wished their father could have shared with them.

For example, you might explore all these areas with questions along the lines of, *"I'm interested in your memories about your own father (or his absence, or a stepfather or father surrogate). I'd like to hear about what stands out the most in your childhood experience with him."* Then, *"What did you decide about how you would like to father your child(ren) based on those experiences?"* Follow up with, *"Reflecting back now, are there any other aspects of your childhood experiences that have influenced your ideas about how you (think about/feel about/act) as a father to your own child(ren)?"*

2. Other dimensions to explore are (a) what the client expects of himself as a father, (b) what he believes others (partner, children, rela-

tives, friends, community, society) expect of him as a father, and (c) times when he has experienced himself living up to (and perhaps falling short of) these expectations. These questions get to the heart of a generative narrative approach, as these conversations will likely deal with what the father deeply believes he can, should, and wants to be as a father.

For example, you may ask some of these types of questions such as, *"Who do you believe has expectations about how you should act and feel as a father?"* Then, *"What do you think those expectations are about?"* And, *"In what ways have you found their expectations have influenced you?"* Follow up with, *"When you might find yourself wanting to live up to those expectations, what have you noticed about how you (think about yourself/feel about yourself/act) as a father?"* *"On those occasions when you have not lived up to what you think a good father should do, how have you decided to improve?"* *"In your mind, what kinds of things do good fathers do with and for their children?"* *"What can you do this week to become more like that kind of father?"*

Generative Parenting Examples. Being a parent constantly confronts a person with opportunities to shape and reshape relationships with children. It takes a clear, ethical commitment and a broad and flexible repertoire of cognitive patterns, behavioral skills, and affective experiences to connect with and influence a child over changing developmental stages and various challenging circumstances. Finding ways to be confident with one's fathering ability is challenging at the best of times. The current generation of fathers was raised in a culture that did not expect men to be highly involved in daily interaction with children to the extent that women were "mentored" by their mothers and the culture into their parenting. Men often perceive differences in women's and men's upbringing as putting them at a disadvantage in the family. Men relate that it can be very frustrating for them to find themselves feeling this disadvantage as they encounter daily interactions with their children (Dienhart, 1995). They feel at a loss and may feel inhibited to take on more involvement for lack of knowledge and/or models of how to be a generative father. It may be helpful to draw their attention to stories where they appreciated the generative parenting demonstrated by others. This may be people in their immediate or extended family, friends, work colleagues, or depictions in popular media.

1. Elicit stories about an observation the man may have of another person he sees as a generative parent. Examples may be male or female, as the purpose in eliciting these types of stories is to have him explore what it is about the parenting he appreciates and perhaps would like to emulate.

For example, the following kinds of questions may help call forth generative narratives: *"I would like to hear about times when you may have noticed someone parenting in a way that you thought (or felt) was admirable."* Then, *"How did your ideas about how you might parent change as a result of seeing (the identified person) parent in . . . (that way)?"* Follow up with, *"In what ways have you noticed yourself trying out . . . (some of the same things identified as admirable)?"* Or, *"What (selected behavior identified as admirable) might you be willing to experiment with this week?"*

2. Introducing media depictions, literature, and everyday stories of men and women parenting may offer fathers ideas and images of generative parenting. The clinician may then explore with a man what meaning these narratives hold for him and how he may see the potential to bring aspects of them into his own experience of being a father. For examples of transformative father narratives, see Brotherson and Dollahite (Chapter 6, this volume), Dollahite et al. (1996), Gerson (1993), Kotre (1985), Meade (1993), and Pittman (1993).[2]

3. Another proactive way for clinicians to bring generative fathering examples together for men to access is to invite individual male clients to form men's groups for exploring parenting experiences and challenges. Though such groups are not offered for parent-education per se, you may perhaps utilize some parent education techniques appropriate for fathers (see Minnesota Fathering Allicance, 1992). Since fatherhood research (Daly, 1993a, 1993b), identifies a kind of isolation men feel as fathers, such groups have the potential to foster generative parenting by bringing men together in a forum where they can share their experiences and learn from each other. A group format may also serve as a forum to use narrative accounts from fathers to explore the potentials of generative fathering and encourage men to support each other in making changes in their family lives.

Fathers' Experiences With Children. Men's experiences of being with and being responsible for their children may range from feelings of delight to marked ambivalence to significant anxiety. We believe it is important to acknowledge the range of experiences and validate the range of feelings. As LaRossa (1988) reminds us, our everyday experiences with children typically depart from the romanticized version we held prior to becoming parents. Narratives about a man's delightful and frustrating experiences with his children can be a way for him to explore his full potential as a generative father.

1. A recommended area of exploration is to elicit personal narratives focusing on a man's preparatory expectations and experiences about becoming a parent. Hearing stories about what he hoped he would think, do, and feel when he became a father can yield ideals and fantasies which then can be explored against his current experiences, actions, and commitments. You may explore what happened for him as his romanticized versions of fatherhood, and possibly his hopes and dreams too, began to fade into the prosaic and often challenging reality of daily parenting. You may also explore the joys that come out of his parenting. Listen to his narrative and pay attention to the choices he has made to move further into or away from generative fathering. Exploring these choices may yield an opportunity to reintroduce some aspects of his hopes and dreams within the now more realistic context of actually raising his children.

For example, you might use the following questions to explore this area: *"I notice in your personal story about your hopes and dreams of being a father that you wanted to be. . . . Have you, in some way, lost touch with some of those hopes and dreams? . . . How?"* Then, *"What aspect of those hopes and dreams might you want to reintroduce into your fatherwork now that you know more about the daily reality of having a growing child in your responsibility?"* *"What do you know about yourself that would allow you to make this happen in your life now?"*

2. Eliciting personal stories about a man's current experiences of fatherwork may reveal anything from the mundane to the special or unusual to truly transcendent moments with his children. Generative parenting may find expression over a wide variety of interactions—play, guidance and life preparation, education, self-care, interpersonal interactions, and so forth. You will want to explore his personal meanings of these kinds of experiences with him, as all of these areas have the potential to be times when he senses for himself the essence of being a generative father. Furthermore, all of these types of experiences and meanings may reveal unique resourcefulness that can be adapted to more problematic areas.

For example, you may explore these ideas with questions like, *"I'd like to hear about some of the variety of experiences you have with your child(ren)."* Then, *"I notice you mention . . . (pull out the prized aspect), and I am wondering what that kind of interaction is like for you?"* Follow up with, *"It seems that you are able to . . . (draw out the resourcefulness), I can see the potential for this to be useful to you in other areas. In what other areas do you think it might help you to more fully realize the kind of fatherwork you want to create in your life?"* *"What can you do this week to make this happen?"*

3. A potentially fruitful area for clinical development of fatherwork is to explore how becoming a parent has changed the man's life, especially his self-image (including his thoughts, feelings, and commitments about himself as a man and the behaviors he expects of himself). Here again, there is the potential to provide a personalized "ethical mirror" by inviting him to reflect on what he values about these changes in his self-image and how he might enhance his valuing of self through his fatherwork.

For example, you might pursue a line of questioning that both reflects backward and projects forward: *"I am curious about what your thoughts, feelings, and commitments were about becoming a father before you had children?"* Then, *"How have those shifted now that you are a parent?"* Or, *"What have you discovered about being a parent that has changed those early images, feelings, and commitments?"* You may want to follow up with, *"Now that you have looked back, what do you think about your potential to recapture any of those early images/feelings by recommitting yourself to better fathering?"* *"What can you do differently this week that moves you in that direction?"*

4. Personal stories about what the man thinks he gives to others by being involved in his child's life can be elicited by asking him to share experiences when he was most aware of the power of his fatherwork to touch others, especially his child.

For example, you could develop the conversation along the following lines: *"I'd like to hear about some ways that you believe being a parent has had an impact on others' lives?"* Or, *"How do you think your fathering affects how your children feel about themselves?"* And, *"When you think about how your fatherwork affects others, how could that influence your choices about your parenting in the future?"* *"If (child's name) were here, how might she/he say this experience influenced her/him? What might she/he want from you in the future that is different from your current parent-child interactions and relationship?*

5. A related approach for introducing ideas of enhanced fatherwork is to ask the man to foretell or create a story about the stories he wants his children to tell of his fatherwork when they become adults. Ask him to imagine, formulate, or identify possible stories his children will tell about him as a father. You can ask him to tell a story representing how he believes his children currently experience him as a father and juxtapose this with the kind of story he would prefer them to be able to tell. You may work with him to fill in some details about the kinds of activities and behaviors they would describe, as well as the kinds of feelings they would relate about their connection to him and what contributed to building

those feelings. Then you would work with him to identify what he might be able to think, do, and feel that may increase the likelihood of his child being able to tell the kind of story he would prefer.

For example, start with a question like, *"I'd be curious to hear what kind of story you think your child(ren) will tell about you as a father when he/she/they are adults looking back on their childhood? Are there other stories you would prefer they would tell? What would those preferred stories say about you as a father?"* Follow up with, *"What kinds of things could you change in the next little while that may allow them to tell those preferred stories?"*

Working With Couples and Mothers

Fatherwork occurs in a family, not an isolated dyad. Fatherwork is embedded in family relationships with women, with other men (father, uncles, brothers), and with child(ren) (Doherty, Chapter 14, this volume). Furthermore, fatherwork is embedded in a cultural milieu that is often nongenerative in spirit and practices (see Dienhart & Daly, Chapter 10, this volume; Gerson, Chapter 3, this volume). Women have a potentially significant influence on how fatherwork is shaped in individual families, whether the couple is living together or not (Dienhart, 1995). Therefore, we think it wise to work with the couple, if at all possible, when you are addressing issues of generative fathering. With the exception of a fathering group, all of the clinical interventions suggested above could be central pieces of couple work if both parents are available and willing to attend. In addition, we appreciate the generative potential of opening dialogue with women about their ideas and expectations regarding men's parenting, as well as joint discussions about the parenting partnership.

Working With Couples. Maintaining a focus on the couple's underlying intent to combine and organize their efforts to parent in the best interest of the children may be a particularly helpful clinical approach. Couple work may focus on what they see as their individual and collective strengths and how they see themselves working together to cover the myriad responsibilities and tasks of daily parenting. You may explore what is working well in their parenting team and how each parent contributes aspects that help make it work. For example, you may ask each partner to relate an example of something they notice and/or particularly appreciate about the other partner's parenting. You can then check in with the partner and explore what it meant to him (or her) to be appreciated for this aspect of his fathering (or her mothering). Then, you could explore whether he (or she) believes there are other areas and/or ways that he (or she) could contribute.

Clinicians working with couples may need to keep an eye on the subtle messages in their interventions that might reinforce stereotypical gender beliefs and behaviors or suggest that the woman's model is the preferred way. Also, it is important to help couples *both* to acknowledge their differences in expressing how to connect with and care for their children *and* to encourage them to balance their individual strengths while developing aspects of interchangeability to cover all the bases of their busy family life.

Working With Women. Dienhart (1995) found that exploring women's "letting-go" experiences and process is important. This may encompass many areas, such as women's standards for how things are done (her way is best); monitoring the man's interactions (she needs to know all that goes on for the child); educating the man as to how to do things (she is really the expert here); and holding onto a feeling that she needs to be the parent of first contact (thus relegating the man to being "second string" on the parenting team). All of these areas may be expressed in a woman's stories about parenting and how she sees the man as being involved (or not). Eliciting narratives that may allow you to work with these areas involves inquiring into the woman's ideas, behaviors, and feelings about parenthood and her expectations of herself as a mother. You can ask her about times when she found herself *both* wanting her partner to get involved *and* monitoring how he was interacting with the child (or performing the task). In following her story, you may ask her to elaborate on the meanings in her own life associated with both these experiences and what she noticed about the impacts on her partner and the child(ren). This exploration should take place against a backdrop of respecting her resourcefulness and desires to parent in a way that includes the potential for her partner's generative involvement.

Conclusions

At this juncture in our cultural and clinical evolution, it seems imperative that clinicians take a generative ethic to their work with fathers. A generative ethic has two implications for clinicians: First, it means clinicians honor the intricate relational web of individual lives; acknowledge the important intergenerational contribution adults must make to children and society; and, advocate a professional moral imperative to promote committed, responsible, and caring fathering. Second, it means adopting a clinical stance to "open space" (Fine & Turner, 1991) in the service of men working to create meaningful shifts in their cognitive, affective, ethical, and behavioral experiences. Opening space means we position ourselves in the therapeutic conversation as participants collaborating with our clients in an original and creative process to generate alternatives in their current view of possibilities, especially possibilities for fully engaging in their fatherwork.

Effective fatherwork demands sustained commitment and the development of broad skill repertoires and potentials. As clinicians working with fathers, we believe it is essential that we invite and listen attentively to men's stories of their fatherwork. By inviting these stories, we can acknowledge and appreciate fathers' critical contributions in families (generally) and in the lives of their children (specifically). In listening to their stories, we have the opportunity to draw out their contributions to their children's lives and point out their resourcefulness in meeting the challenges of parenting. We can also invite men to reflect on their personal ethics and scrutinize their current parenting habits and patterns while challenging them to use their resourcefulness in the service of realizing congruence between their values and their behaviors. It is in this process that we must also acknowledge our potential to respectfully influence fathers to embrace generative fathering—fathering that responds to and actively seeks to meet the critical and changing needs of the next generation.

Notes

1. Please note that we include these questions as illustrations of ways clinicians might explore the suggested areas with fathers. We do not wish to be prescriptive, nor do we suggest that these are the best questions to use. We recognize that an important aspect of clinical work is the creativity and artistry the clinician brings to the encounter. We hope clinicians will consider our suggestions as possibilities and arrive at a selection of questions that fits them as unique professionals and are tailored to the language of their clients.

2. A resource of stories and ideas of generative fathering is also available to family professionals and fathers on the World Wide Web. The website is titled *FatherWork: Stories and Ideas to Encourage Generative Fathering.* (It can be found at http:\\www.fatherwork. byu.edu.) When using these resources, you might use questions similar to those illustrative examples mentioned just above.

13

Reconstructing "Involvement"

Expanding Conceptualizations of Men's Caring in Contemporary Families

ROB PALKOVITZ

Deficit Models, Generative Fathering, and the Concept of Parental Involvement

Variously called involvement, participation, engagement, investment, child care, and child rearing, the concept of parental involvement is defined, conceptualized, and measured in a variety of ways (Palkovitz, in press a). Even when there is agreement of terminology across theoretical or empirical papers, there is little consensus concerning just what involvement is, how to conceptualize it, how to measure it, and how to compare different people's engagement in it. In spite of this, we frequently hear statements to the effect that fathers perform a disproportionately small fraction of the child care in families and the overall conclusion that they are not as involved as mothers in the raising of their children.

The pitfalls of deficit models of fathering have been elaborated in Chapter 1. I believe that much of the thinking that fosters deficit models

AUTHOR'S NOTE: I gratefully acknowledge the brainstorming and insightful discussion of students in a graduate seminar, Intergenerational Relationships and Development: A. Bowers, D. Bardowski, S. Caplan, S. Christiansen, P. Connolly, A. Delaney, N. Hart, L. Johnson, T. Johnson, M. Minker, M. Moskowitz, R. Plaster, N. Schnipper, C. Vari, and C. Vestal. I would also like to acknowledge the expert assistance of Dr. Scott Scheer in preparing Figure 13.1.

of fathering stems from our limited, narrow, and short-sighted conceptualization of involvement. Clearly, where specific measures have been taken, men on average do lag behind women in providing direct child care and related housework. Is this all there is to involvement in parenting? Don't men make significant contributions to the raising of children in other ways beyond the purview of hands-on child care and housework? I am not saying that men have gotten a bad rap only because involvement is too narrowly defined and operationalized, but I am suggesting that as we come to understand the various dimensions of involvement, we may not be so quick to employ deficit models just because one parent outdoes the other on any given measurement of involvement. We need to look at the larger picture. We need to expand and reconstruct our understanding of the concept of involvement.

I am not convinced that it is possible, or even desirable, to generate a set of mutually exclusive and exhaustive categories of involvement. It is necessary, however, to more fully conceptualize, describe, and devise measurement instruments for different types of involvement if we are to come to an understanding of intergenerational relationships, child development outcomes, adult development effects of "involvement" in child rearing, and methods of intervening in families that are not functioning well. There are important constructs concerning involvement that we have overlooked as professionals. But then, any parent could tell us that.

In Chapter 2, Dollahite et al. detail aspects of generative fathering that represent truly innovative scholarship. Borrowing from Snarey (1993) and, of course, Erikson (1950), they define *generative fathering* as fathering that meets the needs of children by working to create and maintain an ongoing ethical relationship between father and child. This conceptualization both parallels and advances work that I have done independently on the concept of *involvement* (Palkovitz, 1980, 1987, 1992, 1994, in press a, in press b). In many ways, generative fathering is similar to involved fathering. The idea is that optimal involvement occurs when both mothers and fathers assess their strengths and weaknesses, the developmental needs of the family, and the resources and deficits that they individually and corporately bring to the family (Palkovitz, 1987, in press b). An ethical investment in care and nurturance of the next generation is based on what is best for the child in the context of the overall family given its current state and history leading up to that point. What is best for a given child at Time 1 may be harmful to the child, the spouse, a sibling, society as a whole, or to the self at Time 2 or if continued for too long. A generative model of parenting would imply that voluntary investments in involvement supersede concerns about what the involvement may cost the individual (Palkovitz, in press b). A broader conceptualization of involvement is cast in the larger picture of how to optimally support, nurture, and bring maturity to others in the family, a characterization consistent with the construct of generative fathering presented in Chapter 2.

In contrast to the prescriptive focus of Chapter 2, the emphasis here is on descriptive synthesis, analysis, and evaluation of the involvement concept. A useful metaphor for the reconstruction of a construct such as involvement would be the remodeling and building of an addition onto a home. What I will do in this chapter is to survey the existing structure, lay out some plans, tear out some of the old walls, and begin to build the new structure. While the project is in progress, it can look overwhelmingly disarrayed, and it may not be advisable to live there during the construction. Until the dust settles, it can make the rest of the house quite messy, too. When looking at the rubble and clutter of a construction project it takes some faith to trust that the finished structure will be worth inhabiting. The reader may experience the same kinds of doubts in this chapter. In my attempts to lead the reader through each of the components in the maze of factors required to reconstruct and expand a conceptualization of involvement (it eventually emerges in Figure 13.1), things may get a little messy. Ways for parents to be involved, the domains of involvement, various continua of involvement, and factors moderating levels of involvement overlap somewhat and the interrelatedness of any of these classifications with all of the others prohibits a neat and linear discussion. This is truly a construct under construction. At the end of the chapter, I advance a promising plan for the emerging structure, but one that still needs some finishing and perhaps further expansion and renovation. Nonetheless, it represents a roomier structure that can be inhabited by aspects of involvement that are currently homeless. Before the renovations begin, I offer a survey of the current structure.

Lamb's Topology of Paternal Involvement

With few exceptions (e.g., Palkovitz, 1980, 1984) prior to 1986, parental involvement was treated as a unidimensional construct. Most recent writers on parental involvement employ Lamb's (1986) tripartite topology of involvement: *interaction* (parent and child interacting one on one), *accessibility* (parent psychologically and physically available to the child), and *responsibility* (parent oversees welfare or care of child). Partly because of the lack of consistent definitions in the literature (Lamb, 1986; McBride, 1989), Lamb set forth this three-part taxonomy "to identify and define the different processes that father involvement in childrearing might entail" (McBride, 1989, p. 15). According to McBride (1989), most father involvement is said to occur on the level of engagement or interaction, consisting of one-on-one interactions between the father and child in activities such as holding, playing with, or talking to. I believe that in reconstructing the concept of involvement we will see that this is a misstatement. This category merely represents what has been empirically observed and reported the most frequently. It is likely that when we consider an expanded conceptualization of involvement this will no longer appear to be the area of greatest paternal involvement.

A second level described by Lamb (1986) is accessibility, characterized by parental availability, but without direct parent-child involvement. McBride (1989) and others have interpreted this category to include activities such as preparing a meal, cleaning the child's room, or just being in the house while the child is in another room. The third of Lamb's categories, responsibility, includes awareness of the child's social, emotional, cognitive, and physical needs. It also involves implementing strategies to meet these needs, such as making appointments with the pediatrician or arranging transportation to soccer practice. Responsibility may entail indirect involvement through parental anxiety and contingency planning.

This three-part categorization has become the standard of contemporary parenting literature. It offers conceptual advancement over older, less differentiated treatments, but the definitions employed leave many issues ambiguous, and the categories do not seem to allow a comprehensive consideration of involvement. Interviews with parents, observations, and reflections on my own parenting experiences suggest that there are multiple dimensions of parental involvement that have not been given serious and systematic attention in the professional literature.

Before I address those aspects of involvement, I feel it is important to state and refute some common misconceptions concerning parental involvement. To return to the reconstruction metaphor, now that we know something about what the existing structure looks like we need to tear out a few walls so that the renovations can begin.

Some Common Misconceptions About Involvement

Misconception 1: More Involvement Is Better. Much of the literature implies that more involvement is better. This little-challenged misconception may be a direct outgrowth of deficit models. In most discussions of family intervention strategies, it is assumed that fathers should always be more involved in child care than they are. Good fathering is assumed to be good enough when it reaches levels similar to mothering. It is difficult to read much of the involvement literature without getting the sense that greater involvement is necessarily better. This may be true for some parents and in some circumstances, but it is critical to note exceptions at either end of a parenting continuum. Parents with substantive deficits (e.g., a history of severe physical, emotional, or substance abuse) or histories of excess involvement (e.g., enmeshment or overprotectiveness) could inhibit the positive development of their children, who would be best served by limited as opposed to greater parental involvement in each of these examples. Although these examples generate a wealth of ethical issues and intervention concerns, the main point is that more involvement is not always better. Rather than assuming that more involvement is better, an advanced understanding of involvement suggests that appropriate involvement is better. There are multiple factors that could make more involvement inappropriate. Specifically, some involvement is probably ill timed or ill motivated (e.g., a burst of vocalization and physical jostling in an attempt to keep a fatigued infant from dozing off). Other actions may be poorly judged (e.g., attempting to suppress a child's expression of pain or fear due to an injury by diverting attention and exaggerated humor). Some attempts at involvement are developmentally inappropriate (either too advanced or too basic to stimulate the current or emerging capabilities of the child). There also may be other conditions that make greater degrees of involvement inappropriate, such as being out of synchrony with the child's interactional rhythms. Developmental and emotional needs or deficits on the part of any participant in an interaction affect the assessment of appropriateness. For example, children who are overly dependent or parents who are overly stressed out may not engage in inappropriate interactions.

For a better understanding of involvement, we should look beyond both more-is-better models and models based on appropriateness to "positive involvement" (Pleck, in press) or "generative involvement," as defined and described in Chapter 2. It should be obvious by this time that appropriate or generative involvement may or may not look like more involvement. It will, however, advance the development of the child and the parent (Palkovitz, in press a) more than a greater amount of inappropriate involvement.

Misconception 2: Involvement Requires Proximity. It is often assumed or stated that to be involved in a relationship you must be physically present, and conversely, that someone who is not physically present can't be involved. As I write this, my thoughts, affections, and some concerns frequently focus on my family, traveling in another state and returning home tonight. No one watching me at my computer would observe (or even suspect) this involvement. During the day, I have done some things because of the absence of family members (e.g., pet care) and made preparations for the family's return (e.g., cleaning, laundry, and "welcome home" surprises) that could be observed. I assert that both the unobservable and the observable activities represent a level of involvement, though my family is currently 200 miles away.

Misconception 3: Involvement Can Always Be Observed or Counted. A corollary misconception is that changes in involvement level are reflected by fluctuations in observable levels of involvement. Any parent can testify, however, that cognitive and affective involvement may not translate directly into observable changes. In fact, increases in involvement (e.g., through increased cognitive and affective activity such as monitoring, planning, and anxiety around the time of a child starting to drive) may be associated with apparent decreases in behavioral involvement (e.g., less chauffeuring). Another example would be where the parent has decided that it is in the best interest of the child to allow him or her to do something independently rather than providing the service for him or her. When the parent stops the overt activity it will appear as a decrease in involvement, but increased monitoring, structuring of the environment, and communication about the area of care may more than compensate for the previous involvement level. (All parents recognize that it is sometimes easier to just do things yourself rather than to delegate responsibility. When you stop doing the task for your child, it actually places greater demands on your time and energy, though it appears to be less involvement by standard ways of measuring involvement.)

Misconception 4: Involvement Levels Are Static and Therefore Concurrently and Prospectively Predictive. It is often assumed that once you measure a particular aspect of how involved a person is, you have a comprehensive view of how involved he or she is now and how involved he or she is likely to be at a later time. For example, a narrow measure (such as time spent in vocalization) is sometimes assumed to represent overall current levels of involvement. Moreover, such a measure is sometimes used to predict future involvement in the same or different categories. *Temporal fluctuations* may be experienced over the short term, however (Thursdays are a particularly busy day for me this semester, but the rest of the week I have more time for family involvement) or over longer periods of time (e.g., a month of particularly demanding deadlines, a year of major commitments, travel, or other drains on resources that would allow greater investment in involvement). Some changes in observed involvement levels are due to change in *developmental status* of parent, child, or both. For example, it is commonly recognized that adolescent children need to establish independence. Parents intentionally alter patterns of involvement with adolescents to promote independence appropriate for their maturity level. Developmental changes in parents can alter involvement levels as well. For example, an aging parent may stop hiking with an adult child for health reasons, although such outdoor activity once constituted a significant proportion of their shared activity.

Misconception 5: Patterns of Involvement Should Look the Same Regardless of Culture, Subculture, or Social Class. Many family professionals still tend to assume that role prescriptions popularized in Western, middle-class, well-educated families are the model for what involved parenting should look like. Involved fathering can take on many forms, however, some of which will be difficult to see with Western eyes. Furthermore, in comparison to some cultures, many U.S. fathers are relatively uninvolved. For example, at the transition to parenthood, many U.S. males appear to be detached in comparison to Garifuna (Black Carib) men in Honduras (Chernela, 1991) and fathers in many less industrialized countries, because few Americans practice the couvade (see Elwood & Mason, 1994).

In other cultures, involved fathering looks distinctly different from anything we would define as involvement. Patriarchy is dominant in Middle Eastern religions and cultures, with some of the greatest extremes appearing among traditional Muslims in the Persian Gulf region (Sharifzadeh, 1992). Muslim fathers make major and minor decisions and are primarily disciplinary agents in their interactions with their children. As such, they would score high in responsibility. But Sharifzadeh (1992) characterizes them as having minimal contact, virtually no caregiving responsibility, and negligible awareness of their children's "intellectual and psychological development" (p. 337). Nhlapo (1993) points out that among African families there are very different definitions and forms of parenting than are customarily thought of in Western literature. Specifically, social parenthood is much more broadly recognized, practiced, and regulated. In this context, fathers demonstrate different norms of involvement than what is viewed to be appropriate in the United States. Mirande (1991) suggests that African American and Latino fathers do not conform to "traditional portrayals found in the literature" (p. 63), a point also articulated well by Allen and Connor in Chapter 4. Some African American men have a different sense of "being there" for their children from that of Anglos (Palkovitz, 1994). Sanchez-Ayendez (1988) has documented that traditional Puerto Rican fathers value *machismo,* and strict discipline, engaging in little direct involvement in child care. Similarly, Asian American men appear to play a minimal role in child rearing (Suzuki, 1985). Shwalb, Imaizumi, and Nakazawa (1987) assert that the Japanese father exercises a weak role in the family in all areas except economic providing.

Clearly, this brief review is neither exhaustive nor representative of individual variations in the cultures discussed. Although it would be a mistake to stereotype individuals in different ethnic and cultural groupings, what can be clearly stated is that each man is displaying a pattern of involvement consistent with his interpretation of the "culture of fatherhood" (LaRossa, 1988) in his own culture and or subculture. To expect to observe the same levels and range of behaviors across cultures is unreasonable.

Misconception 6: Women Are More Involved With Their Children Than Are Men. The truth is that we don't know whether mothers or fathers are more involved with their children. As we move more toward an understanding of involvement in generative parenting and conceptualize involvement to encompass more than the narrow range of measures and concepts that have been employed in the past, we must admit that we don't really know the relative levels of men's and women's overall involvement in parenting. As categories, domains, continua, and moderating factors of involvement are elaborated, the value of overall involvement as a meaningful term comes into question. What we do know is that the genders are differentially involved in different aspects of involvement to varying degrees.

Now that I have torn out some old walls, it is time to assemble the raw materials for the refurbishing. As we move toward a descriptive understanding of involvement, I will assemble components of the construct that need consideration and consolidation in the professional literature.

Dimensions of Involvement

Ways That Parents Can Be Involved in Child Rearing

There are at least 15 major categories of involvement that I can generate (see Table 13.1). These categories are based on my own experiences, qualitative data, and observations coupled with a content analysis of a listing of ways that parents care for children generated with the assistance of students in a graduate seminar. It should be stressed that there are many ways to group the individual examples of involvement listed in this table, and the category headings are intended to be neither mutually exclusive nor exhaustive. With further reflection and content analysis, there may be more appropriate ways to group these categories. The main point of Table 13.1 is to show that it is easy to generate many examples of parental investment in child rearing that would not get credit in typical assessments of involvement, yet to the parent represent significant expenditures of time, affect, energy, and so forth. Laypersons do not think in terms of engagement, accessibility, and responsibility. They tend to list and describe a wide array of ways to be involved without classifying them into categories. In studying the ways that parents view involvement, we will see that the professional literature is too sterile and circumscribed.

Domains of Parental Involvement

Even a partial listing of the ways that parents can be involved in child rearing, such as presented in Table 13.1, makes it clear that parental involvement engages multiple domains of functioning: *cognitive, affective,* and *behavioral.* It is in these three domains that parents *experience* involvement with their children. These domains are summarized in Panel A of Table 13.2.

Of the three domains, the behavioral components are what usually get studied, especially the overtly observable behaviors that exhibit some type of involvement. As any parent can readily testify, however, there are numerous aspects of involvement that occupy the mind and require emotional or affective energy and investment, as well as an investment of the self, in ways that defy observation. Typically, because these things are not studied in empirical research, we do not have good descriptions of the ways that men and women are truly involved in parenting. Our conceptualizations of involvement need to be more inclusive of thought processes and other cognitive components. In interviewing fathers (Palkovitz, 1994), it becomes clear that much of their consciousness, planning, evaluation, and assessment of daily experiences is occupied or influenced by thoughts about their children. Parents' core identities are invested in the fact that they have offspring and that they perform particular functions and roles in carrying out their responsibilities toward their children (Erikson, 1950). The psychological presence of the child in the parent's

Table 13.1 Ways to Be Involved in Parenting

Communication
- Listening
- Talking
- Writing notes
- Making scrapbook
- Calling on phone when away
- Expressing love
- Expressing concerns
- Expressing forgiveness
- Expressing valuing
- Showing genuine interest in day, friends, interests, feelings, thoughts, aspirations, etc.

Teaching
- Advising
- Role modeling
- Problem solving
- Disciplining
- Commenting on child's or parent's progress
- Teaching spiritual development, praying together, etc.
- Fostering independence
- Providing long-term perspective
- Giving choices and respecting selections made
- Assisting in gaining new skills (teach to ride bike, swim, drive, balance checkbook)
- Scolding
- Giving chores
- Teaching responsibility
- Teaching about own and other cultures
- Answering questions
- Encouraging interests, hobbies
- Doing taxes

Monitoring
- Friendships
- Dating partners
- Safety
- Whereabouts
- Health
- Grooming
- Schoolwork
- Checking on sleeping child
- Going to parent/teacher conferences
- Overseeing TV or movie watching and music listening to
- Rides to and from places

Thought Processes
- Worrying
- Planning
- Dreaming
- Hoping
- Evaluating
- Praying for child
- "Being there"

Errands
- Driving
- Picking up items
- Making calls for

Caregiving
- Feeding
- Bathing
- Clothing
- Reaching things for children
- Caring for sick child
- Tucking into bed

Child-Related Maintenance
- Cleaning
- Repairing
- Laundering
- Ironing
- Cooking
- Pet care
- Creating child-centered spaces

Shared Interests
- Developing expertise
- Providing for instruction
- Reading together

Availability
- Attending events
- Leading activities (scouting, PTA, etc.)
- Spending time together
- Allowing/encouraging child to enter into leisure activities
- Being with child when he/she won't go alone
- Baking cookies for child's activities

Planning
- Birthdays
- Vacations
- Education
- Trips
- Holidays
- Saving for future
- Appointments
- Scheduling time with friends

Shared Activities
- Exercising
- Shopping
- Picnicking
- Movie going
- Parks
- Eating meals
- Playing together
- Building forts
- Celebrating holidays
- Working together
- Dancing together
- Chaperoning events

Providing
- Financing
- Housing

(continued)

Table 13.1 Ways to Be Involved in Parenting (continued)

• Clothing	• Alternative care	• Showing patience
• Food	• Insurance	• Praising
• Medical care		
• Education	*Affection*	*Protection*
• Safe transportation	• Loving	• Arranging environment
• Needed documentation	• Hugging	• Monitoring safety
(birth certificates, social	• Kissing	• Providing bike helmets,
security, etc.)	• Cuddling	life jackets, etc.
• Help in finding a job	• Tickling	
• Furnishings	• Making eye contact	*Supporting Emotionally*
• Developmentally appro-	• Smiling	• Encouraging
priate toys or equipment	• Genuine friendship with	• Developing interests
• Extracurricular activities	child	

cognitions is another dimension that needs to be represented in our conceptualizations of involvement. Parents are also affectively involved with their children. Many of parents' emotional experiences, expressions, and restraints are determined by their children's presence or absence and children's behaviors and affect.

Although research has tended to focus on behavioral components of involvement, it is readily apparent that any behavior that can be categorized as parental involvement has co-occurring cognitive and affective components that accompany them. In past research, scholars have primarily focused on the behavioral component when considering a measure of involvement. There are continual interactions taking place between all three domains, however, as parents enact various ways of being involved with their children. As Erikson (1964, p. 147) has observed, "Feelings, thoughts, and acts" are highly interrelated across the life span. More specifically, there are behavioral, affective, and cognitive components to every "way" to be involved, as Snarey (1993) has demonstrated in his seminal longitudinal research on fathering. For example, listening, the first listing under the communication category in Table 13.1, requires behavioral cues and attending and cognitive processing of the information being listened to and has associated affective responses.

Continua of Parental Involvement

Although it is relatively easy to categorize people as parents or nonparents based on a biological occurrence, parenting is not a dichotomous

Table 13.2 An Expanded Conceptualization of Parent Involvement

Panel A: Domains Of Involvement

Domain	Definition/Examples
COGNITIVE:	Reasoning, planning, evaluating, monitoring
AFFECTIVE:	Emotions, feelings, affection
BEHAVIORAL:	Overtly observable manifestations of involvement, such as feeding, talking to, teaching, etc.

Panel B: Simultaneously Occurring Continua

Dimension	Range
APPROPRIATENESS:	Inappropriate-highly appropriate
OBSERVABILITY:	Covert-overt
DEGREE OF INVOLVEMENT:	None, low, moderate, high
TIME INVESTED:	Low-high
SALIENCE OF INVOLVEMENT:	Low-high
PROXIMITY:	Far away-in same room/proximity-touching
DIRECTNESS:	Direct-indirect

Panel C: Factors Moderating Involvement

Factor	Description
TEMPORAL FLUCTUATIONS:	Short term
	Long term
OVERALL CONTEXT:	Developmental status of child and parent
	Life course considerations
	Other ongoing priorities and commitments
	Macrosystem
	Individual strengths and deficits
SPECIFIC CONTEXT OF INVOLVEMENT:	Sole responsibility vs. shared responsibility
INDIVIDUAL DIFFERENCES:	Style and personality
	Subjective experience/evaluation
	Sensitivity to reading signals
	Accumulated effects/history

variable. The parent function is not simply "on" or "off." Parents can be involved in myriad aspects of multifaceted roles to varying degrees at different points in their parenting careers (Palkovitz, in press a). We tend to categorize parents as being relatively involved or uninvolved in their children's lives in a global sense, however. Various dimensions of parental involvement can be conceptualized as existing along a series of *continua*, ranging from noninvolvement through low and moderate levels to high involvement. In fact, as a construct, beyond the sheer degree of participation in specific categories, involvement in an overall sense can be conceptualized to be influenced by a number of co-occurring continua. These are represented in Panel B of Table 13.2. As discussed above, *appropriateness* of involvement and the *observability* of involvement represent two of these continua. We now turn our attention to others.

Parents vary in the *degree* to which they are involved in different aspects of parenting. Time and effort invested in any given child care activity or task may be weakly related or completely unrelated to other areas or means of involvement. For example, it is relatively common for fathers to be more directly involved in play with infants and to share less caregiving responsibility than mothers (Jones, 1985). But the same father who is not directly providing a high degree of child care may in fact do a lot of planning for the child's well being, providing, monitoring, and so forth. In his own, and perhaps his spouse's, estimation, he may be equally involved overall.

Although time spent in particular functions or tasks (e.g., play) may far surpass *time invested* in others (e.g., caregiving), the less time consuming task may be more *salient* to the parent for any number of reasons. In addition, some tasks associated with parental involvement may be salient to the parent because they are aversive (e.g., coping with a toddler's tantrum) and others because they are pleasant (e.g., rocking the same toddler at bedtime). Thus, the subjective realities of involvement may be distinctly different from the overtly observable.

It is also the case that involvement can take place *proximally* or *distally*. Proximal modes of involvement include direct interaction, face-to-face communication, shared activities, and related events. Less directly, distal involvement can include communication by writing or telephone, various forms of child monitoring, or even thinking about or experiencing emotions in regard to children in their physical absence.

We need to recognize that in addition to proximal and distal involvement there are also *direct* and *indirect* types of involvement that affect the climate of the family and the development of both parents and children.

Sometimes involvement does not appear to be very direct. A common example would be working overtime to provide financially for needed or extra goods or services for a child. A less common example of indirect involvement would be that of a father who has moved out of the residence because of substance abuse, but who is actively involved in treatment and counseling and is looking forward to the day when he can engage in supervised visitation. Such a father may be involved in ways that supersede the investment of some coresident parents. Although the child's experience of involvement is different in these two contexts, the fathers are each investing what they can and what they believe to be necessary at that time.

Some events that occur at one time and may not be as directly observable as involvement (e.g., particular thoughts, plans, evaluations, and problem solving) may later be enacted as observable events of involvement. Thus, one type of involvement (mental problem solving) may serve as the antecedent to later observable bouts of involvement, a consequence. Some types of involvement (e.g., evaluation) may yield simultaneous increases in other categories (e.g., communication) and decreases in other categories (e.g., direct service provision).

Conditions Modifying Parental Involvement

It is important to recognize that parental involvement is likely to *vary across time, developmental periods* of both parents and children, and in relation to other components of the social ecology and life circumstances. The overall picture needs to be cast in the framework of *other ongoing priorities and commitments* such as participation in paid and unpaid work. Other moderating effects may be exerted by *life course considerations,* parental *strengths* and *weaknesses, developmental status,* and so forth. For example, a father's involvement with an infant may not appear to be extensive while the father is constructing a home or preparing to go through career hurdles (e.g., tenure decisions). As the individual's and the family's time, developmental status of father and child, priorities, commitments, and demands change, so will the observed levels of father involvement.

Previous research (e.g., Palkovitz, 1980, 1984) has documented that the *specific context* is important in moderating involvement patterns. There are noted differences in parental participation during times of *sole responsibility* versus *shared caregiving* contexts. In some families, there is only one caregiver available. In others, although there are two parents in residence, both parents may not be present at the same time because of shift work or other considerations. Thus, both partners have a significant period of time when they are in charge by themselves—sole responsibility. Some dual-career families may experience less of this time because during the working hours the children are in alternate care. After working hours, both parents may be present, and the responsibilities and opportunities for caregiving are thus divided differently.

It is also the case that different types and levels of involvement are appropriate in different *settings* or contexts. For example, parents would be expected to interact differently with their children in an amusement park than they would in a religious ceremony.

Furthermore, we have not given serious consideration to the fact that there are significant differences between individuals. Although it may be possible to describe general patterns of development that are associated with different levels of parental involvement, it is important to recognize and respect *interindividual differences.* Effective and positive ways of expressing involvement with one child may be less effective or even repulsive to another. Furthermore, different parents construct the meaning and emphases of their roles differently. They enact involvement in parenting differently from others who may be "equally" invested in being an involved parent. In my qualitative work with fathers (Palkovitz, 1994), I address this issue directly and demonstrate that priorities vary widely among "involved" fathers. Even within groups of men who would state or endorse the statement that fathering is their highest priority, there is considerable variation in how they enact paternal behavior ("Fathering comes first, so I work all of the overtime I can get to be a good provider" versus "I have foregone promotions so that I would have more time to invest in relating to my child").

Some fathers may desire greater involvement with their children, but again, there is significant variability in how that involvement may be conceptualized. For some fathers, involvement is best exhibited in "doing stuff" together, with a minimum of conversation or physical contact. For example, a father and his child may go fishing "together," being in different parts of the stream at different times and even competing for the most or the biggest fish, and yet this is genuinely experienced as quality time. Other fathers may prefer to spend time sitting together sharing conversation, emotions, and thoughts over a quiet meal. Individual choice, style, personality attributes, expressiveness, priorities, characteristics of the child, and both parents' and children's desire for intimacy affect observed levels of men's involvement. Individuals vary in their *subjective evaluations* of what is needed, appropriate, or best in any given circumstance. They vary in their *sensitivity* and ability to read interpersonal signals. All of this is moderated by the accumulated effects and *histories* of the individuals and their relationships to one another. The various modifying conditions are summarized in Panel C of Table 13.2.

Few of the above dimensions have been considered in the existing literature, but these are real and salient factors for actual parents. Now that we have assembled the major materials for the reconstruction process, it is time to begin assembly of the component pieces.

Toward a New Conceptualization of Involvement

Figure 13.1 is an attempt to provide a graphic representation (the beginning blueprints for reconstruction?) of the interactions of various components of involvement discussed in this chapter: *ways to be involved, domains* of involvement, *continua* affecting involvement, and the *moderating factors* exerting an influence. I do not claim that I have fully elaborated all of the components of involvement and their interactions. It is likely that this representation will evolve with further reflection, literature review, and quantitative and qualitative data analyses. It represents the beginning of a broader understanding, differentiation, and integration of the components of parental involvement. At this time, I am not prepared to elaborate on the implications for the measurement of parental involvement except to say that I am unaware of any measures that can account for the diversity and complexity of components of involvement represented here. It is my hope that this chapter stimulates discussion, reflection, further reconstruction, and empirical investigation of these issues.

No doubt my restructuring of the involvement concept leaves plenty of room for future remodeling. If we are to make significant progress in our ability to compare parental involvement across contexts (e.g., mothering vs. fathering; nonresident vs. coresident), to study the effects of parental involvement on child development outcomes or adult development (e.g., does greater parental involvement lead to greater developmental change in the parent?), and design effective interventions for at-risk or poorly functioning families, then this type of reconceptualization and further refinement is necessary.

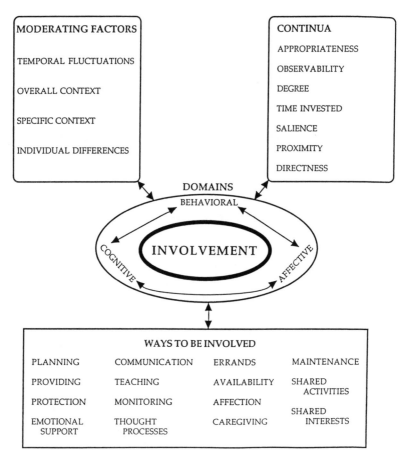

Figure 13.1: Toward a New Conceptualization of Involvement

14

The Best of Times
and the Worst of Times

Fathering as a Contested Arena
of Academic Discourse

WILLIAM J. DOHERTY

It's hard to talk about fathers and fathering in the contemporary United States without being pulled into a whirlpool of political and ideological polarization. On one side are those who emphasize the traditional virtues of the good father as head of the household, breadwinner, and moral authority; the newer virtues of the nurturing father; and the fundamental importance of fathers to the development of children. On the other side are those who emphasize that fathers are relatively uninvolved as parents, that mothers are fully capable of raising healthy children alone, and that fathers often shirk their financial and relational responsibilities to children after divorce. What passes for dialogue across this divide is often reduced to shibboleths such as "fatherless children" and "deadbeat dads."

In academic discourse, the ideological split over fatherhood is frequently a subtext in debates between those who stress the importance of family *structure*—especially two-parent versus one-parent (generally mother-only) families—and those who stress the importance of family *process*—

AUTHOR'S NOTE: This chapter is an adaptation of a previously published chapter in the book *Family: The First Imperative* (1995), Cleveland: O'Neill Foundation and is used by permission of the William J. and Dorothy K. O'Neill Foundation.

how family members relate to one another irrespective of who is present in the household. I return to this issue later in the chapter.

An additional split is evident between those who attribute contemporary family problems nearly entirely to social, economic, and political forces external to the family, and those who point to internal family changes as the main culprit. For example, even if both sides agree that divorce is a serious problem for U.S. families, the first group says that divorce is mainly a problem because of its economic impact, with father absence and nonsupport affecting the welfare of children through their economic impact. The second group says that divorce per se creates long-term problems for children and adults, including economic hardship, and that part of the damage is created by the deterioration of father-child bonds. As a result of all these academic and ideological divisions, debates about family problems often devolve into accusations and acrimony, in both political and professional circles. (See, e.g., the exchange between Glenn, 1993; Popenoe, 1993; and Stacey, 1993.)

The goal of this chapter is to explore how we can engage in constructive, "both-and" discourse about fathers and families. I try to show that people on both sides of the various splits offer important insights and there may be some common ground for consensus building. I then use this both-and approach to examine the paradoxical nature of contemporary U.S. fatherhood, namely, that it is both better than ever and worse than ever.

Bridging the Differences

Despite academic and ideological differences, there is one thing that practically everyone agrees on: Children have become worse off as a group over the past 30 years or so (Horowitz & O'Brien, 1989). It is harder to be a child in the United States now. And most scholars and professionals who have looked at the data agree that childhood problems are disproportionately present in children in one-parent, never-married families and in families that have experienced a divorce. Children in these families are worse off, on the average, on practically every indicator of social and psychological well-being, and their future economic and educational prospects are dimmer (Angel & Angel, 1993; Dawson, 1988). These are the kinds of findings, which have been demonstrated on representative samples of children and hold even after social class factors are controlled, that family structure advocates use to claim that the U.S. family is in serious trouble.

We also know from a large quantity of research that family conflict, particularly interparental conflict, is harmful to children in families of whatever structure. Family process advocates say that focusing on one-parent families blinds us to the everyday negative processes that are harmful to children in two-parent families as well as one-parent families (Kline, Johnston, & Tschann, 1991). Although conceding that single-parent families carry particular risks, these scholars and advocates fault lack of economic and social resources provided for single-parent families, along with gender discrimination against women and the failure of fathers to contribute economically to their children's well-being after a divorce.

From this point of view, if single parents were given adequate material resources and social support, there would be little or no difference for children's well-being between two-parent and single-parent families. It would all come down to the quality of family process. Therefore, we should not be so concerned about high divorce rates, high nonmarital birthrates, and father absence per se, but rather should be putting our emphasis on enhancing the economic and social resources available to single parents and on promoting gender, racial, and economic equality (Stacey, 1993).

I find myself sympathetic to both arguments. I believe that family process is where the good and bad sides of family life are lived out, and that families who lack economic and social support are likely to fare more poorly no matter what their structure. In the case of divorce, recent research shows that a good portion (though not all) of the "damage" of divorce has already occurred before the marital separation, presumably because of preexisting risk factors and poor family process (Cherlin et al., 1991; Doherty & Needle, 1991; Furstenberg & Teitler, 1994). I am also sympathetic to the position that an overemphasis on family structure can lead to scapegoating single parents for their children's problems, thereby making life more difficult than it already is for these families.

On the other hand, those who focus exclusively on family process—and let a thousand structures bloom—ignore the ways in which family structure shapes family process. Certain family structures make certain positive family processes far more difficult to achieve, and they make certain negative family processes more likely to take hold. In this chapter, I argue that the breakdown of father-child relationships is a central problem in contemporary U.S. families. The disintegration of this relationship is a process issue, not a structure issue, but I argue that it is more likely to occur when a marriage between the father and mother does not occur or ends in separation or divorce; in other words, process breakdown is encouraged by family structures in which the father does not reside with his children. In light of this both-and perspective, I attempt in this chapter to discuss problematic aspects of fathering without contributing to the polarization of academic discourse about fathers.

What's Happening to Father-Child Relations?

There is a terrible irony about contemporary father-child relations. On the one hand, there probably has never been a time when more fathers were involved in the daily nurturing of their children, starting from the time of delivery, at which the great majority of fathers are now present (Griswold, 1993). Our era may be the "best of times" for fathering among the segment of families with positive marriages and stable, committed father-child bonds, and among the growing number of families with custodial fathers following a divorce, as DeMaris and Greif document in Chapter 9. On the other hand, we are facing a widespread abdication of fathering by millions of fathers. I return later to why I think these two facts are both true, but first I briefly document my assertions about the "worst of times."

First, in 1993 there were 6.3 million children (9% of all children) living with a single parent (almost always the mother) who had never married, up from 243,000 in 1960. (U.S. Bureau of the Census, 1994). In the great majority of these families, the father is not involved psychologically or socially with the child on a sustained and permanent basis throughout the child's life.

Second, an even greater number of children live in single-parent families created by divorce (about 6.6 million children), with the great majority residing with their mothers. The majority of noncustodial fathers eventually move into a distant relationship with their children. One national study of school-age children found that 2 years after a divorce a majority of children had not seen their father for a year (Furstenberg & Nord, 1985). Although some fathers are quite faithful to their children after divorce, as Pasley and Minton document in Chapter 8, the predominant pattern is one of gradual withdrawal and progressively poorer relationships with their children.

A national longitudinal study by Zill, Morrison, and Coiro (1993) illustrates this sobering situation. They followed a large national probability sample of children and parents from ages 7 to 11 through ages 18 to 22. The authors found increasing alienation of divorced fathers from their children, as measured by the children's reports that they had a poor relationship with the mother or father. Among the 18- to 22-year-olds, 65% of those whose parents had divorced reported a poor relationship with their father, as compared to 29% of those whose parents did not divorce. (The comparable figures for mothers were 30% in the divorced group and 16% in the nondivorced group; all these percentages were adjusted for parent education, sex, race, age, and vocabulary test scores of children.) Thus, divorce has a powerful impact on long-term father-child relationships, considerably more than on mother-child relationships. Remarriage only makes things worse, with 70% of children of divorce and remarriage reporting a poor relationship with their father.

Third, fathers in large numbers fail to provide adequate economic support for their children after a divorce. According to a report on child support by the U.S. Bureau of the Census (1995), only 48% of mothers who are awarded child support receive the full payment due. And the amounts awarded and paid are not adequate to support a child anyway (Rettig, Christensen, & Dahl, 1991). This economic withdrawal frequently leads to a deterioration of the single-parent family's living conditions and threatens their financial survival. This economic abandonment is even more true of fathers whose children are born outside of marriage. In 1993, 38.4% of children living with divorced mothers and 66.3% of those living with mothers who had never married were living below the poverty line, as compared to 10.6% of children living in two-parent families (U.S. Bureau of the Census, 1994).

In sum, because of large increases in divorce and in nonmarital childbearing, many fathers are far less involved with their children's everyday lives and far less financially supportive than they were in the recent past. Increasingly more children do not live with their fathers, relate to their fathers on a regular basis, or enjoy the economic support of their fathers. In my view, this situation is a rending of the moral fabric of family life and thus of society as a whole, as a generation of men fail to engage in responsible generativity toward the next generation (Dollahite et al., Chapter 2, this volume; Erikson, 1950; Snarey, 1993).

What Are the Roots of Disintegrating Father-Child Relations?

It would be partly accurate but simplistic to say that the cause of disintegration in father-child relations is the changes in family structures. Family structures have changed without a notable decline in mothers' responsibility for, and generativity toward, their children, although divorce does appear to hurt that relationship as well (Zill et al., 1993). Nor is it enough to say that the cause is that fathers do not generally live with their children after divorce or when never married. Living arrangements, although important, cannot alone account for poor relationships. Although there is a dearth of studies in this area, noncustodial mothers appear to do better in maintaining ties to their children. For instance, more noncustodial mothers than fathers live in the same state as their children do (U.S. Bureau of the Census, 1995) and have more contact with their children (Amato & Rezac, 1994).

Although fathers, more than mothers, tend to withdraw physically and emotionally from their children in nonmarital family structures—thus suggesting that gender norms may be more important than family structure in affecting fathers' behavior—recent evidence suggests a different scenario for economic support. For the first time, the U.S. Bureau of the Census (1995) has documented the child support payments of noncustodial mothers as well as noncustodial fathers. The report found that noncustodial mothers are even worse than noncustodial fathers in paying the amounts awarded by the courts, with 57.3% of mothers not paying the full amount, compared with 47.7% of fathers. (Although these rates are based on court awards, which are calibrated partly to the noncustodial parent's income, it should be kept in mind that a higher percentage of women, mostly poor, do not receive child support awards at all.) If mothers who are not living with their children are not better than fathers in supporting their children economically, then we can hypothesize that the nonresidential family structure itself, not gender norms for fathering, is a primary influence on fathers' abandonment of their financial responsibilities for children outside of marriage. In other words, there are more deadbeat dads only because there are more noncustodial fathers than mothers. It may be that this kind of family structure, with its coparental tensions and generally infrequent contact with children, makes it difficult for nonresidential parents to pay what they owe.

If responsible and generative fathering is threatened in the contemporary United States, I believe the roots are a combination of the widely recognized changes in family structure (nonmarital childbearing and divorce) along with an underrecognized but powerful cultural norm; namely, that men's relations with their children are dependent to a significant extent on their relations with the child's mother. In other words, we assume culturally that a mother is committed to continual presence and support in her child's life no matter what happens to her relationship with the father. She is to act like a mother no matter what. For fathers, on the other hand, the prevailing cultural assumption in the United States is that fatherhood and marriage are, to use Frank Furstenberg's (1988a) term, a "package deal." Even in married-couple families, studies have demonstrated that fathers' nurturing involvement with their children is more dependent on the quality of the marriage than is true for mothers; mothers' relations with their children are less contingent on the quality of their marriage (Snarey, 1993). It appears, then, that the adult virtue of generative care builds upon the foundation of intimacy, as Erikson (1959) theorized, and this is especially true for men.

The upshot is that if the marital relationship is disrupted, or if a marriage partnership is never created, the father's relationship with the child becomes optional or elective, both psychologically and economically. The powerful cultural norms that create an expectation for responsible and generative mothering, no matter what happens to the father, tend to release a man into a parental netherworld if he is divorced and a noncustodial parent, and especially if he was never married to the mother.

A root cause of the disintegration of father-child relations, then, is the disintegration of male-female relations in contemporary society. Marriage has become increasingly fragile in the United States over the past 30 years, with divorce rates doubling and 60% of newly married couples likely to end their marriage by divorce or permanent separation, and far less likelihood that unmarried couples will marry in the event of a pregnancy (Martin & Bumpass, 1989). Intimate partnerships between men and women are far more fragile than in the past, and this fragility in turn affects the endurance of father-child relations when the mother-father relationship dissolves.

Taking the issue one step farther back, what historical processes have led to this situation? The historical record shows that until the 19th century in the United States, children stayed with the father in the event of a divorce (Rotundo, 1993). The father was the moral overseer and teacher of the child in these relatively patriarchal family systems. The mother's primary leadership ended when the child was weaned and could talk. A father abandoning his children, although it did occur, was held in the highest contempt. It was during the 19th century that gender role shifts and economic changes brought an amazing reversal of norms for postdivorce parenting. Now, it was the mother who was deemed the parent most responsible for socializing children. Fathers, who by then were heavily involved in the industrial workforce, were relegated to the breadwinner role. The doctrine of the separate spheres for men and women took hold, particularly in middle-class U.S. life: Women were to stay home and provide nurturing and socialization, whereas men were to work outside the home and provide economic support, disciplinary backup, and sex role modeling for their sons (Griswold, 1993; Rotundo, 1993).

Released from the expectation that they would provide daily oversight for children, men were allowed to pursue their economic and recreational interests as the first class of liberated individuals in the modern world (Fox-Genovese, 1990). As long as they supported their families economically, men, at least in the middle classes, could pursue their own agenda in the world, whereas women were still expected to put the needs of their children and husband above all else. Families were fairly stable under this system, as long as men and women performed their prescribed roles reasonably well.

The emancipation of women, however, began to erode this arrangement in the latter part of the 19th century, the time when divorce rates began to concern observers of U.S. social trends. Women began to enter the workplace and the professions in greater numbers, and women's suffrage became the political issue of the day in the early 20th century. This period also marks the coming of age of a new norm of marriage—the companionate marriage—in which the reigning ideal called for men and women to be friends, confidants, and equals. The liberation of women from traditional constraints was leading to a revised cultural norm of male-female relations (Doherty, 1992; Rotundo, 1993). But the father's breadwinner role was still intact until later in the century.

The second wave of feminism in the late 1960s, along with major structural changes in the U.S. and world economies, brought about the most important change in the culture of fatherhood in over a hundred years. Specifically, the decline in the purchasing power of the male breadwinner's wages and the entry of mothers into the labor force meant that men could no longer claim the privilege of being the sole breadwinner in the family. As a result, women were no longer as economically dependent on men. Combined with an even-stronger cultural emphasis on equal, companionate marriages and women's increasing demands that men share household and child care responsibilities, the loss of men's unique breadwinner role represents a fundamental shift in U.S. fatherhood (Griswold, 1993, Chapter 5, this volume).

Historically, then, fathers moved from the primary agent of socialization and economic support for children, to a helper in socialization but still the primary economic support, and finally to a helper with no unique role other than perhaps a sense of being a male role model for children. The "new father" of the 1980s and 1990s is expected to be a nurturing and socializing father, but expertise in child rearing was given away to mothers more than a century ago. Although many fathers are trying to embrace the nurturing role more fully than their fathers did, they have few role models and little in the way of strong incentives. The result is raised expectations for fathers' involvement, especially by women, but only modest behavioral changes in the direction of more active, daily care of children (Lamb, 1987). If this confusion is true for men in marriage, men outside of marriage are bereft of any cultural standards and role models for committed fathering (Blankenhorn, 1995; Seltzer & Brandreth, 1994). And because men are still given cultural permission to "do their own thing" as individuals, and many men experience strain in maintaining their noncustodial relationships with their children (Umberson & Williams, 1993), most of the incentives are for letting go of these ties.

Conclusion: Beyond Polarization

I have argued that the most immediate cause of the breakdown of father-child relations is the breakdown of male-female relations in marriage, leaving noncustodial fathers (and custodial mothers) without a cultural image of generative fathering outside of a marriage-based family in which fathers are the main breadwinners. The breakdown in male-female relations in turn stems from new cultural expectations for marriage, new feminist-inspired expectations for equality and partnership, and economic and social changes that have taken away men's unique breadwinner role and thus women's dependence on them. As Blankenhorn (1995) has documented, we have not yet evolved a set of powerful cultural norms for how to be a good father outside of a committed partnership with the mother and outside of a unique breadwinner role with live-in children.

One of the reasons we do not have a new cultural norm for fathering is that there has been a marked decline in community in the United States over the last century. The nation has moved increasingly in the direction of individualism and away from community expectations for private behavior (Bellah et al., 1985). Thus, fathers have been relatively free to create their own way to be a father to their nonresident children, even if the result was unconscionable neglect. Only in recent years, with feminists leading the way, have communities begun to get serious about nonresident fathers' responsibilities for the economic support of their children, as witnessed by mandatory child support collection procedures. There has been no corresponding urgency, however, about fathers' socioemotional responsibilities to their nonresident children, in part, I believe, because of a reluctance to imply that single-parent mothers cannot do an adequate job on their own. Indeed, there is a tendency for some writers to suggest that fathers are important only for their paychecks (e.g., Zinn, 1987).

This discussion of cultural norms should not be taken to mean that men as a group are passive responders to cultural forces shaped by others. Fathers participate in creating and changing the culture of fatherhood by embracing certain themes of their era and ignoring others. Fathers were not forced into the labor and delivery room starting in the 1970s; they went willingly and in large numbers, helping to create a new cultural norm that generative fathering begins before the baby is born. Contemporary fathers appear to be reevaluating their relative commitments to work and family, as many corporations are discovering. If nonresidential fathering is problematic in the United States, it is partly because fathers have not yet figured out a way to do it with the responsibility and generativity they increasingly demonstrate when they live with their children. The historical record suggests that contemporary fathers are more ideologically committed to generative fathering than any generation in history (Pleck & Pleck, 1995), but the deterioration in male-female relations in marriage and coparenting has short-circuited what should be the golden era of generative fathering in the United States.

One encouraging sign about the possibility of a cultural shift to promote generative fathering is the growing national movement in the area of "responsible fathering," in which groups from various parts of the political spectrum are focusing on promoting better fathering (Levine & Pitt, 1995). Volumes such as the present one also reflect a growing ability of scholars to focus in nonpolemical ways on defining, studying, and promoting good fathering. I offer a caveat, however, for these movements and discussions: Unless we deal with male-female relations, and with marriage, we will be avoiding what I believe is the heart of the problem with fathering today.

This brings me back to the issue of how we can discuss difficult issues, such as father-child relations outside of marriage, without lapsing into two misleading positions: either that children who grow up without a resident, married, and involved father are doomed to serious problems, or that the involvement of fathers with their children is only essential in the economic arena—and if the state did more to support single mothers, even this economic support would not be that important. The first position risks elevating fathers to the status of saviors of children; the second risks trivializing the importance of father-child relations.

We must find a different path if we are to find ways to avert the continuing disintegration of father-child relations in the United States. I believe we must elevate this problem to the highest levels of our national priorities, because although many children are now receiving quite wonderful fathering from men who are committed nurturers, we are also raising millions of children with a sense of abandonment by one of the two major figures in their lives. We must find ways both to promote improved male-female partnerships for child rearing in marriage and to help men manage committed fathering outside of marriage, because not all fathers will marry and not all marriages will endure.

At the academic and professional level, it is imperative that we move beyond the polarization between those who champion the "irreplaceable dad" and those who bemoan the "deadbeat dad," between those who would reassert traditional, prefeminist gender roles as a way to revive fatherhood in the United States and those who see talk about the importance of fathers as a threat to the viability of single-parent, mother-headed families, and between those who believe that structure is destiny and those who believe that structure is irrelevant. No one side is complex enough for the challenge of understanding fathering and promoting the well-being of families in this contentious, high-stakes era in U.S. family history.

15

Questions and Activities for Teaching About Generative Fathering in University Courses

DAVID C. DOLLAHITE
STEPHANIE N. MORRIS
ALAN J. HAWKINS

This chapter was written with university faculty and students in mind. Because many readers of this book will be in university settings, we wanted to find ways to facilitate constructive discourse about generative fathering in the university classroom in addition to summarizing some of the main ideas of this volume. In Chapter 14, Doherty called for constructive, nonpolemical scholarly discourse on fathering. Consistent with that call, in this chapter we provide specific applications of the ideas in this volume to teaching a university course. This chapter is like an instructor's manual for a textbook in that it provides suggested questions for classroom discussion and student activities for each of the other 14 chapters. We assume that teachers who choose this book for a course have some appreciation for the ideas of generative fathering, or at least potential interest in exploring ways to invite discussion about these ideas in university courses on such topics as fathering, parenting, gender issues, adult development, and work and family.

First, we present an overview of the generative fathering perspective presented in the chapters in this volume. Then, we suggest ways to apply these ideas to theory, research, and practice. We chose to concentrate these questions and activities in this last chapter (rather than at the end of each) to avoid intruding on the ideas of each chapter. The questions and activities are designed to draw forth reasoned discourse and creative learning, which invite students to consider ways to understand and encourage generative fathering.

An Ethic of Generative Fathering

We hope this volume demonstrates the value to scholars, practitioners, and policymakers of moving toward a widely shared ethic of good fathering that is (a) grounded in children's needs and a respect for men's lives and special capabilities; (b) able to challenge men to give their best to the next generation; and (c) broad enough to apply meaningfully across time, circumstances, and cultures. We realize that this volume has only dealt with a limited range of the issues and challenging circumstances that confront fathers and those who work with them, but we think these ideas have relevance to many situations. Table 15.1 summarizes the general ideas of this volume in what we call an ethic of generative fathering.

Chapter-Focused Questions and Activities

Questions and Activities on Theory Building

The chapters in Part I of this volume are focused on building a perspective of generative fathering (theory). In the classroom, theory is often discussed in ways that are abstract and sometimes at odds with the reality and needs of people being discussed. This can be frustrating for students and teachers alike, especially when students are involved in or interested in applications such as therapy, teaching, and family life education. Yet, appropriate use of theory greatly improves research and practice (Lavee & Dollahite, 1991). Talking about theory from a generative fathering perspective invites students to think about the meaning and implications of ideas for individuals, families, and communities.

Table 15.1 Volume Summary: An Ethic of Generative Fathering

An ethic of generative fathering invites scholars; practitioners, and students to:

1. Assume that most fathers accept the obligation to meet the needs of the next generation.

2. Assume that good fathering is consistent with mens' healthy development.

3. Assume that most fathers want to provide resources and opportunities for their children.

4. Assume that most fathers love and care for their children deeply.

5. Assume that most men have the capabilities to care for children in meaningful ways.

6. Appreciate the varied capabilities that men bring to their fathering.

7. Recognize that manifestations of generative fathering vary across time and context.

8. Realize that fathering occurs in a context of constraints on fathers, mothers, and children.

9. Engage in respectful, accurate, and constructive discourse about fathers and fathering.

10. Identify the factors that lead to good fathering across culture and circumstance.

11. Work to improve cultural and institutional supports for good fathering.

12. Call forth and facilitate fathers' obligations to care for the next generation.

13. Care for the next generation in their personal lives.

Chapter 1: Beyond a Role-Inadequacy Perspective of Fathering (Hawkins & Dollahite)

Discussion Questions

1. What are the advantages and disadvantages of a nondeficit perspective in understanding fathers and their relationships with children?

2. What are the strengths and weaknesses of a social role metaphor?

3. What are the other limitations of the role-inadequacy perspective besides those included in Chapter 1?

4. When is it appropriate to use conceptual frameworks like the role-inadequacy perspective to understand fathering?

Student Activity 1: Deficit or Nondeficit—That Is the Question. Gather information about father-child relationships from TV, movies, observations, interviews, books, historical accounts, songs, photo albums, or paintings. Use a role-inadequacy perspective to analyze the father-child interactions. Explore the limitations and strengths of this way of seeing and knowing. Then, approach this information from a nondeficit, generative fathering perspective. For example, you could watch mothers and fathers interact with children. First, look at the interaction from the role-inadequacy perspective. Ask the question: How are the men uninvolved or deficient? Then, ask questions from a generative fathering perspective, such as: What cultural factors constrain fathers from being involved? What are the indications that they do want to be involved? What are fathers actually doing to meet a child's needs? Explore the differences in the explanations each approach makes about the interaction.

Chapter 2: Fatherwork: A Conceptual Ethic of Fathering as Generative Work (Dollahite, Hawkins, & Brotherson)

Discussion Questions

1. What metaphors, other than work, could be helpful in understanding and encouraging good fathering?

2. How is a conceptual ethic grounded in identifying and meeting the needs of the next generation different from theory based on other criteria, such as descriptive accuracy, predictive power, or accounting for variance?

3. What other kinds of "work" could be added to the conceptual ethic of fathering as generative work?

4. How does an ethical obligation for a father to meet the needs of his child(ren) relate to his ethical obligation to meet the needs of the child(ren)'s mother?

Student Activity 2: Building Onto the Fatherwork Framework. Simultaneously interview two fathers accompanied by two of their children. Ask them a series of questions to find out (a) what children think they need from their fathers, (b) what fathers think their children need from them, and (c) what fathers and children can do together to facilitate good fathering. You may consider talking with fathers and their children in a public setting (i.e., park, mall, bus, playground, swimming pool). Analyze what you find out in relation to the conceptual ethic of fathering as generative work. Build your ideas into or rework the framework.

Chapter 3: An Institutional Perspective on Generative Fathering: Creating Social Supports for Parenting Equality (Gerson)

Discussion Questions

1. What are examples of society-level changes that would facilitate generative fathering and what can you personally do to invite these changes?

2. What should be the balance between family adaptation and societal change in trying to encourage generative fathering?

3. How could changes in technology help institutions support generative fathering?

4. How are the concepts of egalitarian parenting, equal parenting, and coparenting similar to and different from each other?

Student Activity 3: Role Play on Societal Influences. Create a role play centering on a problem or challenging circumstance (e.g., children's illnesses or special needs) including two parents, a child, and two members of the community representing institutions that impact parents and families (i.e., employer, coworker, schoolteacher, principal, religious leader, social worker, government employee, etc.). Act out two versions of the scenario: (a) one in which the family and community members relate in ways that do not support generative fathering and egalitarian gender relationships, and (b) one in which they relate in a way that is ideal in terms of both generative fathering and egalitarian gender relationships.

Chapter 4: An African American Perspective on Generative Fathering (Allen & Connor)

Discussion Questions

1. In what important ways are men (other than biological fathers) engaged in generative fathering in African American and other racial or ethnic communities?

2. What are the different forms of generative fathering in African American and other racial or ethnic communities?

3. How can generative fathering practiced in African American or other racial or ethnic communities inform conceptualizations of good fathering in the broader culture?

4. How is the ecosystemic framework particularly suited to understanding African American men's generative fathering?

Student Activity 4: Fathering and Ethnicity in Film. Watch two films that depict families from two different racial or ethnic communities. (You may wish to ask members of these ethnic communities to suggest films with accurate portrayals.) Note specific illustrations of the strengths and uniqueness of the adult men you observed. Then, to check the accuracy of these films, talk with members of these two racial or ethnic groups about your perceptions of fathering from these films. Relate what you saw and learned to the ideas about African American fathering found in Chapter 4. Come to class prepared to show a scene from a film and discuss it from a generative fathering perspective.

Chapter 5: Generative Fathering:
A Historical Perspective (Griswold)

Discussion Questions

1. How can taking a perspective based on an ethic of generative fathering rather than a role-inadequacy perspective change the way fathers are understood historically?
2. How can manifestations of generative fathering over the past 200 years inform our conceptualizations of contemporary fathering?
3. Of what value is an historical perspective in building accurate and helpful theory about good fathering?
4. How can (or should) scholars and students avoid judging previous generations of fathers against contemporary notions of fathering?

Student Activity 5: Future History of Fathering. Project yourself into the future and imagine yourself as an historian in the year 2020. Write a brief history of fathering from the 1990s to 2020. Focus on the influence of technological innovations (e.g., Internet, transportation, home offices), economic changes (e.g., career shifting, unemployment), media (e.g., television, film, magazines), and cultural expectations on gender and multicultural relations. Speculate on how a future historian looking back on the 1990s would (or would not) see manifestations of generative fathering in the many kinds of fathering that exist today.

Questions and Activities on Research

The chapters in Part II of this volume are devoted to empirical explorations of generative fathering in a variety of challenging circumstances (research). Like theory discussions, talking about research can be unappealing to students. Research can also distance students from the people being studied and from application. Our approach to and goals for research are generally consistent with the "action-oriented" research discussed by Small (1995). We believe that by staying focused on solutions to tangible problems and keeping the needs of the next generation prominent, research can be more applicable and interesting for students. Research to explore and go beyond deficit perspectives while learning about generative fathering under challenging circumstances can be exciting for students.

Chapter 6: Generative Ingenuity in Fatherwork
With Young Children With Special Needs
(Brotherson & Dollahite)

Discussion Questions

1. In what ways do disabilities, medical challenges, or chronic illnesses provide unique opportunities for men to manifest generative fathering?
2. What unique challenges and opportunities do fathers of special needs children face in developing generative ingenuity compared to other fathers?
3. What are the advantages of narrative accounts, compared to other forms of data, to help us understand generative ingenuity in a variety of challenging circumstances?
4. What can fathers of special-needs children teach us about generative fathering in other challenging circumstances?

Student Activity 6: Narrative Accounts of Fathering. The authors of Chapter 6 suggest that narrative accounts (stories) are a good way to collect information about good fathering. Write about an experience you have had that captures the essence of your relationship with your father. Use as much detail as possible so that the reader can know of at least: (a) your age when the experience occurred; (b) the physical and emotional and relational context for the experience; and (c) what happened and how this experience illustrates the nature of your relationship with your father. Then, create a story that describes a future father-child encounter with one of your children as you imagine yourself as the father. Finally, connect your narratives to some of the ideas presented in the various chapters of this volume.

Chapter 7: Teen Dads: A Generative Fathering Perspective
Versus the Deficit Myth (Rhoden & Robinson)

Discussion Questions

1. What constraints are there in doing research with teenage fathers?
2. What are the advantages of studying teenage fathers who are succeeding in their efforts to care for the next generation?
3. Using Eriksonian theory, how is teenage fathering an apt circumstance for studying how identity, intimacy, and generativity are interwoven?
4. How would program evaluation research on programs for teenage fathers be different using a non-deficit, generative fathering perspective?

Student Activity 7: Evaluate a Teenage Parenting Program. Interview a teenage father to learn about his experiences and needs. Then, locate a teenage parenting program in a nearby city (or one described in the literature). Conduct an evaluation of the program based on how well it (a) meets the needs of the father you interviewed, (b) moves beyond a deficit perspective, and (c) facilitates generative fathering. Suggest possible ways that fathers are excluded and included by these programs. As part of your evaluation, think of creative ways to conceptualize and measure teenage father involvement and the constraints that teenage fathers face in their efforts to be involved in the lives of their children.

Chapter 8: Generative Fathering After Divorce and Remarriage: Beyond the "Disappearing Dad" (Pasley & Minton)

Discussion Questions

1. The authors of Chapter 8 note several constraints to generative fathering in marital transitions (e.g., legal barriers, ex-spouse relationships, economic factors, geographic and logistical difficulties). How can we account for these constraints in research?

2. When studying fathers in marital transition who are trying to stay connected to their children, how can we find out what children need and what fathers can provide in this challenging circumstance?

3. How do typical operationalizations of father involvement inhibit our abilities to see generative fathering in marital transition? How would our operationalizations need to change to improve our view of generative fathering in marital transition?

4. How can an exclusive focus on the father-child dyad mislead us about fathering in marital transition?

Student Activity 8: Issues in Marital Transition. From the information in this chapter, create a list of issues and constraints fathers must deal with in marital transition. Then, gather some information about fathers in marital transition and compare it with the ideas in the chapter. Recognizing that fathers, mothers, and children do encounter a lot of stress during times like these, we suggest an unobtrusive approach to gathering information from fathers in marital transition. There are a number of ways to gather information about and from fathers without directly interviewing them. Some of these include (a) accessing one of the Internet bulletin boards or World Wide Web home pages that focus on men in marital transition, (b) observing divorce or custody proceedings in court, (c) asking permission to attend a support group for fathers in transition, or (d) getting written information from community agencies designed to serve this population.

Chapter 9: Single Custodial Fathers and their Children:
When Things Go Well (DeMaris & Greif)

Discussion Questions

1. In what ways do researchers use a model of "good mothering" to understand good single custodial fathering?
2. In what ways is generative fathering in single-parent situations different from and similar to generative fathering in other situations?
3. What constraints are there for studying single custodial fathers?
4. How would children and adolescents being reared mainly by single custodial fathers define a "successful" experience? How would it differ for boys and girls?

Student Activity 9: Resources for Single Custodial Fathers. Interview a few fathers and their children and ask them about their situations and needs. Determine what community resources are available and create a list of resources, activities, and information to help meet their needs. This list might include (a) good child care providers, (b) community programs that provide services like car pooling and after-school care, (c) work organizations in the area with family- or father-friendly policies, (d) other fathers who want to interact, (e) on-line sites focused on single custodial fathering, (f) good parks to take kids, (g) inexpensive and enjoyable activities, and (h) a list of books fathers could read individually or with children. Offer to provide a copy of the list to the fathers you interview and make it available to local parent-child agencies and parent educators.

Chapter 10: Men and Women Cocreating Father Involvement
in a Nongenerative Culture (Dienhart & Daly)

Discussion Questions

1. What are the advantages and disadvantages of using qualitative research to study father involvement in nongenerative cultures?
2. How can research identify ways that mothers may discourage fathers' involvement?
3. What cultural, social, personal, and relational factors have contributed to the tendency of many men to reject their fathers as examples of good fathering?

4. How can scholars account for the changing cultural expectations of fathers?

Student Activity 10: Couple Interview on Coinvolvement. Talk to a couple committed to coinvolvement with their children about how outside institutions (church, work, recreation, government, school), family members, and friends both hinder and support their coparenting. Ask about what they have done or can do to invite change in institutions, personal attitudes, and expectations that impact their lives. Incorporate ideas from Chapter 10 and write a report for your class.

Questions and Activities on Application to Practice and Scholarship

The chapters in Part III of this volume illustrate how an ethic of generative fathering can be applied in education and clinical activities (application to practice) and to research (application to scholarship). This section is focused on application of the ideas of generative fathering to practice in the education, intervention, and scholarly communities. Palmer (1983) argues for education reaching out to unite individuals with their communities. Scholars and teachers have responsibilities to their professional community and to the local community in which they reside. Teaching an ethic of generative fathering focused on working to meet the needs of the next generation suggests that educational approaches and activities extend beyond the boundaries of the campus. This is consistent with our assumption that most faculty and students in the social sciences want to take their ideas, research findings, and enthusiasm to improve and strengthen individuals, families, and communities.

Chapter 11: Promoting Generative Fathering
Through Parent and Family Education (Palm)

Discussion Questions

1. How can educators help make parent and family education more inviting to fathers?
2. How can parent and family educators adapt current programs to be respectful of and comfortable for both fathers and mothers?
3. How can we evaluate programs according to their value, appeal, effectiveness, approach, and presentation for men?
4. How can parent and family educators encourage men to communicate with one another about fathering within the constraints of their lives?

Student Activity 11: Evaluation of Educational Media. Use of educational technology and media is one of the frontiers of parent and family education with fathers. Evaluate educational media in one of the following ways: First, log on to one of the internet sites that deals with fathering such as "Dad's Pages," "Father Pages," "Father's Manifesto," "Dad's Workshop," "The Fathers' Resource Center,' or "FatherWork" (our personal favorite!). Evaluate these sites in relation to the criteria for parent education for fathers provided in Chapter 11. If you were asked to design an on-line site for fathers, how would you approach it? Who would be your target audience? How would you improve on the sites that exist? How would you incorporate ideas of generative fathering into the site? Alternatively, evaluate two parent-training films and determine if the films (a) depict fathers in nondeficit ways, (b) suggest approaches that are gender-specific or gender-neutral, or (c) deal with any of the ideas on generative fathering discussed in this volume. Then, either (a) write a detailed outline for an educational film including the main ideas you would want to cover and the specific ways you would portray examples of generative fathering, or (b) actually make a generative fathering training video.

Chapter 12: A Generative Narrative Approach
to Clinical Work With Fathers (Dienhart & Dollahite)

Discussion Questions

1. How could other clinical approaches (e.g., cognitive, structural, Jungian) be used to encourage generative fathering in therapy?

2. In what ways are prevailing methods of doing therapy consistent with or contrary to the ethic of fathering as generative work?

3. In what ways can emotion-focused clinicians working with fathers avoid continually expecting, asking for, and rewarding verbal emotional disclosure?

4. How can a therapist working with couples meet many women's preferences for emotion-focused approaches and many men's preferences for cognitive or behavioral approaches?

Student Activity 12: Clinical Case Scenario. Create a clinical case scenario for a role play concerning some problem related to fathering (perhaps a circumstance discussed in one of the chapters in this volume). Include parts for each family member and the therapist. Generate an approach to assessment, intervention, and evaluation based on the ideas discussed in Chapter 12 (and another chapter, if applicable). Act out the first session of therapy in class or write what could be the transcript of the first session.

Chapter 13: Reconstructing "Involvement":
Expanding Conceptualizations of Men's Caring
in Contemporary Families (Palkovitz)

Discussion Questions

1. If we were to assume that fathers are positively involved with children in different ways than mothers, how would we notice those differences in our research?

2. In what ways do some behavioral coding schemes make men look uninvolved by employing mainly "maternally oriented" assumptions of involvement (e.g., direct, face-to-face, verbal)?

3. What kinds of measurement strategies would be most effective in capturing the dimensions of involvement that the chapter author discusses?

4. How can researchers better capture the overlapping activities and identities (marital, parental, occupational) of fathers?

Student Activity 13: Measuring Father Involvement. Talk with different people about how a full assessment of fathers' involvement with children could be done and develop ideas toward better measures of father involvement. Choose three people, a father, a researcher, and a family member of the father or an involved professional. Compare and contrast the ideas from the three discussions and draw out the ideas most relevant to the dimensions of father involvement discussed in Chapter 13. Then, formulate some broad principles covering effective assessment of father involvement in the lives of children.

Chapter 14: The Best of Times and the Worst of Times:
Fathering as a Contested Arena of Academic Discourse (Doherty)

Discussion Questions

1. What principles and guidelines could be created to avoid polemical debate and encourage constructive discourse about fathering?

2. How can we talk about family process and family structure in relationship to fathering in ways that facilitate constructive discourse?

3. How can scholars and practitioners attend to the important ways that couple relationships are a context for fathering?

4. What is the relationship between individual responsibility and cultural norms in supporting generative fathering?

Student Activity 14: Encouraging Constructive Discourse. In class, create lists of words and phrases that discourage and encourage constructive discourse from the perspectives of opposing philosophies and ideologies (e.g., feminism and masculinism, conservative and liberal, ethnocentrism and multiculturalism, modernism and postmodernism, etc.). Then, make a list of the kinds of facilities that could facilitate more constructive discourse that moves beyond polemical, offensive language and concepts. Generate a set of guidelines and principles to facilitate respectful and constructive discourse across ideological and political positions.

General and Integrative Questions and Activities

Here, we suggest questions and activities to help students integrate ideas of generative fathering, consider possible research questions, and reflect on how university courses and students can facilitate understanding and encouraging generative fathering.

Discussion Questions

1. What could be added to the ideas in Table 15.1 about the generative fathering perspective?
2. How does the concept of generative fathering connect with issues such as wage garnishment, fathers' rights, and gatherings such as the Men's Movement, the Promise Keepers, and the Million Man March?
3. What additional types of research could be conducted to understand and encourage generative fathering in other challenging circumstances?
4. How does postmodernism serve to both facilitate and constrain teaching about an ethical approach to generative fathering?

Student Activity 15: Extended Abstract of Unwritten Chapter. Write an extended abstract for an unwritten chapter in this volume that would add significantly to our understanding of and ability to encourage generative fathering. In conceptualizing the chapter, include one or more of the following: (a) focus on an area where a nondeficit approach would be especially helpful; (b) link your chapter to as many chapters in the volume as possible; (c) integrate theory, research, and practice of generative fathering in the circumstance you chose; and (d) expand or challenge the ethic of generative fathering discussed in this volume.

Student Activity 16: Design a University Course. Design a university course that would be ideally suited to building a generative fathering perspective, exploring generative fathering under challenging circumstances, and encouraging generative fathering in community and professional settings. Consider readings, assignments, in-class and out-of-class activities, projects, exams, class discussion and climate, the role of faculty and students, and outreach. Consider constraints in the university context to teaching from a generative fathering perspective. Consider these questions: How would you decide if examples of theory, research, or application are consistent with the generative fathering perspective? What kinds of goals and commitments would faculty and students in this course have?

Conclusion

It is our desire that theory, research, practice, and teaching that seeks to explore and encourage generative fathering be given a place in university courses. We hope that the questions and activities in this chapter will be helpful in stimulating a new generation of students and faculty focused on exploring and encouraging generative fathering.

References

Ahlander, N. R., & Bahr, K. S. (1995). Beyond drudgery, power, and equity: Toward an expanded discourse on the moral dimensions of housework in families. *Journal of Marriage and the Family, 57*, 54-68.

Ahrons, C. R., & Miller, R. B. (1993). The effect of the postdivorce relationship on paternal involvement: A longitudinal analysis. *American Journal of Orthopsychiatry, 63*, 441-450.

Ahrons, C. R., & Rodgers, R. (1987). *Divorced families: A multidisciplinary development view.* New York: Norton.

Ahrons, C. R., & Wallisch, K. (1987). Parenting in the binuclear: Relationships between biological and stepparents. In K. Pasley & M. Ihinger-Tallman (Eds.), *Remarriage and stepparenting: Current research and theory* (pp. 225-256). New York: Guilford.

Allen, W. (1976). The search for applicable theories of black family life. *Journal of Marriage and the Family, 40*, 111-129.

Allen, W. (1981). Moms, dads, and boys: Race and sex differences in the socialization of male children. In L. Gary (Ed.), *Black men* (pp. 99-114). Beverly Hills, CA: Sage.

Allen, W. D., & Doherty, W. J. (1995). Being there: The perception of fatherhood among a group of African-American adolescent fathers. In H. McCubbin, E. Thompson, A. Thompson, & J. Futrell (Eds.), *Resiliency in ethnic minority families* (Vol. 2, pp. 207-244). Madison: University of Wisconsin Press.

Amato, P. R., & Rezac, S. J. (1994). Contact with non-resident parents, interparental conflict, and children's behavior. *Journal of Family Issues, 15*, 191-207.

Ameatea, E. S., Cross, E. G., Clark, J. E., & Bobby, C. L. (1986). Assessing the work and family role expectations of career-oriented men and women: The Life Role Salience Scales. *Journal of Marriage and the Family, 48*, 831-838.

Anderson J. (1930). *Parent Education: The First Yearbook.* Washington, DC,: National Congress of Parents and Teachers.

Anderson J. (1933). *Happy Childhood.* Minneapolis: University of Minnesota Press.

Angel, R., & Angel, J. L. (1993). *Painful inheritance: Health and the new generation of fatherless families.* Madison, Wisconsin: University of Wisconsin Press.

Arcus, M., Schvaneveldt, J. & Moss, J. (1993). The nature of family life education. In M. Arcus, J. Schvaneveldt, & J. Moss (Eds.), *Handbook of family life education: Foundations of family life education* (Vol. 1, pp. 1-25). Newbury Park, CA: Sage.

Arditti, J. A. (1992). Factors related to custody, visitation, and child support for divorced fathers: An exploratory analysis. *Journal of Divorce and Remarriage, 17,* 186-195.

Arditti, J. A., & Keith, T. Z. (1993). Visitation frequency, child support payment, and the father-child relationship postdivorce. *Journal of Marriage and the Family, 55,* 699-712.

Arendell, T. (1992). After divorce: Investigations into father absence. *Gender & Society, 6,* 562-586.

Arendell, T. (1995). *Fathers and divorce.* Thousand Oaks, CA: Sage.

Asante, M. (1989). *Afrocentricity.* Trenton, NJ: Africa World Press.

Atkinson, R. (1995). *The gift of stories: Practical and spiritual applications of autobiography, life stories, and personal mythmaking.* Westport, CT: Bergin & Garvey.

Backett, K. (1982). *Mothers and fathers.* New York: St. Martin's.

Backett, K. (1987). The negotiation of fatherhood. In C. Lewis & M. O'Brien (Eds.), *Reassessing fatherhood: New observations on father and the modern family* (pp. 74-90). Newbury Park, CA: Sage.

Bahr, K. (1992). Family love as a paradigmatic alternative in family studies. *Family Perspective, 26,* 281-303.

Barret, R., & Robinson, B. (1982). A descriptive study of teenage expectant fathers. *Family Relations, 31,* 349-352.

Barret, R., & Robinson, B. (1990). The role of adolescent fathers in parenting and childrearing. *Adolescent Mental Health, 4,* 189-200.

Baruch, G. K., & Barnett, R. C. (1986). Father's participation in family work and children's sex-role attitudes. *Child Development, 57,* 1210-1223.

Beck, U. (1992). *Risk society.* Newbury Park, CA: Sage.

Becvar, D. S., & Becvar, R. J. (1993). *Family therapy: A systemic integration.* Boston: Allyn & Bacon.

Bellah, R. N., Madsen, R., Sullivan, W. M., Swidler, A., & Tipton, S. M. (1985). *Habits of the heart: Individualism and commitment in American life.* Berkeley: University of California Press.

Benokraitis, N. (1985). Fathers in the dual-earner family. In S. M. Hanson & F. W. Bozett (Eds.), *Dimensions of fatherhood* (pp. 243-268). Beverly Hills: Sage.

Bergman, S. (1991). *Men's psychological development: A relational perspective* (Work in Progress No. 48). Wellesley, MA: The Stone Center, Wellesley College.

Berry, W. (1986). *The unsettling of America: Culture and agriculture.* San Francisco: Sierra Club Books.

Bertoia, C., & Drakich, J. (1993). The father's rights movement: Contractions in rhetoric and practice. *Journal of Family Issues, 14,* 592-615.

Bigner, J. (1994). *Parent-child relations: An introduction to parenting.* New York: Macmillan.

Biller, H. B. (1993). *Fathers and families: Parental factors in child development.* Westport, CT: Auburn House.

Billingsley, A. (1993). *Climbing Jacob's ladder.* New York, NY: Simon & Schuster.

Billingsley, A., & Greene, M. (1973–1974). Family life among the free black population in the 18th century. *Journal of Social and Behavioral Sciences, 19,* 172-180.

Blacher, J. (1984). Sequential stages of parental adjustment to the birth of a child with handicaps: Fact or artifact? *Mental Retardation, 22,* 55-68.

Blankenhorn, D. (1995). *Fatherless America: Confronting our most urgent social problem.* New York: Basic Books.

Blassingame, J. (1972). *The slave community.* New York, NY: Oxford University Press.

Bloch, R. (1978). American feminine ideals in transition: The rise of the moral mother, 1785–1815. *Feminist Studies, 4,* 101-126.

Bohen, H. H., & Viveros-Long, A. M. (1981). *Balancing jobs and family life: Do flexible work schedules help?* Philadelphia: Temple University Press.

Borrows, J. A. (1996). *Generative fathering among the Canadian Chippewa: Narrative accounts of the circle of life.* Unpublished masters thesis, Brigham Young University.

Boszormenyi-Nagy, I., & Sparks, G. M. (1984). *Invisible loyalties: Reciprocity in intergenerational family therapy.* New York: Brunner/Mazel.

Bowman, P. (1993). The impact of economic marginality on African-American husbands and fathers. In H. McAdoo (Ed.), *Family ethnicity* (pp. 120-137). Newbury Park, CA: Sage.

Bowman, P., & Saunders, R. (1988, December). *Black fathers across the life cycle: Provider role strain and psychological well-being.* Paper presented at the 12th Empirical Conference on Black Psychology, Ann Arbor, MI.

Bowman, T. (1992). Group leadership issues. In L. Johnson & G. Palm (Eds.), *Working with fathers: Methods and perspectives* (pp. 101-112). Stillwater, MN: nu ink.

Braver, S. L., Fitzpatrick, P. J., & Bay, R. C. (1991). Noncustodial parents' report of child support payment. *Family Relations, 40,* 180-185.

Braver, S. L., Wolchik, S. A., Sandler, I. N., Fogas, B., & Zvetina, D. (1991). Frequency of visitation by divorced fathers: Differences in reports by fathers and mothers. *American Journal of Orthopsychiatry, 61,* 448-454.

Bray, J. H., & Berger, S. H. (1993). Developmental issues in stepfamilies research project: Family relationships and parent-child interactions. *Journal of Family Psychology, 7,* 76-90.

Braybrooke, D. (1987). *Philosophy of science.* Englewood Cliffs, NJ: Prentice Hall.

Breines, W. (1992). *Young, white, and miserable: Growing up female in the fifties.* Boston: Beacon.

Brim, O. (1965). *Education for childrearing.* New York: Russell Sage Foundation.

Bristol, M. M. (October 1984, October). *Families of developmentally disabled children: Health adaptations and the double ABDX model.* Paper presented at the Family Systems and Health Pre-Conference Workshop, National Council on Family Relations, San Francisco.

Bristol, M. M., & Gallagher, J. J. (1986). Research on fathers of young handicapped children: Evolution, review, and some future directions. In J. J. Gallagher & P. M. Vietze (Eds.), *Families of handicapped persons: Research, programs, and policy issues* (pp. 81-100). Baltimore, MD: Brooks.

Brod, H. (1987). The case for men's studies. In H. Brod (Ed.), *The making of masculinities: The new men's studies* (pp. 39-62). Boston: Allen & Unwin.

Brody,, G., & Forehand, R. (1990). Interparental conflict, relationship with the noncustodial father, and adolescent post-divorce adjustment. *Journal of Applied Developmental Psychology, 11,* 139-147.

Broman, C. (1988). Satisfaction among blacks: The significance of marriage and parenthood. *Journal of Marriage and the Family, 50,* 45-51.

Brotherson, S. E. (1995). *Using fathers' narrative accounts to refine a conceptual model of generative fathering.* Master's thesis, Brigham Young University, Provo, Utah.

Brown, S. V. (1983). The commitment and concerns of black adolescent parents. *Social Work Research and Abstracts, 19,* 27-34.

Buber, M. (1970). *I and thou* (W. Kaufman, Trans.). New York: Scribner.

Buchannan, C. M., Maccoby, E. E., & Dornbusch, S. M. (1991). Caught between parents: Adolescents' experience in divorced homes. *Child Development, 62,* 1008-1029.

Buchannan, C. M., Maccoby, E. E., & Dornbusch, S. M. (in press). *The divided child: Adolescents' adjustment after divorce.* Cambridge, MA: Harvard University Press.

Buehler, C., & Ryan, C. (1994). Former-spouse relations and noncustodial father involvement during marital and family transitions: A closer look at remarriage following divorce. In K. Pasley & M. Ihinger-Tallman (Eds.), *Stepparenting: Issues in theory, research, and practice* (pp. 127-150). New York: Greenwood.

Card, J., & Wise, L. (1978). Teenage mothers and teenage fathers: The impact of early childbearing on the parents' personal and professional lives. *Family Planning Perspectives, 10,* 199-205.

Carnes, M. C. (1989). *Secret ritual and manhood in Victorian America.* New Haven, CT: Yale University Press.

Cazenave, N. (1979). Middle-income black fathers: An analysis of the provider role. *Family Coordinator, 28,* 583-593.

Cherlin, A. J. (1978). Remarriage as an incomplete institute. *American Journal of Sociology, 84,* 634-650.

Cherlin, A. J., & Furstenberg, F. F. (1986). *The new American grandparent: A place in the family, a life apart.* New York: Basic Books.

Cherlin, A. J., Furstenberg, F. F., Chase-Landale, P. L., Kiernan, K. E., Robins, P. K., Morrison, D. R., & Teitler, J. O. (1991). Longitudinal studies of effects of divorce on children in Great Britain and the United States. *Science, 252,* 1386-1389.

Chernela, J. M. (1991). Symbolic inaction in rituals of gender and procreation among the Garifuna (Black Caribs) of Honduras. *Ethos, 19,* 52-67.

Chesler, P. (1986). *Mothers on trial: The battle for children and custody.* New York: McGraw-Hill.

Chinen, A. (1992). *Once upon a mid-life.* New York: G. P. Putnam.

Chodorow, N., & Contratto, S. (1982). The fantasy of the perfect mother. In B. Thorne & M. Yalom (Eds.), *Rethinking the family: Some feminist questions* (pp. 54-75). New York: Longman.

Cohen, T. F. (1987). Remaking men: Men's experiences becoming and being husbands and fathers and their implications for reconceptualizing men's lives. *Journal of Family Issues, 8,* 57-77.

Cohen, T. F. (1994). What do fathers provide? Reconsidering the economic and nurturant dimensions of men as parents. In J. C. Hood (Ed.), *Men, work and family* (pp. 1-22). Newbury Park, CA: Sage.

Coltrane, S. (1989). Household labor and the routine production of gender. *Social Problems, 36,* 473-490.

Coltrane, S. (1996). *Family man: Fatherhood, housework, and gender equity.* New York: Oxford University.

Coltrane, S., & Hickman, N. (1992). The rhetoric of rights and needs: Moral discourse on the reform of child custody and child support laws. *Social Problems, 39,* 400-420.

Comer, J. (1989). Black fathers. In S. Cath, A. Gurwitt, & L. Gunsberg (Eds.), *Fathers and their families* (pp. 365-383). Hillsdale, NJ: Analytic Press.

Connolly, L. (1978). Boy fathers. *Human Development, 7,* 40-43.

Connor, M. (1986). Some parenting attitudes of young black fathers. In R. Lewis & R. Salt (Eds.), *Men in families* (pp. 159-168). Beverly Hills, CA: Sage.

Connor, M. (1995). Level of satisfaction in African-American marriages: A preliminary investigation. In H. McCubbin, E. Thompson, A. Thompson, & J. Futrell (Eds.), *Resiliency in ethnic minority families* (Vol. 2, pp. 159-177). Madison: University of Wisconsin Press.

Cook, J. A. (1988). Dad's double binds: Rethinking fathers' bereavement from a men's studies perspective. *Journal of Contemporary Ethnography, 17,* 285-308.

Cooke, B., & Thomas, R. (1985). *Profile of Parent Education.* White Bear Lake: Minnesota Curriculum Services Center.

Cooney, T. M., & Uhlenberg, P. (1990). The role of divorce in men's relations with their adult children. *Journal of Marriage and the Family, 52,* 677-688.

Corneau, G. (1991). *Absent fathers, lost sons: The search for masculine identity.* Boston: Shambala.

Council on Quality Education. (1981). *A study of policy issues related to early childhood and family education in Minnesota.* St. Paul: Minnesota Department of Education.

Cowan, C. P., & Cowan, P. A. (1992). *When partners become parents: The big life change for couples.* New York: Basic Books.

Cowan, R. S. (1983). *More work for mother: The ironies of household technology from the open hearth to the microwave.* New York: Basic Books.

Crawley, B. (1988). Black Families in a neo-conservative era. *Family Relations, 37,* 415-419.

Crawley, B., & Freeman, E. (1993). Themes in the life views of older and younger African American males. *Journal of African American Male Studies, 1,* 15-29.

Cummings, S. T. (1976). The impact of the child's deficiency on the father: A study of fathers of mentally retarded and chronically ill children. *American Journal of Orthopsychiatry, 46,* 246-255.

Cyba, E. (1992). Women's attitudes towards leisure and the family. *Society and Leisure, 15,* 79-94.

Daly, K. J. (1993a). Reshaping fatherhood: Finding the models. *Journal of Family Issues, 14,* 510-530.

Daly, K. J. (1993b). Through the eyes of others: Reconstructing the meaning of fatherhood. In T. Haddad & L. Lam (Eds.), *Reconstructing Canadian men and masculinity* (pp. 203-221), Toronto: Canadian Scholars.

Daly, K. J. (1994). Uncertain terms: The social construction of fatherhood. In M. L. Dietz, R. Prus, & W. Shaffir (Eds.), *Doing everyday life: Ethnography as human lived experience* (pp. 170-185). Toronto: Copp Clark Pitman.

Danzinger, S. K., & Radin, D. (1990). Absent does not equal uninvolved: Predictors of fathering in teen mother families. *Journal of Marriage and the Family, 52,* 636-642.

Darling, R. B., & Darling, J. (1982). *Children who are different: Meeting the challenge of birth defects in society.* St. Louis, MO: C. V. Mosby.

Davidson, L., & Duberman, L. (1982). Friendship: Communication and interactional patterns in same-sex dyads. *Sex Roles, 8,* 809-822.

Dawson, D. A. (1991). Family structure and children's health and well-being: Data from the 1988 National Health Interview Survey on Child Health. *Journal of Marriage and the Family, 53,* 573-584.

Day, J. M. (1991). Narrative, psychology, and moral education. *American Psychologist, 46,* 167-168.

Day, R. D., & Mackey, W. C. (1989). An alternative standard for evaluating American fathers. *Journal of Family Issues, 10,* 401-408.

De Anda, D. (1984). Bicultural socialization: Factors affecting the minority experience. *Social Work, 29*(2), 101-107.

De La Cancela, V. (1994). "Coolin'": The psychosocial communication of African and Latino men. In D. Jones (Ed.), *African American males: A critical link in the African American family* (pp. 33-44). New Brunswick, NJ: Transaction.

DeMaris, A. (1992). *Logit modeling: Practical applications.* Newbury Park, CA: Sage.

DeMaris, A. (1995). A tutorial in logistic regression. *Journal of Marriage and the Family, 57,* 956-968.

DeMaris, A., & Greif, G. L. (1992). The relationship between family structure and parent-child relationship problems in single father households. *Journal of Divorce and Remarriage, 18,* 55-77.

Demo, D. H., & Acock, A. C. (1993). Family diversity and the division of domestic labor: How much have things really changed? *Family Relations, 42,* 323-331.

Demos, J. (1982). The changing faces of fatherhood: A new exploration in family history. In S. Cath, A. Gurwitt, & J. M. Ross (Eds.), *Father and child: Developmental and clinical perspectives* (pp. 425-450). Boston: Little, Brown.

DeWitt, P. M. (1994). The second time around. *American Demographics, 16,* 11-14.

Dienhart, A. (1995). *Men and women co-constructing fatherhood through shared parenthood: Beyond the dominant discourse?* Unpublished doctoral dissertation, University of Guelph, Guelph, Ontario.

Doherty, W. J. (1991). Beyond reactivity and the deficit model of manhood: A commentary on articles by Napier, Pittman, and Gottman. *Journal of Marital and Family Therapy, 17,* 29-32.

Doherty, W. J. (1992). Private lives, public values. *Psychology Today, 25,* 32-37, 82.

Doherty, W. J. (1995). *Soul searching: Why psychotherapy must promote moral responsibility.* New York: Basic Books.

Doherty, W. J., & Needle, R. (1991). Psychological adjustment and substance use before and after a parental divorce. *Child Development, 62,* 328-337.

Dollahite, D. C. (1991). Family resource management and family stress theories: Toward a conceptual integration. *Lifestyles: Family and Economic Issues, 12*(4), 361-377.

Dollahite, D. C., Hawkins, A. J., & Brotherson, S. E. (1996). *Narrative accounts, generative fathering, and family life education. Marriage and Family Review, 24,* 333-352.

Dollahite, D. C., & Rommel, J. I. (1993). Individual and relationship capital: Implications for theory and research on families. *Journal of Family and Economic Issues, 14,* 27-48.

Dudley, J. R. (1991). Increasing our understanding of divorced fathers who have infrequent contact with their children. *Family Relations, 40,* 279-285.

Duffy, A. (1988). Struggling with power: Feminist critiques of family inequality. In N. Mandell & A. Duffy (Eds.), *Reconstructing the Canadian family: Feminist perspectives* (pp. 111-139). Toronto: Butterworths.

Earls, F., & Siegal, B. (1980). Precocious fathers. *American Journal of Orthopsychiatry, 50,* 469-480.

Ehrensaft, D. (1990). *Parenting together: Men and women sharing the care of their children.* Urbana: University of Illinois Press.

Elshtain, J. B. (1993, November). *Families, communities, and habits of the heart.* Paper presented at the Annual Conference of the National Council on Family Relations, Baltimore, MD.

Elwood, R. W., & Mason, C. (1994). The couvade and the onset of paternal care: A biological perspective. *Ethology and Sociobiology, 15,* 145-156.

Emery, R. E. (1994). *Renegotiating family relationships: Divorce, child custody, and mediation.* New York: Guilford.

Emery, R. E., Hetherington, E. M., & DiLalla, L. F. (1984). Divorce, children, and social policy. In H. W. Stevenson & A. E. Siegel (Eds.), *Child development research and social policies* (Vol. 1, pp. 189-226). Chicago: University of Chicago Press.

Erikson, E. H. (1950). *Childhood and society.* New York: Norton.

Erikson, E. H. (1959). *Identity and the life cycle.* New York: Norton.

Erikson, E. H. (1964). *Insight and responsibility: Lectures on the ethical implications of psychoanalytic insight.* New York: Norton.

Erikson, E. H. (1968). *Identity, youth and crisis.* New York: Norton.

Erikson, E. H. (1969). Adult stage: Generativity versus stagnation. In R. Evans (Ed.), *Dialogue with Erik Erikson* (pp. 50-53). New York: Dutton.

Erikson, E. H. (1974). *Dimensions of a new identity.* New York: Norton.

Erikson, E. H. (1975). *Life history and the historical moment.* New York: Norton.

Erikson, E. H. (1980). On the generational cycle. *International Journal of Psychoanalysis, 61,* 212-223.

Erikson, E. H. (1982). *The life cycle completed.* New York: Norton.

Erikson, E. H., & Erikson, J. M. (1981). On generativity and identity. *Harvard Educational Review, 51*(2), 249-269.

Erikson, E. H., Erikson, J. M., & Kivnick, H. (1986). *Vital involvement in old age: The experience of old age in our time.* New York: Norton.

Erikson, J. M. (1988). The woven life cycle. In J. M. Erikson, *Wisdom and the senses: The way of creativity* (pp. 74-112). New York. W. W. Norton.

Faludi, S. (1991). *Backlash: The undeclared war against American women.* New York: Crown.

Family and Medical Leave Act. (1993). 29 U.S.C. §2601.

Family Resource Coalition. (1993). *Best practices project* [Packet for focus groups]. Chicago: Author.

Ferree, M. M. (1990). Beyond separate spheres: Feminism and family research. *Journal of Marriage and the Family, 52,* 866-884.

Führmann, G., & McGill, J. C. (1996, January). *Parallel parenting: When cooperation just won't work.* Workshop presented at the Second International Congress on Parent Education Programs, Association of Family and Conciliation Courts, Clearwater Beach, FL.

Fine, M. A., & Fine, D. R. (1992). Recent changes in laws affecting stepfamilies: Suggestions for legal reform. *Family Relations, 41,* 334-340.

Fine, M., & Turner, J., (1991). Tyranny and freedom: Looking at ideas in the practice of family therapy. *Family Process, 30,* 307-320.

Firestone, J., & Shelton, B. A. (1994). A comparison of women's and men's leisure time: Subtle effects of the double day. *Leisure Sciences, 16,* 45-60.

Fox-Genovese, E. (1991). *Feminism without illusions: A critique of individualism.* Chapel Hill: University of North Carolina Press.

Fox-Genovese, E. (1996). *"Feminism is not the story of my life": How today's feminist elite has lost touch with the real concerns of women.* New York: Doubleday.

Frank, S. M. (1995). *Life with father: Parenthood and masculinity in the nineteenth-century American north.* Unpublished doctoral dissertation, University of Michigan.

Frey, K. S., Greenberg, M. T., & Fewell, R. R. (1989). Stress and coping among parents of exceptional children: A multidimensional approach. *American Journal of Mental Retardation, 94,* 240-249.

Fry, P. S., & Trifiletti, R. J. (1983). Teenage fathers: An exploration of their developmental needs and anxieties and the implications for clinical-social intervention services. *Journal of Psychiatric Treatment and Evaluation, 5,* 219-227.

Furman, B., & Ahola, T. (1992). *Solution talk: Hosting therapeutic conversations.* New York: Norton.

Furstenberg, F. F., Jr. (1988a). Good dads—bad dads: Two faces of fatherhood. In A. Cherlin (Ed.), *The changing American family and public policy* (pp. 193-218). Washington, DC: Urban Institute.

Furstenberg, F. F., Jr. (1988b). Marital disruptions, child custody, and visitation. In A. J. Kahn & S. B. Kamerman (Eds.), *Child support: From debt collection to social policy* (pp. 277-305). Newbury Park, CA: Sage.

Furstenberg, F. F., Jr. (1990). Divorce and the American family. *Annual Review of Sociology, 16,* 379-403.

Furstenberg, F. F., Jr., & Cherlin, A. J. (1991). *Divided families: What happens to children when parents part.* Cambridge, MA: Harvard University Press.

Furstenberg, F. F., Jr., & Harris, K. M. (1993). When and why fathers matter: Impacts of father involvement on the children of adolescent mothers. In R. I. Lerman & R. S. Ooms (Eds.), *Young unwed fathers* (pp. 117-138). Philadelphia: Temple University Press.

Furstenberg, F. F., Jr., Nord, C. W., Peterson, J. L., & Zill, N. (1983). The life course of children after divorce. *American Sociological Review, 48,* 656-668.

Furstenberg, F. F. Jr., & Teitler, J. O. (1994). Reconsidering the effects of marital disruption: What happens to children of divorce in early adulthood? *Journal of Family Issues, 15,* 173-190.

Galinsky, E., Bond, J. T., & Friedman, D. E. (1995). *The changing workforce: Highlights of the national study.* New York: Families and Work Institute.

Gallagher, J. J., Cross, A. H., & Scharfman, W. (1981). Parental adaptation to a young handicapped child: The father's role. *Journal of the Division for Early Childhood, 3*(1), 3-14.

Garbarino, J. (1993). Reinventing fatherhood. *Families in Society, 74,* 51-54.

Genovese, E. (1974). *Roll, Jordan, roll.* New York: Pantheon.

Gerson, K. (1993). *No man's land: Men's changing commitments to family and work.* New York: Basic Books.

Gilbert, L. A., Holahan, C. K., & Manning, L. (1981). Coping with conflict between professional and maternal roles. *Family Relations, 30,* 419-426.

Giles-Sims, J. (1984). The stepparent role: Expectations, behavior, sanctions. *Journal of Family Issues, 5,* 116-130.

Gilligan, C. (1982). *In a different voice.* Cambridge, MA: Harvard University Press.

Giveans, D. (1988). From where I stand. *Nurturing Today, 10*(1), 2.

Glenn, N. D. (1993). A plea for objective assessment of the notion of family decline. *Journal of Marriage and the Family, 55,* 542-544.

Glick, P. (1988). Demographic pictures of black families. In H. McAdoo (Ed.), *Black Families* (2nd ed., pp. 111-132). Newbury Park, CA: Sage.

Goolishian, H., & Anderson, H. (1988). Human systems as linguistic systems: Preliminary and evolving ideas about the implications for clinical theory. *Family Process, 27,* 371-393.

Gottman, J. (1994). *Why marriages succeed or fail.* New York: Simon & Schuster.

Greif, G. L. (1979). Fathers, children, and joint custody. *American Journal of Orthopsychiatry, 49,* 311-319.

Greif, G. L. (1985). *Single fathers.* New York: Lexington/Free Press.

Greif, G. L. (1995). Single fathers with custody following separation and divorce. *Marriage and Family Review, 20*(1/2), 213-231.

Greif, G. L., & DeMaris, A. (1989). Single fathers in contested custody suits. *Journal of Psychiatry and Law, 17,* 223-238.

Greif, G. L., & DeMaris, A. (1990). Single fathers with custody. *Families in Society, 71,* 259-266.

Greif, G. L., & DeMaris, A. (1991). When a single custodial father receives child support. *American Journal of Family Therapy, 19,* 167-176.

Greif, G. L., & DeMaris, A. (1995). Single fathers with custody: Do they change over time? In W. Marsiglio (Ed.), *Fatherhood: Contemporary theory, research, and social policy* (pp. 193-210). Thousand Oaks, CA: Sage.

Greif, G. L., DeMaris, A., & Hood, J. C. (1993). Balancing work and single fatherhood. In J C. Hood (Ed.), *Men, work, and family* (pp. 176-194). Newbury Park, CA: Sage.

Greif, G. L., & Kritall, J. (1993). Common themes in a group of noncustodial parents. *Families in Society, 74,* 240-245.

Griswold, R. L. (1982). *Families and divorce in California, 1850-1890: Victorian illusions and everyday realities.* Albany: State University of New York Press.

Griswold, R. L. (1993). *Fatherhood in America: A history.* New York: Basic Books.

Grossman, F. (1972). *Brothers and sisters of retarded children: An exploratory study.* Syracuse, NY: Syracuse University Press.

Grossman, F. K., Pollack, W. S., & Golding, E. (1988). Fathers and children: Predicting the quality and quantity of fathering. *Developmental Psychology, 24,* 82-91.

Guttman, H. (1976). *The black family in slavery and freedom, 1750-1925.* New York: Pantheon.

Guttman, J. (1989). The divorced father: A review of the issues and the research. *Journal of Comparative Family Studies, 20,* 247-261.

Haas, L. (1990). Gender equality and social policy: Implications of a study of parental leave in Sweden. *Journal of Family Issues, 11,* 401-423.

Haas, L., & Hwang, P. (1995). Company culture and men's usage of family leave benefits in Sweden. *Family Relations, 44,* 28-36.

Hardy, K. (1989). The theoretical myth of sameness. In G. Saba, B. Karrer, & K. Hardy (Eds.), *Minorities and family therapy* (pp. 17-33). New York: Haworth.

Harris, S. (1992). Black male masculinity and same-sex friendships. *Western Journal of Black Studies, 16*(2), 74-81.

Harris, W. (1976). Work and the family in black Atlanta. *Journal of Social History, 9,* 319-330.

Harrison, C. E. (1982). "Teenage pregnancy. " In D. J. Parron & I. Eisenburg (Eds.), *Infants at risk for developmental dysfunction* (pp. 43-55). Washington, DC: National Academy Press.

Haskins, R., Richey, T., & Wicker, F. (1987). *Paying and visiting: Child support enforcement and fathering from afar.* Unpublished manuscript.

Hawkins, A. J., Christiansen, S. L., Sargent, K. P., & Hill, E. J. (1993). Rethinking fathers' involvement in child care: A developmental perspective. *Journal of Family Issues, 14,* 531-549.

Hawkins, A. J., Dollahite, D. C., & Rhoades, C. J. (1993). Turning the hearts of the fathers to the children: Nurturing the next generation. *BYU Studies, 33*(2), 273-291.

Hawkins, A. J., & Eggebeen, D. J. (1991). Are fathers fungible? Patterns of coresident adult men in maritally disrupted families and young children's well being. *Journal of Marriage and the Family, 53,* 958-972.

Hawkins, A. J., Roberts, T., Christiansen, S. L., & Marshall, C. (1994). An evaluation of a program to help dual-earner couples share the second shift. *Family Relations, 43,* 213-220.

Heath, D. T., & McKenry, P. C. (1993). Adult family life of men who fathered as adolescents. *Families in Society, 74,* 36-45.

Heesacker, M., & Prichard, S. (1992). In a different voice revisited: Men, women, and emotion. *Journal of Mental Health Counseling, 14,* 274-290.

Henderson, K. A., & Dialeschki, M. D. (1991). A sense of entitlement to leisure as constraint and empowerment for women. *Leisure Sciences, 13,* 51-65.

Hendricks, L. E. (1980). Unwed adolescent fathers: Problems they face and their sources of social support. *Adolescence, 15,* 861-869.

Hendricks, L. E. (1988). Outreach with teenage fathers: A preliminary report on three ethnic groups. *Adolescence, 23,* 711-720.

Hetherington, E. M., Arnett, J., & Hollier, E. A. (1988). Adjustment of parents and children to remarriage. In S. A. Wolchick & P. Karoly (Eds.), *Child of divorce: Empirical perspectives on adjustment* (pp. 67-107). New York: Gardner.

Hetherington, E. M., & Clingempeel, W. G. (1992). Coping with marital transitions. *Monographs of the Society for Research in Child Development, 57*(2-3).

Hetherington, E. M., Cox, M., & Cox, R. (1976). Divorced fathers. *Family Coordinator, 25,* 417-428.

Hetherington, E. M., Cox, M., & Cox, R. (1982). Effects of divorce on parents and children. In M. E. Lamb (Ed.), *Nontraditional families* (pp. 233-288). Hillsdale, NJ: Lawrence Erlbaum.

Hill, R., Billingsley, A., Engram, E., Malson, M., Rubin, R., Stack, C., Stewart, J., & Teele, J. (1993). *Research on the African American family: A holistic perspective* Westport, CT: Auburn House.

Himmelfarb, G. (1994, Fall). A de-moralized society. *Public Interest,* pp. 57-80.

Hochschild, A. R. (1989). *The second shift.* New York: Avon.

Hoffman, C. D. (1995). Pre- and post-divorce father-child relationships and child adjustment: Noncustodial fathers' perspectives. *Journal of Divorce and Remarriage, 23*(1/2), 3-20.

Hoffman, L. (1990). Constructing realities: An art of lenses. *Family Process, 29,* 1-12.

Holden, G. (1988). Adults' thinking about a child-rearing problem: Effects of experience, parental status, and gender. *Child Development, 59,* 1623-1632.

Horowitz, F. D., & O'Brien, M. (1989). In the interest of the nation: A reflective essay on the state of our knowledge and the challenges before us. *American Psychologist, 44,* 441-445.

Hosmer, D. W., & Lemeshow, S. (1989). *Applied logistic regression.* New York: John Wiley.

Hudson, W. (1982). *Clinical measurement package: A field manual.* Chicago: Dorsey.

Hunter, A., & Davis, J. (1993, November). *The socio-political construction of black manhood: Implications for research on African-American men in families.* Paper presented at the 1993 Annual Conference of the National Conference on Family Relations in Baltimore, MD.

Hunter, A., & Davis, J. (1994). Hidden voices of black men: The meaning, structure, and complexity of manhood. *Journal of Black Studies, 25*(1), 20-40.

Hyde, B., & Texidor, M. (1988). A description of the fathering experience among black fathers. *Journal of Black Nurses Association, 2,* 67-78.

Ihinger-Tallman, M., Pasley, K., & Buehler, C. (1993). Developing a middle-range theory of father involvement postdivorce. *Journal of Family Issues, 14,* 550-571.

Issacs, M. B. (1988). The visitation schedule and child adjustment: A three-year study. *Family Process, 27,* 251-256.

Jackson, J. (1974). Ordinary black husbands: The truly hidden men. In D. Aldridge (Ed.), *Black male-female relationships* (pp. 105-111). Dubuque, IA: Kendall/Hunt.

Jacobs, J. W. (1982). The effect of divorce on fathers: An overview of the literature. *American Journal of Psychiatry, 139,* 1235-1241.

Johnson, L., & Palm, G. (1992a). Planning programs: What do fathers want? In L. Johnson & G. Palm (Eds.), *Working with fathers: Methods and perspectives* (pp. 59-77). Stillwater, MN: nu ink.

Johnson, L., & Palm, G. (1992b). What men want to know about parenting In L. Johnson & G. Palm (Eds.), *Working with fathers: Methods and perspectives* (pp. 129-155). Stillwater, MN: nu ink.

Johnson, L., & Palm, G. (1992c). *Working with fathers: Methods and perspectives.* Stillwater, MN: nu ink.

Johnson, L., & Palm, G. (1995). *Understanding male involvement and promoting healthy male socialization* (Workshop materials for Winter/Spring 1995 Early Childhood Family Education Regional In-Service Trainings). Minnesota Department of Education.

Johnston, J. R. (1992). *High-conflict and violent divorcing parents in family court: Findings on children's adjustment and proposed guidelines for the resolution of custody and visitation disputes* (Final report to the statewide office of Family Court Services). San Francisco: Judicial Council of California.

Johnston, J. R. (1995). Research update: Children's adjustment in sole custody compared to joint custody families and principles for custody decision making. *Families and Conciliation Courts Review, 33,* 415-435.

Johnston, J. R., & Campbell, L. E. G. (1993). Parent-child relationships in domestic violence families disputing custody. *Families and Conciliation Courts Review, 31,* 282-298.

Johnston, J. R., Gonzales, R., & Campbell, L. E. G. (1987). Ongoing postdivorce conflict and childhood disturbance. *Journal of Abnormal Child Psychology, 15,* 493-509.

Jones, J. (1985). *Labor of love, labor of sorrow: Black women, work, and the family from slavery to the present.* New York: Basic Books

Jones, S. L. (1991). Unemployed fathers and their children: Implications for policy and practice. *Child and Adolescent Social Work, 8,* 101-116.

Josselson, R. (1993). A narrative introduction. *Narrative Study of Lives, 1,* ix-xv.

Josselson, R. J., & Lieblich, A. (1993). *The narrative study of lives* (Vol. 1). Newbury Park, CA: Sage.

Kaplan, S., & Kaplan, E. (1988). *Black presence in the era of the American Revolution* (Rev. ed., pp. 209-211). Amherst: University of Massachusetts Press.

Kaufman, M. (1987). The construction of masculinity and the triad of men's violence. In M. Kaufman (Ed.), *Beyond patriarchy: Essays by men on pleasure, power, and change* (pp. 1-44). Toronto: Oxford University Press.

Keen, S., & Valley-Fox, A. (1989). *Your mythic journey: Finding meaning in your life through writing and storytelling.* New York: Jeremy P. Tarcher/Perigee.

Kelland, C. B. (1927, January). It's fun being a father. *American Magazine, 103,* 146.

Kelly, J. (1991). Parent interaction after divorce: Comparison of mediated and adversarial divorce processes. *Behavioral Sciences and the Law, 9,* 387-398.

Keibel, L. (1980). *Women of the republic: Intellect and ideology in revolutionary America.* Chapel Hill: University of North Carolina.

Kiselica, M., Rotzien, A., & Doms, J. (1994). Preparing teenage fathers for parenthood: A group psychoeducational approach. *Journal for Specialists in Group Work, 19,* 83-94.

Kiselica, M., & Sturmer, P. (1993). Is society giving teenage fathers a mixed message? *Youth and Society, 24,* 487-501.

Klinman, D., & Kohl, R. (1984). *Fatherhood U.S.A.* New York: Garland.

Kline, M., Johnston, J. R., & Tschann, J. M. (1991). The long shadow of marital conflict: A model of children's postdivorce adjustment. *Journal of Marriage and the Family, 53,* 297-309.

Kline, M., Tschann, J., Johnston, J. R., & Wallerstein, J. S. (1989). Children's adjustment in joint and sole physical custody families. *Developmental Psychology, 25,* 430-438.

Konen, D. (1992). Women Facilitators. In L. Johnson & G. Palm (Eds.), *Working with Fathers: Methods and perspectives* (pp. 113-128). Stillwater, MN: nu ink.

Kotre, J. (1984). *Outliving the self: Generativity and the interpretation of lives.* Baltimore, MD: Johns Hopkins University Press.

Kraemer, S. (1991). The origins of fatherhood: An ancient family process. *Family Process, 30,* 377-392.

Kramer, L., & Washo, C. A. (1993). Evaluation of a court-mandated prevention program for divorced parents: The Children First program. *Family Relations, 42,* 179-186.

Krause-Eheart, B. (1981, April). *Special needs of low-income mothers of developmentally delayed children.* Paper presented at the National Conference of the Society for Research in Child Development, Boston.

Kristenson, N. (1984). *Guide for developing early childhood family education programs.* White Bear Lake: Minnesota Curriculum Services.

Kruk, E. (1991). Discontinuity between pre- and postdivorce father-child relationships: New evidence regarding paternal disengagement. *Journal of Divorce and Remarriage, 16,* 195-227.

Kruk, E. (1992). Psychological and structural factors contributing to the disengagement of noncustodial fathers after divorce. *Family and Conciliation Courts Review, 30,* 81-101.

Lamb, M. E. (1979). *The role of the father in child development.* New York: John Wiley.

Lamb, M. E. (1981a). Developing trust and perceived effectance in infancy. In L. P. Lipsitt (Ed.), *Advances in infancy research* (Vol. 1, pp. 101-127). Norwood, NJ: Ablex.

Lamb, M. E. (1981b). Fathers and child development: An integrative overview. In M. E. Lamb (Ed.), *The role of the father in child development* (2nd ed., pp. 1-70). New York: John Wiley.

Lamb, M. E. (1981c). *The role of the father in child development* (2nd ed.). New York: John Wiley.

Lamb, M. E., (1986). The changing roles of fathers. In M. E. Lamb (Ed.), *The father's role: An applied perspective* (pp. 3-27). New York: John Wiley.

Lamb, M. E. (1987). Introduction: The emergent father. In M. E. Lamb (Ed.), *The father's role: A cross-cultural perspective* (pp. 3-25). Hillsdale, NJ: Lawrence Erlbaum.

Lamb, M. E. (1995). The changing roles of fathers. In J. L. Shapiro, M. J. Diamond, & M. Greenberg (Eds.), *Becoming a father* (pp. 18-35). New York: Springer.

Lamb, M. E., & Meyer, D. J. (1991). Fathers of children with special needs. In M. Seligman (Ed.), *The family with a handicapped child* (2nd ed., pp. 151-179). Boston: Allyn & Bacon.

Lamb, M. E., Pleck, J., Charnov, E., & Levine, J. (1987). A biosocial perspective on paternal behavior and involvement. In J. Lancaster, J. Altmann, A. Rossi, & L. Sherrod (Eds.), *Parenting across the lifespan: Biosocial dimensions* (pp. 111-142). New York: Aldine de Gruyter.

Lamb, M. E., Pleck, J. H., & Levine, J. A. (1986). Effects of paternal involvement on fathers and mothers. In R. A. Lewis & M. B. Sussman (Eds.), *Men's changing roles in the family* (pp. 67-83). New York: Haworth.

LaRossa, R. (1988). Fatherhood and social change. *Family Relations, 37,* 451-457.

LaRossa, R. (in press). *The modernization of fatherhood: A social and political history.* Chicago: University of Chicago Press.

Larson, T. (1988). Employment and unemployment of young black males. In J. Gibbs, (Ed.), *Young, black, and male in America: An endangered species* (pp. 97-128). New York, Auburn House.

Lavee, Y., & Dollahite, D. C. (1991). The linkage between theory and research in family science. *Journal of Marriage and the Family, 53,* 361-373.

Lears, T. J. J. (1983). From salvation to self-realization: Advertising and the therapeutic roots of the consumer culture, 1880-1930. In T. J. J. Lears & R. W. Fox (Eds.), *The culture of consumption: Critical essays in American history, 1880-1980* (pp. 3-37). New York: Pantheon.

Leashore, B. (1986). Social policies, black males, and black families. In R. Staples (Ed.), *The black family* (5th ed., pp. 334-340). Belmont, CA: Wadsworth.

Lee, D. (1976). *Valuing the self: What we can learn from other cultures.* Englewood Cliffs, NJ: Prentice Hall.

Lemann, N. (1991). *The promised land: The great black migration and how it changed America.* New York: Knopf.

LeMasters, E. E., & DeFrain, J. (1983). *Parents in contemporary America: A sympathetic review* (4th ed). Homewood, IL: Dorsey.

Levant, R. F. (1988). Education for fatherhood. In P. Bronstein & C. P. Cowan (Eds.), *Fatherhood today: Men's changing role in the family* (pp. 253-275). New York: John Wiley.

Levant, R. F. (1992). Toward the reconstruction of masculinity. *Journal of Family Psychology, 5,* 379-402.

Levinas, E. (1969). *Totality and infinity* (A. Lingis, Trans.). Pittsburgh, PA: Duquesne University Press.

Levinas, E. (1985). *Ethics and infinity.* Pittsburgh, PA: Duquesne University Press.

Levinas, E. (1987). *Time and the other* (R. A. Cohen, Trans.). Pittsburgh, PA: Duquesne University Press.

Levine, J. A. (1976). *Who will raise the children? New options for fathers (and mothers).* New York: J. B. Lippincott.

Levine, J. A. (1991, June 11). Babies and briefcases: Creating a family-friendly workplace for fathers. *Hearings before the Select Committee on Children, Youth, and Families* (102nd Cong., 1st session). Washington, DC: Government Printing Office.

Levine, J. A. (1993). Involving fathers in Head Start: A framework for public policy and program development. *Families in Society, 74,* 4-19.

Levine, J. A., & Pitt, E. W. (1995). *New expectations: Community strategies for responsible fatherhood.* New York: Families and Work Institute.

Lewis-Rowley, M., Brasher, R., Moss, J., Duncan, S., & Stiles, R. (1993). The evolution of education for family life. In M. Arcus, J. Schvaneveldt, & J. Moss (Eds.), *Handbook of family life education: Foundations of family life education* (Vol. 1, pp. 26-49). Newbury Park, CA: Sage.

Lillie, T. (1993). A harder thing than triumph: Roles of fathers of children with disabilities. *Mental Retardation, 31,* 438-443.

Lonsdale, G. (1978). Family life with a handicapped child: The parents speak. *Child: Care, Health, and Development, 4,* 99-120.

Lynd, R. S., & Lynd, H. M. (1956). *Middletown: A study in modern American culture.* New York: Harcourt, Brace, World.

Maccoby, E. E., Depner, C., & Mnookin, R. H. (1990). Coparenting in the second year after divorce. *Journal of Marriage and the Family, 52,* 141-155.

Maccoby, E. E., & Mnookin, R. H. (1992). *Dividing the child: Social and legal dilemmas of custody.* Cambridge, MA: Harvard University Press.

Mahoney, M. J. (1991). *Human change processes: The scientific foundations of psychotherapy.* Delran, NJ: Basic Books.

Mair, M. (1988). Psychology as storytelling. *International Journal of Person Construct Psychology, 1,* 125-137.

Majors, R. (1987). *Cool pose: A new approach toward a systematic understanding and studying of black male behavior.* Unpublished doctoral dissertation, University of Illinois, Urbana.

Majors, R., & Billson, J. (1993). *Cool pose: The dilemmas of black manhood in America.* New York: Touchstone.

Marsh, M. (1988). Suburban men and masculine domesticity, 1870-1915. *American Quarterly, 40,* 165-188.

Marsh, M. (1989). From separation to togetherness: The social construction of domestic space in American suburbs, 1840-1915. *Journal of American History, 76,* 506-527.

Marsh, M. (1990). *Suburban lives.* New Brunswick, NJ: Rutgers University Press.

Martin, T. C., & Bumpass, L. L. (1989). Recent trends in marital disruption. *Demography, 26,* 37-51.

Masheter, C. (1991). Postdivorce relationships between exspouses: The roles of attachment and interpersonal conflict. *Journal of Marriage and the Family, 55,* 103-110.

May, J. (1991). *Fathers of children with special needs: New horizons.* Bethesda, MD: Association for the Care of Children's Health.

McAdams, D. P. (1985). *Power, intimacy, and the life story: Personological inquiries into identity.* Homewood, IL: Dorsey.

McAdoo, H. (Ed.). (1988). *Black families* (2nd ed.). Newbury Park, CA: Sage.

McAdoo, J. (1981). Involvement of fathers in the socialization of black children. In H. McAdoo (Ed.), *Black families* (pp. 225-237). Beverly Hills, CA: Sage.

McAdoo, J. (1986). Black fathers' relationships with their preschool children and the children's development of ethnic identity. In R. Lewis & R. Salt (Eds.), *Men in families* (pp. 169-180). Beverly Hills: Sage.

McAdoo, J. (1988). The role of black fathers in the socialization of black children. In H. McAdoo (Ed.), *Black families* (pp. 257-269). Newbury Park, CA: Sage.

McAdoo, J. (1993). The roles of African American Fathers: An ecological perspective. *Families in Society, 74,* 28-35.

McBride, B. A. (1989). Interaction, accessibility, and responsibility: A view of father involvement and how to encourage it. *Young Children, 44,* 13-19.

McBride, B. A. (1990). The effects of parent education/play group program on father involvement in child rearing. *Family Relations, 39,* 250-256.

McBride, B. A. (1991). Parental support and paternal stress: An exploratory study. *Early Childhood Research Quarterly, 6,* 137-149.

McBride, B., & Palm, G. (1992, August). *Intervention programs for fathers: Outcome effects on paternal involvement.* Paper presented at the Annual Convention of the American Psychological Association, Washington, DC.

McBride, J., Robertson, M., & Lane, W. (1996, January). *911 families: Can a co-parenting model work for them?* Workshop presented at the Second International Congress on Parent Education Programs, Association of Family and Conciliation Courts, Clearwater Beach, FL.

McCoy, J. E., & Tyler, F. B. (1985). Selected psychosocial characteristics of black unwed adolescent fathers. *Journal of Adolescent Health Care, 6,* 12-16.

McIssac, H. (Ed.). (1996). Parent education in divorce and separation [Special issue]. *Family and Conciliation Courts Review, 34*(1).

McIvor, M. (1990). *Family literacy in action: A survey of successful programs.* Syracuse, NY: New Readers.

McKelvey, R. D., & Zavoina, W. (1975). A statistical model for the analysis of ordinal level dependent variables. *Journal of Mathematical Sociology, 4,* 103-120.

McLoyd, V. (1990). The impact of economic hardship on black families and children. *Child Development, 61,* 311-346.

Meade, M. (1993). *Men and the water of life: Initiation and the tempering of men.* San Francisco: HarperSanFrancisco.

Meyer, D. J. (1986). Fathers of children with handicaps: Developmental trends in fathers' experiences over the family life cycle. In R. R. Fewell & P. F. Vadasy (Eds.)., *Families of handicapped children: Needs and supports across the lifespan* (pp. 35-73). Austin, TX: Pro-Ed.

Meyer, D., Vadasy, P., & Fewell, R. (1982). Involving fathers of handicapped infants: Translating research into program goals. *Journal of the Division for Early Childhood, 5,* 64-72.

Mills, C. W. (1959). *The sociological imagination.* London: Oxford University Press.

Minton, C., & Pasley, K. (1996). Fathers' parenting role identity and father involvement: A comparison of nondivorced and divorced nonresident fathers. *Journal of Family Issues, 17,* 26-45.

Mintz, S., & Kellogg, S. (1988). *Domestic revolutions: A social history of American family life.* New York: Free Press.

Mirande, A. (1991). Ethnicity and fatherhood. In F. W. Bozet & S. M. H. Hanson (Eds.), *Fatherhood and families in cultural context* (pp. 53-82). New York: Springer.

Nhlapo, R. T. (1993). Biological and social parenthood in African perspective: The movement of children in Swazi family law. In J. Eekelaar & P. Sarcevic (Eds.), *Parenthood in modern society* (pp 35-50). Dordecht, The Netherlands: Martinus Nijhoff.

Norton M. B. (1980). *Liberty's daughters: The revolutionary experience of American women, 1750-1800.* Boston: Little, Brown.

Nydegger, C. N., & Mitteness, L. S. (1991). Fathers and their adult sons and daughters. *Marriage and Family Review, 16*(3-4), 249-256.

Nye, F. I. (1976). *Role structure and analysis of the family.* Beverly Hills, CA: Sage.

Oliver, W. (1989). Black males and social problems: Prevention through Afrocentric socialization. *Journal of Black Studies, 20,* 15-39.

Osherson, S. (1994). Groups for fathers: What do fathers most want to talk about? In F. Litman & D. Whyte (Eds.), *A view from all sides.* (pp. 54-56). Boston: Center for Parenting Studies, Wheelock College.

Palkovitz, R. (1980). Predictors of involvement in first time fathers. *Dissertation Abstracts International, 41,* 096. (University Microfilms No. 705-801).

Palkovitz, R. (1984). Parental attitudes and fathers' interactions with their five-month-old infants. *Developmental Psychology, 20,* 1054-1060.

Palkovitz, R. (1987). Consistency and stability in the family microsystem environment. In D. L. Peters & S. Kontos (Eds.), *Annual advances in applied developmental psychology* (Vol. 2, pp. 40-67). New York: Ablex.

Palkovitz, R. (1992, April). *Parenting as a generator of adult development: Is the child parent to the adult?* Paper presented at the Conference on Human Development, Atlanta, GA.

Palkovitz, R. (1994, November). *Men's perceptions of the effects of fathering on their adult development and lifecourse.* Paper presented at the National Council on Family Relations, Minneapolis, MN.

Palkovitz, R. (in press a). Parenting as a generator of adult development: Conceptual issues and implications. *Journal of Social and Personal Relationships.*

Palkovitz, R. (in press b). The recovery of fatherhood? Invited chapter to appear in A. Carr & M. S. Van Leeuwen (Eds.), *Religion, feminism and the family.* New York: Westminster/John Knox.

Palm, G. (1988, May). *Creating new approaches for working with fathers.* Paper presented at the Family Resource Coalition Conference, Chicago.

Palm, G. (1993). Involved fatherhood: A second chance. *Journal of Men's Studies, 2*(2), 139-155.

Palm, G. (1994). *Involving men in parenting programs.* Minneapolis, MN: Family Information Services.

Palm, G. (1995). *Raising the standards for good fathering.* Minneapolis, MN: Family Information Services.

Palm, G., & Johnson, L. (1992). Building intimacy and parenting skills through father-child activity time. In L. Johnson & G. Palm (Eds.), *Working with fathers: Methods and perspectives* (pp. 79-100). Stillwater, MN: nu ink.

Palm, G., & Joyce, W. (1994, November). *Attachment from a father's perspective.*: Paper presented at National Council on Family Relations Annual Conference in Minneapolis, MN.

Palm, G., & Palkovitz, R. (1988). The challenge of working with new fathers: Implications for support providers. In R. Palkovitz & M. Sussman (Eds.), *Transitions to parenthood* (pp. 357-376). New York: Haworth.

Palmer, P. J. (1983). *To know as we are known: A spirituality of education.* San Francisco: Harper & Row.

Palus, C. J. (1993). Transformative experiences of adulthood: A new look at the seasons of life. In J. Demick, K. Bursik, & R. DiBiase (Eds.), *Parental development* (pp. 39-58). Hillsdale, NJ: Lawrence Erlbaum.

Panzarine, S., & Elster, A. B. (1983). Coping in a group of expectant adolescent fathers: An exploratory study. *Journal of Adolescent Health Care, 4,* 117-120.

Parke, R. D. (1981). *Fathers.* Cambridge, MA: Harvard University Press.

Parke, R. D. (1990). In search of fathers: A narrative of an empirical journey. In I. E. Sigel & G. H. Brody (Eds.), *Methods of family research: Biographies of research projects: Vol. 1. Normal Families* (pp. 153-188). Hillsdale, NJ: Lawrence Erlbaum.

Parmerlee-Greiner, P. (1993). Boulder Valley Schools teen parenting program. *Journal for Vocational Special Needs Education, 15,* 26-30.

Parry, A., & Doan, R. E. (1994). *Story re-visions: Narrative therapy in the postmodern world.* New York: Guilford.

Pasley, K. (1985). Stepfathers. In S. H. Hanson & F. W. Bozett (Eds.), *Dimensions of fatherhood* (pp. 288-306). Beverly Hills, CA: Sage.

Pasley, K., Dollahite, D., & Ihinger-Tallman, M. (1993). Bridging the gap: Clinical applications of research findings on the spouse and stepparent roles in remarriage. *Family Relations, 42,* 315-322.

Pauker, J. D. (1971). Fathers of children conceived out of wedlock: Pregnancy, high school, psychological test results. *Developmental Psychology, 4,* 215-218.

Pearson, J., & Anhalt, J. (1992). *Impact on child access and child support* (Final report of the visitation enforcement program). Denver, CO: Center for Policy Research.

Pearson, J., Thoennes, N., & Anhalt, J. (1993). Child support in the United States: The experience in Colorado. *Family and Conciliation Courts Review, 31,* 226-243.

Peck, J. R., & Stephens, W. B. (1960). A study of the relationship between the attitudes and behavior of parents and that of their mentally defective child. *American Journal of Mental Deficiency, 64,* 839-844.

Pedersen, F. A., Rubenstein, J. L., & Yarrow, L. J. (1979). Infant development in father-absent families. *Journal of Genetic Psychology, 135,* 51-61.

Peters, M. (1988). Parenting in black families with young children: A historical perspective. In H. McAdoo (Ed.), *Black families* (pp. 228-241). Newbury Park, CA: Sage.

Pittman, F., (1993). *Man enough: Fathers, sons, and the search for masculinity*. New York: G. P. Putnam.

Pleck, E. H., & Pleck, J. H. (1995, November). *Fatherhood ideals in the United States: Historical dimensions*. Paper presented at the National Council on Family Relations, Portland, OR.

Pleck, J. H. (1985). *Working wives, working husbands*. Beverly Hills, CA: Sage.

Pleck, J. H. (1987). American fathering in historical perspective. In M. Kinmel (Ed.), *Changing men: New directions in research on men and masculinity*. (pp. 83-97) Newbury Park, CA: Sage.

Pleck, J. H. (1993). Are "family supportive" employer policies relevant to men? In J. C. Hood (Ed.), *Men, work and family* (pp. 217-237). Newbury Park, CA: Sage.

Pleck, J. H. (in press). Paternal involvement: Levels, sources, and consequences. In M. E. Lamb (Ed.), *The role of the father in child development* (3rd ed.). New York: John Wiley.

Pogrebin, L. (1987). *Family politics: Love and power are an intimate frontier*. New York: McGraw-Hill.

Polkinghorne, D. E. (1988). *Narrative knowing and the human sciences*. Albany: State University of New York Press.

Popenoe, D. (1988). *Disturbing the nest*. New York: Aldine de Gruyter.

Popenoe, D. (1993). American family decline, 1960-1990: A review and appraisal. *Journal of Marriage and the Family, 55*, 527-542.

Press, S. J., & Wilson, S. (1978). Choosing between logistic regression and discriminant analysis. *Journal of the American Statistical Association, 73*, 699-705.

Price-Bonham, S., & Skeen, P. (1979). A comparison of white and black fathers with implications for parent education. *Family Coordinator, 28*, 53-59.

Pruett, K. D. (1988). *The nurturing father*. New York: Warner.

Pruett, K. D. (1989). The nurturing male: A longitudinal study of primary nurturing fathers. In S. Cath, A. R. Gurwitt, & L. Gunsberg (Eds.), *Fathers and their families* (pp. 389-405). Hillsdale, NJ: Analytic Press.

Pruett, K. D. (1993). The paternal presence. *Families in Society, 74*, 46-50.

Pruett, K. (1995). The paternal presence. In J. L. Shapiro, J. J. Diamond, & M. Greenberg (Eds.), *Becoming a father: Contemporary, social, developmental, and clinical perspectives* (pp. 36-42). New York: Springer.

Ramsey, S. (1994). Stepparents and the law: A nebulous status and a need for reform. In K. Pasley & M. Ihinger-Tallman (Eds.), *Stepparenting: Issues in theory, research, and practice* (pp. 217-239). New York: Greenwood.

Restrepo, D. (1995). *Gender entitlements in Colombian families*. Unpublished doctoral dissertation, University of Guelph, Ontario.

Rettig, K. D. (1993). Problem-solving and decision-making as central processes of family life: An ecological framework for family relations and family resource management. *Marriage and Family Review, 18* (3/4), 187-222.

Rettig, K. D., Christensen, D. H., & Dahl, C. M. (1991). Impact of child support guidelines on the economic well-being of children. *Family Relations, 40*, 167-175.

Riessman, C. K. (1993). *Narrative analysis*. Newbury Park, CA: Sage.

Risman, B. J. (1986). Can men "mother"? Life as a single father. *Family Relations, 35*, 95-102.

Ritner, G. (1992). *Fathers' liberation ethics: A holistic ethical advocacy for active nurturant fathering*. Lanham, MD: University Press of America.

Rivara, F., Sweeney, P., & Henderson, B. (1986). Black teenage fathers: What happens when the child is born? *Pediatrics, 78*, 151-158.

Roberts, G. (1983). *Conceptual framework for parent education*. White Bear Lake: Minnesota Curriculum Service Center.

Robinson, B. (1988). *Teenage fathers.* Lexington, MA: Lexington.

Robinson, B., & Barret, R. (1986). *The developing father: Emerging roles in contemporary society.* New York: Guilford.

Robinson, B., Barret, R., & Skeen, P. (1983). Locus of control of unwed adolescent fathers versus adolescent nonfathers. *Perceptual and Motor Skills, 56,* 397-398.

Rogers, R. H., & White, J. M. (1993). Family development theory. In P. G. Boss, W. J. Doherty, R. LaRossa, W. R. Schumm, & S. K. Steinmetz (Eds.), *Sourcebook of theories and methods: A contextual approach* (pp. 225-254). New York: Plenum.

Rosenblatt, P. C. (1994). *Metaphors of family systems theory: Toward new constructions.* New York: Guilford.

Rothenberg, A. (1981). *Parent making: A practical handbook for teaching parent classes about babies and toddlers.* Menlo Park, CA: Banster.

Rothstein, A. A. (1978). Adolescent males, fatherhood, and abortion. *Journal of Youth and Adolescence, 7,* 203-214.

Rotundo, E. A. (1985). American fatherhood. *American Behavioral Scientist, 29,* 7-24.

Rotundo, E. A. (1993). *American manhood: Transformations in masculinity from the revolution to the modern era.* New York: Basic Books.

Rubin, L. B. (1994). *Families on the fault line.* New York: HarperCollins.

Ruddick, S. (1989). *Maternal thinking: Toward a politics of peace.* Boston: Beacon.

Russell, C. S. (1980). Unscheduled parenthood: Transition to "parent" for the teenager. *Journal of Social Issues, 36,* 46-63.

Russell, G. (1982). Shared-caregiving families: An Australian study. In M. E. Lamb (Ed.), *Nontraditional families: Parenting and child development.* (pp. 139-171) Hillsdale, NJ: Lawrence Erlbaum.

Sadler, L. S., & Catrone, C. (1983). The adolescent parent: A dual developmental crisis. *Journal of Adolescent Health Care, 4,* 100-105.

Sanchez-Ayendez, M. (1988). The Puerto Rican American family. In C. H. Mindel, R. W. Habenstein, & R. W. Wright (Eds.), *Ethnic families in America: Patterns and variations* (pp. 173-195). New York: Elsevier.

Schuldberg, D., & Guisinger, S. (1991). Divorced fathers describe their former wives: Devaluation and contrast. *Journal of Divorce and Remarriage, 14*(3/4), 61-87.

Seeley, J., Sim, R. A., & Loosely, E. W. (1956). *Crestwood Heights.* Toronto: University of Toronto.

Segal, L. (1990). *Slow motion: Changing masculinities, changing men.* New Brunswick, NJ: Rutgers University Press.

Seltzer, J. A. (1991). Relationship between fathers and children who live apart: The father's role after separation. *Journal of Marriage and the Family, 53,* 79-101.

Seltzer, J. A., & Bianchi, S. M. (1988). Children's contact with absent parents. *Journal of Marriage and the Family, 50,* 663-677.

Seltzer, J. A., & Brandreth, Y. (1994). What fathers say about involvement with children after separation. *Journal of Family Issues, 15,* 49-77.

Seltzer, J. A., Schaeffer, N. C., & Charng, W. (1989). Family ties after divorce: The relationship between visiting and paying child support. *Journal of Marriage and the Family, 51,* 1013-1032.

Shannon, L. B. (1978). *Interactions of fathers with their handicapped preschoolers.* Unpublished doctoral dissertation, University of Kentucky.

Sharifzadeh, V. (1992). Families with middle eastern roots. In E. W. Lynch & M. J. Hanson (Eds.), *Developing cross-cultural competence* (pp. 319-351). Baltimore, MD: Brooks.

Shaw, S. (1992). Dereifying family leisure: An examination of women's and men's everyday experiences and perceptions of family time. *Leisure Sciences, 14,* 271-286.

Shwalb, D. W., Imaizumi, N., & Nakazawa, J. (1987). The modern Japanese father: Roles and problems in a changing society. In M. E. Lamb (Ed.), *The father's role: Cross-cultural perspectives* (pp. 247-269). Hillsdale, NJ: Lawrence Erlbaum.

Slife, B. D., & Williams, R. N. (1995). *What's behind the research? Discovering hidden assumptions in the behavioral sciences.* Thousand Oaks, CA: Sage.

Small, S. A. (1995). Action-oriented research: Models and methods. *Journal of Marriage and the Family, 57,* 941-955.

Smith, D. B. (1980). *Inside the great house: Planter family life in eighteenth century Chesapeake society.* Ithaca: NY: Cornell University Press.

Snarey, J. (1993). *How fathers care for the next generation: A four-decade study.* Cambridge, MA: Harvard University Press.

Stacey, J. (1993). Good riddance to "the family": A response to David Popenoe. *Journal of Marriage and the Family, 55,* 545-547.

Staples, R. (1994). Changes in black family structure: The conflict between family ideology and structural conditions. In R. Staples (Ed.), *The black family* (5th ed., pp. 11-19). Belmont, CA: Wadsworth.

Staples, R., & Johnson, L. (1993). *Black families at the crossroads.* San Francisco: Jossey-Bass.

Stoneman, Z., & Brody, G. H. (1982, August). *Observational research on retarded children, their parents, and their siblings.* Paper presented at the NICHHD Lake Wilderness Conference, University of Washington, Seattle, WA.

Sum, A., & Fogg, N. (1990, January/February/March). The changing economic fortunes of young black men in America. *Black Scholar,* pp. 47-55.

Suzuki, B. H. (1985). Asian-American families. In J. H. Henslin (Ed.), *Marriage and family in a changing society* (pp. 104-119). New York: Macmillan.

Taggart, M. (1985). The feminist critique in epistemological perspective: Questions of context in family therapy. *Journal of Marital and Family Therapy, 11,* 113-126.

Tannen, D. (1990). *You just don't understand.* New York: William Morrow.

Tasch, R. (1952). The role of the father in the family. *Journal of Experimental Education, 20,* 339-346.

Taylor, R., Chatters, L., Tucker, B., & Lewis, E. (1990). Black families. *Journal of Marriage and the Family, 52,* 993-1014.

Taylor, R., Leashore, B., & Toliver, S. (1988). An assessment of the provider role as perceived by black males. *Family Relations, 37,* 426-431.

Tepp, A. V. (1983). Divorced fathers: Predictors of continued paternal involvement. *American Journal of Psychiatry, 140,* 1465-1469.

Thevenin, T. (1993). *Mothering and fathering: The gender differences in child rearing.* Garden City Park, NY: Avery.

Thomas, P. (1987). *Down these mean streets.* New York: Knopf.

Thompson, L. (1991). Family work: Women's sense of fairness. *Journal of Family Issues, 12,* 181-196.

Thompson, L., & Walker, A. (1989). Gender in families: Women and men in marriage, work, and parenthood. *Journal of Marriage and the Family, 51,* 845-871.

Toffel, R. (1994). *Why parents disagree and what you can do about it.* New York: Avon.

Tropf, W. (1984). An exploratory examination of the effects of remarriage on child support and personal contacts. *Journal of Divorce, 7*(3), 57-73.

Turbiville, V. P. (1994). *Fathers, their children, and disability: Literature review.* Lawrence: Beach Center on Families and Disability, University of Kansas.

Turbiville, V. P., Turnbull, A. P., & Turnbull, III, H. R. (1995). Fathers and family-centered early intervention. *Infants and Young Children, 7*(4), 12-19.

Turner, R. H. (1978). The role and the person. *American Journal of Sociology, 84,* 1-23.

Umberson, D., & Williams., C. L. (1993). Divorced fathers: Parental role strain and psychological distress. *Journal of Family Issues, 14,* 378-400.

U.S. Bureau of the Census. (1987, July). *Money income and poverty status of families and persons in the United States: 1986* (Series P-60, No. 157). Washington, DC: Government Printing Office.

U.S. Bureau of the Census. (1990). Remarriage among women in the United States: 1985. *Studies in Household and Family Formation* (Series P-23, No. 169). Washington, DC: Government Printing Office.

U.S. Bureau of the Census. (1991). Family disruption and economic hardship: The short-run picture for children. *Current Population Reports* (Series P-70, No. 23). Washington, DC: Government Printing Office.

U.S. Bureau of the Census. (1992). Marriage, divorce and remarriage in the 1990s. *Current Population Series* (Series P-23, No. 180). Washington, DC: Government Printing Office.

U.S. Bureau of the Census. (1994). *The diverse living arrangements of children, Summer, 1991.* Washington, DC: Government Printing Office.

U.S. Bureau of the Census. (1995a). Child support for custodial mothers and fathers: 1991. *Current Population Reports* (Series P60-187). Washington, DC: Government Printing Office.

U.S. Bureau of the Census. (1995b). *Household and family characteristics: March 1994* (Series P20-483). Washington, DC: Government Printing Office.

Vaz, R., Smollen, P., & Miller, C. (1983). Adolescent pregnancy: Involvement of the male partner. *Journal of Adolescent Health, 4,* 246-250.

Verhoff, J., Douran, E., & Kulka, R. (1981). *The inner American: A self-portrait from 1957-1976.* New York: Basic Books.

Van Nostrand, C. (1993). *Gender-responsible leadership.* Newbury Park, CA: Sage.

Wallerstein, J. S., & Blakeslee, S. (1989). *Second chances: Men, women, and children a decade after divorce.* New York: Ticknor & Fields.

Wallerstein, J. S., & Kelly, J. B. (1980). *Surviving the breakup: How children and parents cope with divorce.* New York: Basic Books.

Walter, J. L., & Peller, J. E. (1992). *Becoming solution-focused in brief therapy.* New York: Brunner/Mazel.

Webster's ninth new collegiate dictionary. (1983). Markham, Ontario: Thomas Allen.

Weissbourd, B. (1987). *A brief history of family support programs.* In S. Kagan, D. Powell, B. Weisbound, & E. Zigler (Eds.), *America's family support programs* (pp. 38-56). New Haven, CT: Yale University Press.

Westbrook, R. (1990, December) "I want a girl, just like the girl that married Henry James": American Women and the problem of political obligation in World War II. *American Quarterly, 42,* 558.

White, J., & Parham, T. (1990). *The psychology of blacks: An African American perspective.* Englewood Cliffs, NJ: Prentice Hall.

White, M., & Epston, D. (1990). *Narrative means to therapeutic ends.* New York: Norton.

White House Conference on Child Health and Protection. (1934). *The adolescent in the family: A study of personality development in the home environment.* New York: Appleton-Century.

Wiegerink, R., Hocutt, A., Posante-Loro, R., & Bristol, M. (1980). Parent involvement in early education programs for handicapped children. *New Directions for Exceptional Children, 1,* 67-85.

Wikler, L. (1981). Chronic stresses of families of mentally retarded children. *Family Relations, 30,* 281-288.

Williams, R. N. (1992). The human context of agency. *American Psychologist, 57,* 752-760.

Willie, C. (1976). *A new look at black families.* New Bayside, NY: General Hall.

Wilson, J. Q. (1993, Summer). On gender. *Public Interest,* pp. 3-26.

Wilson, R., & Melendez, S. (1986). *Fifth annual status report on minorities in higher education.* Washington, DC: American Council on Education, Office of Minority Concerns.

Wilson, W. (1987). *The truly disadvantaged: The inner city, the underclass, and public policy.* Chicago: University of Chicago Press.

Yogev, S. (1981). Do professional women have egalitarian marital relationships. *Journal of Marriage and the Family, 43,* 865-872.

Zill, N., Morrison, D. R., & Coiro, M. J. (1993). Long-term effects of parental divorce on parent-child relationships, adjustment, and achievement in young adulthood. *Journal of Family Psychology, 7,* 91-103.

Zinn, M. B. (1987). *Diversity in American families.* New York: Harper & Row.

Author Index

Subject Index

parent family education program
  definition of, 132, 168-170
  educators in, 170, 172, 175, 176-182,
    237-238
  evolution of the field, 11, 83, 168-172
  goals for mothers and fathers, 169-172,
    173-174, 237-238, 181
  services, 169-172, 175, 176, 177-179, 238
parenting
  balancing work and, 41-42, 140
  coparenting, 12, 39, 46, 47, 49, 50, 60,
    61, 84, 151-153, 156, 161, 179,
    182-226, 232
  divorce and, 88, 118, 122, 125-128,
    129, 131-133, 134-135, 137-140,
    218-223
  employment and, 47, 140, 154-155,
    159-160
  equal opportunities for men in, 36-51,
    85-86
  effect of living arrangements on,
    219-223
  predictors of successful experiences in,
    140-144, 236
parents
  as equals, 2, 36-51, 60, 85-86, 153,
    231-232
paternal pathology, 5
play
  with children, 11, 13, 44, 21, 75, 77,
    79-82, 83, 92, 102, 161-162, 175,
    178, 203, 209, 212, 214
politics
  effect on fathering, 81-82
Puritan fathers
  spiritual and intellectual contributions
    of, 72-74

recreation (*see* leisure)
relationship
  between mother and child, 26, 220-221
  between mother and father, 26, 41,
    64-65, 72, 83, 97-98, 102, 179, 182,
    197-198, 225-227, 236
  between mothers and fathers and effect
    on children, 41, 44, 49-50, 61,
    64-65, 222-223, 225-227, 239, 218

coparenting, 12, 46, 49, 50, 61, 84, 151-
    153, 156, 161, 179, 182, 232, 237
  egalitarian, 41, 44, 45, 46, 49-50, 60,
    61, 85-86, 232
relationship work
  encourage understanding, 29, 186
  facilitate attachments, 29, 186
  of generative fathering, 27, 28, 29, 32,
    90, 95, 186
religion, 31, 82
remarriage, 88, 118, 128-133, 182, 235
republican mother, 74
role-inadequacy perspective (RIP), 1, 2,
    3-4, 7-16, 230

separate spheres, 223
sexual desire, 75
single-custodial father
  discomfort as a, 139-140
social institutions, xv, 36-40, 50-51,
    231-232, 237
social role
  concept of, 14-15
  fathering as a, 2, 3, 14-16, 17, 21, 23,
    157-158, 230
  rescripting, 9
stepparenting, 128-133
stereotypes
  of African American men, 53, 57-58,
    59, 69, 207
  of men, xii, 3-7, 11, 36, 48, 118-119,
    178, 180, 187, 207, 217, 223, 224
  of teenage fathers, 87, 106-107, 108-111
  of women, 49, 163, 187, 198, 207,
    223, 224
stewardship work
  generative ingenuity and, 99-100
  generative work and, 28, 32, 90, 95, 186
  providing opportunities for children
    through, 28, 186
  providing resources through, 28, 186

teaching in university courses, 228-241
teenage fathers
  challenges of, 112-113
  and the deficit perspective, 87,
    107-108, 234-235

About the Contributors

William D. Allen is a doctoral student and teaches in the Family Social Science department at the University of Minnesota in St. Paul, MN. He has completed the Marriage and Family Therapy program and worked as a therapist for a local agency working with a diverse, urban clientele. His research interests include the family experiences of African Americans with a particular focus on the role of black men in families.

Sean E. Brotherson received bachelor's degrees in family sciences and English in 1993 from Brigham Young University. He completed a master's degree in family sciences at Brigham Young University in 1995, where his thesis was on using fathers' narrative accounts to refine a conceptual model of generative fathering. He is now pursuing a doctorate degree in the Human Development and Family Science program at Oregon State University. His research interests include fatherhood, qualitative research, marital quality, and gerontology.

Michael Connor received his PhD from the University of Hawaii in clinical psychology in 1972. Originally a professor of psychology at California State University, Long Beach, he is a founding faculty member of the new campus located at Monterey Bay, CA. He is a licensed clinical psychologist; his activities with fatherwork include research, presenting workshops, developing courses, and an advocacy-oriented private practice.

Kerry Daly is an Associate Professor in the Department of Family Studies at the University of Guelph. He received his PhD in sociology from McMaster University, Hamilton, Ontario. His research interests focus on the social meaning of time, the social construction of fatherhood, constraints associated with father involvement, and the nature of adoptive relationships.

Alfred DeMaris is a Professor in the Department of Sociology at Bowling Green State University. He holds a doctorate in sociology from the University of Florida and a masters in statistics from Virginia Polytechnic Institute. His research interests are primarily in family social psychology and quantitative methods. He has coauthored a number of articles and book chapters on single fathers with Geoffrey L. Greif, and has authored other works on premarital cohabitation, marital violence, and relationship dissolution.

Anna Dienhart is an Assistant Professor in the Department of Family Studies at the University of Guelph. She received her PhD in family relations and human development, with a speciality in marriage and family therapy, from the University of Guelph. She also has a master of science in management (business economics) from the University of California at Los Angeles. Her current research interests focus on gender relations in family and society, gender considerations in therapy, and the social construction of fatherhood.

William J. Doherty is a Professor in the Department of Family Social Science at the University of Minnesota, where he is also Director of the Marriage and Family Therapy Program. He has scholarly, clinical, ethical, and personal interests in generative fathering.

David C. Dollahite is an Assistant Professor of Family Sciences at Brigham Young University and a clinical member of the American Association for Marriage and Family Therapy. He received a BA in family living and an MS in marriage and family therapy from BYU and a PhD in family social science from the University of Minnesota. His scholarship has focused generally on theory development and conceptual linkages between research, theory, and practice in family science. He is currently interested in understanding and encouraging generative fathering.

Kathleen Gerson is Professor of Sociology and Director of Undergraduate Studies in Sociology at New York University. She has written two books on gender issues involved with balancing work and family demands, as well as numerous articles on gender, work, and family change. She is now at work on a study of how children growing up in diverse types of families have responded to the gender revolution at home and at the workplace.

Geoffrey L. Greif is Associate Dean and Professor, School of Social Work, University of Maryland at Baltimore. He is the author of numerous book chapters, professional articles, and books dealing with the topic of single fathers. Two new books, one on parents who lose contact with their children after divorce, and one on academically successful African American male college students, are in progress.

Robert L. Griswold received his PhD from Stanford University and is a Professor of History at the University of Oklahoma. He has published many articles and books on American family history. He is a member of the Editorial Advisory Committee for the *Journal of Family History*. He is currently researching a book tentatively titled *Youth Sport, Gender, and American Culture, 1945–2000*.

Alan J. Hawkins is an Associate Professor of Family Sciences at Brigham Young University. He received a BS in psychology and a master of organizational behavior from Brigham Young University, and a PhD in human development and family studies from Pennsylvania State University. His teaching, scholarship, and family life education focus on understanding and encouraging good fathering, and on sharing domestic labor.

Carmelle Minton, MS, is a doctoral student in human development and family studies at the University of North Carolina at Greensboro. Her expertise is in men's roles, focusing on fathers' parenting role identity and father involvement in different social contexts. Her current efforts address the effects of the coparental relationship and the legal system on fathering in postdivorce families.

Stephanie N. Morris is a graduate student in family sciences at Brigham Young University. She received a BS in psychology from BYU in 1994. Her scholarship interests include on-line family life education with fathers, the connections between communities and families, and ethical issues in family science. She assisted in the creation of the FatherWork web site (http://fatherwork.byu.edu).

Rob Palkovitz is Associate Professor of Individual and Family Studies at the University of Delaware, where his teaching and research interests focus on the developmental outcomes of life course transitions. He was trained as a developmental psychologist. His dissertation research, launched during his first transition to parenthood, focused on predictors of father involvement. He has been studying various aspects of intergenerational relationships and development ever since.

Glen F. Palm is an Associate Professor in Child and Family Studies at St. Cloud State University in St. Cloud, MN. He teaches classes in child development and parent and family education, coordinates the parent education licensure program, and supervises student teachers in parent education. He has worked as a parent educator with fathers' groups for the last 17 years in Early Childhood Family Education programs in Minnesota and coedited a book based on that topic. He also writes a regular column for Family Information Services, titled "Working With Fathers."

Kay Pasley, EdD, is Associate Professor of Human Development and Family Studies at the University of North Carolina at Greensboro. She received her doctoral degree in 1974 from Indiana University. She has studied remarriage and stepfamilies since 1977 and has written extensively in this area with Marilyn Ihinger-Tallman. Her current research interests include fathering in marital transition and discovering the meanings men attach to fathering and how they redefine themselves following divorce and remarriage. She also continues to explore the marital dynamics in remarriage and stepfamilies.

J. Lyn Rhoden is a Visiting Assistant Professor in the Department of Human Services at the University of North Carolina at Charlotte. Her research publications and interests include marital quality and family relations, especially in the context of changing contemporary family configurations, gender, race, and class.

Bryan E. Robinson, PhD, is a Professor of Child and Family Development at the University of North Carolina at Charlotte. He is a licensed marriage and family therapist with interest in work and family dynamics. He is author or coauthor of 20 books and more than 100 articles in professional journals and popular magazines. He has written scripts for national television programs on child development and has appeared on national radio and television discussing children's needs.